AF412235

Making Spaniards

Also by Alejandro Quiroga

LOS ORÍGENES DE NACIONALCATOLICISMO: Pemartin y la Dictadura de Primo de Rivera

THE REINVENTION OF SPAIN: Nation and Identity since Democracy (*with Sebastian Balfour*)

Making Spaniards

Primo de Rivera and the Nationalization of the Masses, 1923–30

Alejandro Quiroga

Cañada Blanch Centre for Contemporary Spanish Studies

palgrave
macmillan

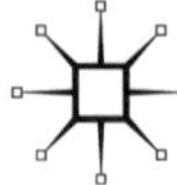

© Alejandro Quiroga 2007

All rights reserved. No reproduction, copy or transmission of this publication may be made without written permission.

No paragraph of this publication may be reproduced, copied or transmitted save with written permission or in accordance with the provisions of the Copyright, Designs and Patents Act 1988, or under the terms of any licence permitting limited copying issued by the Copyright Licensing Agency, 90 Tottenham Court Road, London W1T 4LP.

Any person who does any unauthorised act in relation to this publication may be liable to criminal prosecution and civil claims for damages.

The author has asserted his right to be identified as the author of this work in accordance with the Copyright, Designs and Patents Act 1988.

First published 2007 by
PALGRAVE MACMILLAN
Houndmills, Basingstoke, Hampshire RG21 6XS and
175 Fifth Avenue, New York, N.Y. 10010
Companies and representatives throughout the world

PALGRAVE MACMILLAN is the global academic imprint of the Palgrave Macmillan division of St. Martin's Press, LLC and of Palgrave Macmillan Ltd. Macmillan® is a registered trademark in the United States, United Kingdom and other countries. Palgrave is a registered trademark in the European Union and other countries.

ISBN-13: 978-0-230-01968-3   hardback
ISBN-10: 0-230-01968-4   hardback

This book is printed on paper suitable for recycling and made from fully managed and sustained forest sources. Logging, pulping and manufacturing processes are expected to conform to the environmental regulations of the country of origin.

A catalogue record for this book is available from the British Library.

Library of Congress Cataloging-in-Publication Data

Quiroga, Alejandro, 1972–
    Making Spaniards : Primo de Rivera and the nationalization of the
        masses, 1923–1930 / Alejandro Quiroga.
            p. cm.
    Includes bibliographical references and index.
    ISBN-0-230-01968-4 (alk. paper)
        1. Primo de Rivera, Miguel, 1870–1930. 2. Spain--Politics and
government--1923–1930. 3. Nationalism--Spain--History--20th
century. I. Title.
DP236.P7Q57 2007
946'.074092--dc22   2007018726
[B]

10   9   8   7   6   5   4   3   2   1
16   15   14   13   12   11   10   09   08   07

Printed and bound in Great Britain by
Antony Rowe Ltd, Chippenham and Eastbourne

Contents

List of Illustrations

The Spanish masses will consent to be shaped, for they are a noble race

(Lieutenant Colonel Emilio Rodríguez Tarduchy, member
of the Junta de Propaganda Patriótica)

*You keenly personify the most dangerous trend for the preservation of
national unity, which regionalisms and political autonomies are bound
to destroy, for the masses' ideas are simplistic and do not understand the
subtleties of sharp minds*

(General Miguel Primo de Rivera to Francesc Cambó)

Foreword

Authoritarian regimes such as the Dictatorship of Primo de Rivera were widespread throughout Europe of the 1920s and 1930s. In most countries, they emerged, like fascism, as a result of the post-war collapse of old regimes. Yet they displayed an extraordinary degree of heterogeneity. Indeed, such is the complexity of the different manifestations of both authoritarianism and fascism that there has been a proliferation of explanatory models and ideal types. Like nationalism, no one model satisfactorily covers the multitude of forms they have taken. Nor do existing models account adequately for the shifting balance between conservatism and fascism typical of all regimes from fascist to authoritarian conservative. Nevertheless, the key to understanding their success is the historical context – the aftermath of the First World War, the punitive Versailles settlement, the resentment of demobilized veterans, the cleavages within the new nations, economic recession, the crisis of liberalism, the contradictions of modernization and much else besides.

It should also be remembered that at the end of the nineteenth century, liberal capitalism seemed to have triumphed. Most of Europe had embraced some form of representative government, as limited or diluted as it was in countries like Spain and Italy. Liberal values based on ideological pluralism, capitalism and individual rights were almost everywhere in the ascendant. Yet less than thirty years later, most of Europe had succumbed to authoritarian or totalitarian governments. To make sense of this extraordinary lurch to the far right, we need to distinguish authoritarianism from fascism, though both embraced a number of common features. Authoritarian regimes were repressive, anti-liberal, anti-Marxist, pro-military and nationalist. They adopted corporatism, launched a cult of the leader, in some cases promoted a cult of violence and machismo, and often created single parties. But they differed fundamentally from fascist regimes in that they were largely, though not exclusively, anti-modern. Authoritarian regimes took power at a time of a liberal crisis of state mainly to defend the existing social and political order against revolution, not to transform it. They were not as heterogeneous as fascist movements, understandably so because they were defensive and reactive rather than revolutionary. No single party emerged with such a mass following as the Nazis and the Italian fascists. The key issue is that the state was dominated by traditional political, clerical and economic elites acting through a strong man, whether a king or a general, rather than by the fascist party.

The Dictatorship of Primo de Rivera is a prime illustration of the heterogeneity of the authoritarian model. Although its sources of power and legitimacy lay in the traditional elites, the Dictatorship set out to transform Spain by modernizing its economy and society. Until recently, it was regarded by historians as a brief, six-year interregnum between the constitutional monarchy of the Restoration system and the Spanish Republic. No one questions the fact that the Dictatorship failed to replace the constitutional monarchy which it helped to destroy. On the other hand, there has been some recognition of the achievements of Primo de Rivera's programme of public works inasmuch as they helped to lay the basis for industrial modernization. Yet new studies have demonstrated the extent to which the dictator undertook a revolutionary path in seeking to indoctrinate the masses into a modern, nationalist ideology closely akin to fascism.

Alejandro Quiroga's book is a lucid and innovative account of that effort to 'make the new Spaniard', examining the process of programming from above, as Primo de Rivera set out to create the structures and agencies to carry out the task of nationalization. The book analyses the discourse of this programme of indoctrination, its symbols, rituals and quasi-religious myths. It also evaluates the impact this programme had on society. His conclusion is a convincing one: far from garnering support for National-Catholic values among the masses, the dictator's programme mobilized and brought together opposition against the elites and their institutions, paving the way for the Second Republic. But equally, as Quiroga stresses, the Dictatorship established the ideological foundations of the Franco regime. Thus his book demonstrates the enormous influence this short-lived regime had on society. It also makes an important contribution to the study of the political phenomenon of authoritarian regimes in Europe of the 1920s and 1930s as a whole.

Sebastian Balfour
Professor of Contemporary Spanish Studies
London School of Economics and Political Science

Acknowledgements

This book has been a long time in the making and the volume of my debts is commensurate with the time scale. Along the way I enjoyed financial assistance from the Universidad Autónoma de Madrid and the Government Department at the London School of Economics that enabled me to spend much needed time in the archives of Madrid, Alcalá de Henares, Barcelona and London. I am especially indebted to Professor Sebastian Balfour, for his trust and encouragement throughout the years. This book began as a PhD thesis under his supervision and his support has been unfailing at all stages. Goyo Alonso too has always been there to help. My debt to him goes a long way back – for his constant help and extraordinary generosity as a scholar over the many years of our friendship.

I should like to express my thanks to all those colleagues and friends in Britain and Spain who helped me in various ways. I would especially like to mention Rodney Barker, Marta Bizcarrondo (†), Martin Blinkhorn, Gerald Blaney, Jaime Briones, Fergus Campbell, Martin Farr, Eduardo González Calleja, Helen Graham, Miguel Guerrero, John Hutchinson, Tim Kirk, Rudolf Muhs, Diego Muro, Paul Preston, Luc Racaut, Francisco Romero, Sandra Souto, Guy Theaker and Chiara Thumiger. My colleagues at the University of Newcastle provided a stimulating and stable environment in which to work, as well as always being ready to give their personal advice. My warmest gratitude is to Mari Carmen Fernández de Soto, whose support has made the completion of this book possible.

List of Abbreviations

ACNP	Asociación Católica Nacional de Propagandistas
AGM	Academia General Militar
CEDA	Confederación Española de Derechas Autónomas
CNCA	Confederación Nacional Católica Agraria
CNT	Confederación Nacional del Trabajo
CSG	Central School of Gymnastics
FCS	Federación Cívico Somatenista
FET y de las JONS	Falange Española Tradicionalista y de las Juntas Ofensivas Nacional Sindicalistas
JONS	Juntas Ofensivas Nacional Sindicalistas
JPPC	Junta de Propaganda Patriótica y Ciudadana
NCOs	Non-commissioned officers
PCE	Partido Comunista de España
PNV	Partido Nacionalista Vasco
PSOE	Partido Socialista Obrero Español
SNEFP	Servicio Nacional de Educación Física y Premilitar
SNEFCP	Servicio Nacional de Educación Física Ciudadana y Premilitar
TNE	Tiro Nacional de España
UGT	Unión General de Trabajadores
UMN	Unión Monárquica Nacional
UP	Unión Patriótica

Introduction

It is difficult to exaggerate the political and social cataclysm produced in Europe by the First World War. Empires collapsed, borders were redrawn, new states were created, millions were forced to leave their homes, revolution triumphed in Russia, working-class movements increased their mass support, popular pressure to democratize nineteenth-century elitist political systems dramatically grew and revolutionary upheavals broke out all around the continent. The ruling classes and important sectors of the bourgeoisie felt under threat. They knew the pre-1914 regimes would not hold under increasing popular demands for radical change and some of them resorted to dictatorships to stop the advance of the left. In the 1920s Hungary, Italy, Spain, Greece, Portugal, Poland and Yugoslavia became counterrevolutionary dictatorships. In the 1930s, Germany, Austria, Romania and the Baltic republics followed suit.

Together with pure physical repression, these regimes appealed to nationalist ideas in order to gain mass support, legitimize themselves and undermine the popular allure of the left. By diverting public attention towards external 'threats' and the 'enemy within', the European political elites aimed at producing a 'negative integration', that is, the indoctrination of the lower and middle classes in nationalist ideas emphasizing foreign and domestic foes. This was not new. It had been a constant strategy throughout Europe since the turn of the century, notoriously in Germany, and the process only intensified after the First World War.[1] As the old nineteenth-century mechanisms of social control became increasingly inefficient in politically mobilized societies, the European dictatorships found political indoctrination in nationalist values to be the most useful tool to integrate the masses into politics without having to pay the toll of democratization. The authoritarian regimes not only used the traditional state agencies to transmit nationalist ideas to the population, such as the education system and the army, they also set up unprecedented propaganda machines, official parties and national militias and organized thousands of patriotic ceremonies in an attempt to produce an anti-democratic mass mobilization. The nationalization of the masses, the historical process of homogenizing the population under a common national identity, gained momentum in the interwar period when the continent was in the middle of a 'European civil war' between right and left.[2]

Spain was one of the first European countries to be submerged under the tide of counterrevolutionary dictatorships. Spain had not entered the Great War but the effects of the conflict were felt all the same in the shape of an increasingly militant working-class movement, socio-economic dislocation, nationalist agitation and colonial crises. Since 1917, the growth of the labour movement, popular bottom-up pressure to change the oligarchic liberal monarchy, the increasing support of regionalist movements in Catalonia and nationalist options in the Basque Country and a series of disastrous colonial campaigns in Morocco had generalized the belief that the Restoration political system was in a state of permanent crisis. Many in the upper and middle classes began to look for an authoritarian solution outside the system that could guarantee their privileged position and halt the left. By the summer of 1923 the fact that diverse military generals were plotting to overthrow the government was no secret. On 13 September 1923, Captain General of Catalonia Miguel Primo de Rivera staged a coup d'état in Barcelona. The following day, King Alfonso XIII backed the insurrection, dismissed the civilian government and named Primo de Rivera president of a Military Directory formed to rule the country with extraordinary powers. Although Primo first declared that his was to be a temporary, three-month government, his Dictatorship lasted more than six years and deeply transformed Spanish society.

This book analyses the official nationalist doctrine developed during the Dictatorship of Primo de Rivera and its transmission throughout Spanish society. It sets out to explain the ideological evolution of conservative Spanish nationalism in the 1920s and the process of nationalization of the masses undertaken by the regime. My aim is to explore the crucial role played by the state in shaping an authoritarian national identity, and in particular its procedures for developing a political discourse, for implementing nationalist policies and for transferring national ideals into society. This study focuses on the main agencies that the Primo de Rivera regime used in the process of mass nationalization, namely the army, the education system, the official party and the militia. The study of these agencies allows us to assess the process of political indoctrination and nationalization of society implemented by the Dictatorship.

This book argues that the Primo de Rivera regime attempted to implement an authoritarian nationalist political project to construct a modern corporative nation-state which could appeal to the majority of Spaniards during the 1920s. In order to achieve its goal, the Dictatorship carried out a process of mass indoctrination from above, seeking to replace the hegemonic liberal Spanish national identity with a new authoritarian one. At the ideological level, the book argues, the organic intellectuals of the *primorriverista* regime outlined the principles of an extreme-right nationalism that eventually became the doctrinal basis of the Franco dictatorship. The *primorriverista* political discourse equated Catholicism with Spanishness and started a process of 'sacralization' of politics in which the myth of the nation became the supreme political value. This new organic canon of Spain had its political implications, both in terms of the actions taken against those considered to be 'internal enemies' of the nation (for example republicans, liberals, anarchists, Catalan regionalists and Basque nationalists) and the reform of state agencies in order to improve their capacity as propagandist devices. Thus nationalist policies and the nationalization of the masses attempted by the Dictatorship are examined here in direct relation to the *primorriverista* official doctrine.

The book is divided into two main thematic sections. The first part covers the making of the nationalist doctrine by the ideologues of the regime. The second part concentrates on the process of nationalization, analysing the transmission of the official idea of Spain into society by the state agencies.

Following a first chapter on Spanish nationalism and the question of the nationalization of the masses prior to 1923, Chapter 2 deals with the official discourse during the Military Directory (1923–1925). It examines Primo's idea of the Spanish nation and the governmental policies seeking to undermine Catalan and Basque nationalists' and regionalists' power during the first two years of the Dictatorship. Chapter 3 focuses on the *primorriverista* nationalist doctrine formulated during the Civil Directory (1926–1930). It shows how the regime's ideologues created an anti-liberal canon of the nation, combining different alternative conservative models of Spanish nationalism and radical right-wing European thought. This chapter also analyses the *primorriverista* nationalist doctrine within its European context, comparing the *primorriverista* nationalist discourse to its Italian and French counterparts.

The second part of the study concentrates on the main agencies used by the state to transmit the ideological premises of the regime. Chapter 4 looks at the role of the army as an institution of nationalization in the military barracks. I explore here the *primorriverista* reforms of the military education system at both officer and rank-and-file levels and the recruitment system. These transformations are extremely revealing of the regime's aims as they were specifically designed to improve the patriotic indoctrination of recruits during their military service. But Primo de Rivera went beyond the classical use of the army as an agency of nationalization and took the military outside the barracks to promote the regime's 'patriotic teachings' among civilians all around Spain. The dictator not only replaced civil governors by military governors in every province of the country but also created the figure of the 'governmental delegates' (*delegados gubernativos*), military officers ascribed to all Spanish districts (*partidos judiciales*) with the specific orders to control political opposition, organize mass rallies of support for the regime, propagate the official doctrine in public ceremonies and educate the population in 'patriotic values'. Chapter 5 focuses on the role of these military governmental delegates and the regime's attempts to create a nationwide system of pre-military, gymnastic and political education for teenagers and children.

Chapter 6 studies the *primorriverista* transformation of the primary education system and its political consequences. Changes in the national curricula, the creation of espionage networks to punish rebel teachers, the development of state schools and the expansion of Castilian language became the hallmarks of a reform aimed at increasing the nationalization of the masses under *primorriverista* principles. Chapter 7 focuses on the implementation of nationalist policies in secondary education and the reaction it provoked from the Catholic Church. Special attention is paid here to the implementation of official linguistic policies and the political implications of the process of nationalization in Catalonia.

The last two chapters examine the role of the militia, the *Somatén Nacional*, and the official party, the *Unión Patriótica* (Patriotic Union, UP). Chapter 8 analyses the use of the *Somatén Nacional* not only as an auxiliary armed force of middle-class citizens created by Primo to defend the Dictatorship and its 'social order', but also as an agency conceived to indoctrinate citizens in militarist values and to organize parades and nationalist rituals all over Spain. A similar 'educational mission' is to be found in the *Unión Patriótica*. Organized from above as a catch-all party, the UP sought to channel popular support for the Dictatorship, while at the same time providing an instrument of social control over the masses. Chapter 9 explores how the Dictatorship used the state-sanctioned party to indoctrinate the population in *primorriverista* nationalist values as a way of creating popular consensus and social cohesion.

By taking this top-down approach to the process of nationalization, the book focuses on the state as the 'maker' of the nation. Thus I do not analyse some other autonomous factors, independent of the state, which also intervene in the process of nationalization. The popular culture which originated in civil society (literature, theatre, bullfighting, *zarzuela*, flamenco and so on) will not be addressed here. This study does not constitute a cultural history of the period in question. Nor will a great deal be said about the role of ideologies promoted by political groups and cultural associations other than the *primorriveristas*, even though the former played a part in the process of generating 'alternative nationalizations' to the official one.

This book is a study of the ideological and political implications of the process of mass nationalization implemented by Primo de Rivera. It argues that his Dictatorship developed the principles of a *fascisticized* nationalism in line with the European radical right that eventually constituted the ideological principles of the Franco dictatorship. In the short term, however, the *primorriverista* bid to carry out a process of indoctrination of the masses from above led to a 'negative nationalization', in which increasing opposition to the state agents propagating the official canon of the nation was accompanied by the rejection of the very idea of the nation defended by those agents. Thus the regime's policies had the unintended consequence of discrediting the authoritarian canon of Spain and contributed to the popular consolidation of a democratic idea of the nation, hence paving the way for the establishment of the Second Republic in 1931.

1
The Roots of National-Catholicism

Nations are the work of God

(Antonio Cánovas)[1]

On 13 September 1923, Miguel Primo de Rivera staged a military coup and launched a manifesto to the nation. In it, the Captain General of Catalonia justified his action against the constitutional government as the only way to save 'the Fatherland from a dishonourable end'.[2] In his view, trade unionists, Catalan and Basque nationalists and incompetent civilian politicians had constantly threatened the patria since Spain lost the remnants of its empire to the USA in 1898. After a quarter of a century of continuous disasters and decadence, Primo stated, the army had to intervene to avoid national disintegration. Although there had been a long history of military intervention in Spanish political life, the 13 September 1923 coup was different. Whilst in the nineteenth century military officers would stage coups in order to put one particular political group in power, Primo's intervention led to the formation of a Military Directory to rule the country. For the first time, the army took power as an institution.

There were also novelties at the discursive level. The *primorriverista* discourse, oversaturated in nationalism since day one of the Dictatorship, combined old and new elements. Many of Primo's ideas had their roots in the nineteenth century, yet his nationalist postulates were part of a new discourse elaborated as a response to the rapid and accelerating process of modernization that Spain was undergoing from the start of the twentieth century. Actions soon followed words. In the first weeks after the coup, the Military Directory imprisoned hundreds of politicians, trade unionists and regional nationalists accused of being enemies of the fatherland. At the heart of these actions lay the belief that the body of the nation had been contaminated by anti-Spanish elements which had to be eradicated.

But repression was not enough. Primo also introduced changes in schools, the military, central and municipal public administrations and the media in order to improve the transmission of a Spanish national identity to the masses. The indoctrination of citizens in nationalist values was at the top of the *primorriverista* agenda since the very beginning of the Dictatorship. Implicit in this position was the idea that the Restoration (1875–1923), the constitutional system that Primo brought down, had failed to indoctrinate the masses effectively. State agencies needed to be reformed because in the past they had been unsuccessful in their task of 'making' Spaniards.

The creation of the modern Spanish nations (1808–1898)

In Spain, the co-existence of two opposing concepts of the modern nation can be traced back to the first decades of the nineteenth century, when the liberal and the traditionalist models of the patria as an imagined political and cultural community were first formulated. Hence, the confrontation between the liberal and the traditionalist conceptions of the nation was to play an outstanding role throughout the nineteenth and twentieth centuries. The modern liberal concept of Spain was created during the Peninsular War (1808–1814). The invasion of Napoleonic troops mobilized an important sector of the population in the struggle against the French and triggered the liberal revolution. In 1810, the National Assembly convened in Cadiz, assumed national sovereignty and defended a modern canon of Spain as a political community of citizens endowed with equal rights. The constitution, passed by the National Assembly in March 1812, established the 'Spanish nation' as the ultimate sovereign and recognized Spain as a national, constitutional, parliamentarian and Catholic body. Wartime also witnessed the invention of traditions to justify the abandoning of the absolutist regime. Liberals recreated and vindicated a medieval popular inheritance to define the national community in terms of a common history and culture. Thus Aragon's medieval parliaments and the Castilian *Comuneros'* opposition to Habsburg rule were highlighted as historical episodes in order to illustrate the 'traditional' origins of Spanish liberalism. In turn, this new vindication of the 'popular' and 'democratic' institutions justified liberal political views, which were intended to create new participatory bodies within a modern state. In other words, from its conception, the liberal idea of Spain incorporated an important 'organicist' understanding of the nation as a community shaped by history and culture, which implied the need to position liberalism within popularly accepted traditions.

During the Isabeline era (1833–1868) moderate liberals in power elaborated a nationalist mythology following the canons established in Cadiz. The fight against the French was then named the 'War of Independence' and became a pillar of national myth-making. The large number of monuments erected to the 'martyrs' of the struggle and the conversion of 2 May into a national holiday are two good examples of this. Scholars and artists also played a prominent role in the propagation of the moderate nationalist discourse. The 'people' became the main character in literature and academic books, which underlined the historical continuity of the Spanish *Volkgeist*. The practical goal of this production of general histories of Spain was to legitimize the construction of the liberal state and contemporary bourgeois social values. At the political level, the moderate discourse defended a uniform centralized state as the best way to cement the liberal order, and maintained a strong identification between Catholicism and Spanish national identity.

A political alternative to the moderate canon of Spain came from progressive liberals and republicans. They interpreted the medieval parliaments, the *fueros* (local charters), and religious tolerance as the hallmarks of the Spanish nation's 'Golden Age'. Conversely, the Habsburg rule, 'foreign' absolutism, and religious intolerance had in their view paved the way for Spanish decadence. Finally, freedom, democracy and, in some versions, republicanism were the redemptive ideals of the liberal-progressive model. Unlike the moderates, progressive liberals supported the construction of a decentralized state. They justified this political position by idealizing the medieval local statutes and municipalities, as the 'historical protectors' of the so-called 'regional freedoms'. Consequently, when advocating a decentralized state, democrats also claimed to be preserving the 'traditional' political structure of the nation.[3] But ideological intentions and political realities proved difficult to marry. When progressive liberals were in power (1868–1874) the political system remained highly unstable and the federal project during the First Republic (1873–1874) could never be properly developed.

A competing concept of the nation is to be found in traditionalist thought. It also has its early formulations in the 'War of Independence', when defenders of the *ancien régime* defined the Spanish nation as intrinsically Catholic and mobilized the population to fight the 'atheist invader'. The *Serviles*, Fernando VII supporters, first, and the Carlists, later, considered liberal ideas as 'anti-Spanish' and against the country's 'traditions'. These alleged 'traditions' were nothing but a modern invention of those reactionary forces. In fact, the *Serviles* copied the traditionalist discourse elaborated in France during the Revolution and used the anti-liberal rhetoric as an ideological tool to defend the 'Altar and the Crown'.[4] But whatever the novelty of these postulates, the truth is that the reactionaries of the early nineteenth century laid the foundations of traditionalist thought and many of their ideas were used to build the Catholic model of Spain fifty years later.

It was not until the second half of the nineteenth century, however, that reactionary thinkers realized the potent appeal of nationalist legitimacy and fully formulated the traditionalist version of the nation. In this model, expressed in the works of the historians Víctor Gebhart, Antonio Merri y Colón and, above all, Marcelino Menéndez Pelayo, Catholic unity was the common denominator of the foundation of the Spanish nationality and legitimized the monarchy as the national political institution par excellence. Traditionalist historians explained the pinnacle of Spanish power in the sixteenth and seventeenth centuries as a consequence of the struggle against foreign heresy in Europe and the evangelization of the Americas. They also held French rationalism and German Krausism responsible for the introduction of revolutionary ideas that had supposedly destroyed the unity of Spanish culture. Contrary to the liberal model, traditionalists found the Spanish 'Golden Era' during the time of the first Habsburgs and blamed Bourbon reformism for the nation's decadence. Their redemptive ideal was a community politically and religiously united, led by a strong crown and an independent Catholic Church.[5]

This theocratic and romantic conception of the nation was adopted by all those traditionalist groups opposed to the liberal state, such as Carlists, Catholic Integrists, and significant sectors of the Spanish ecclesiastical hierarchy. Concerning the state structure, the traditionalists advocated a decentralized Spain, where regions would maintain their medieval privileges. Then the restoration of the *ancien régime* would entail the reinstatement of old territorial statutes. This in turn would signal the return to the nation's 'Golden Era'.[6] Against liberal centralization and throughout the nineteenth century, the defence of the *fueros* increasingly became a propagandist tool to mobilize support for the traditionalist cause, gaining significant success in the rural areas of Navarre, the Basque region and Catalonia.

During the Restoration (1875–1923), the right wing of the Conservative party defended a very similar version of the Spanish nation, within the liberal monarchic system. Antonio Cánovas, the architect of the Restoration and Conservative leader, understood nations as biological organisms with their own 'national character' shaped through the centuries by tradition and culture. This historicist-romantic conception did not completely rule out the liberal idea of a shared will and communal consciousness in the formation of nations, but it certainly gave more importance to divine intervention. Beyond all geographical, cultural, racial and linguistic aspects, 'nations were the work of God', Cánovas stated in a lecture in 1882.[7] The sacred nature of the fatherland was always present in the conservative idea of Spain.

Unlike the traditionalists, however, these sectors of the right were intensely centralist. Following the moderate-liberals' route, they aimed for the end of medieval regional privileges and attempted to unify legislation and the state administration during the last quarter of the nineteenth century. This process of centralization ran parallel to the emergence of a Castilian-centred interpretation of Spanish history, which became dominant at the turn of the century. According to this view, Castile had been the leading region in the formation of Spain and, therefore, the 'national psychology' was of Castilian origin. Also detectable in art and literature, the historical centrality of Castile in the nation-building process became a cultural artefact at the service of political nationalism.[8]

By the end of the nineteenth century the traditionalist–liberal divide was clearly established in Spain. This was not an exceptional case. In France, the Dreyfus affair clearly showed the clash of two conflicting concepts of the nation. In Italy, the idea of the existence of two antagonistic nations within one state remained well into the twentieth century.[9] In fact, opposing visions of the nation were part of the ideological processes of nation-building all around Europe in the nineteenth century. In all cases, elites elaborated different concepts of nations and transmitted them to the masses in order to mobilize supporters.

Nation-building in the nineteenth century

The process of nation-building is a complex one. In it very different elements intervene, ranging from socio-economic developments (industrialization, the establishment of a bourgeoisie, the creation of a mass education system and so on) to political aspects (the consolidation of a modern liberal state, war, the inclusion of the population in the system via political representation etc.), from cultural factors (the spread of printing and the press, and the emergence of patriotic literature and songs) to symbolism (flags and anthems, for instance). In recent years historians have discussed the process of nation-building and the weaknesses and strengths of the process of nationalization of the masses in nineteenth-century Spain. Initially, many saw the emergence of Catalan and Basque nationalisms at the end of the nineteenth century as a clear sign of the failure of the Spanish elites to integrate the population into the national ideal.[10]

In recent years, the original interpretation of the process of mass nationalization as weak and unsuccessful has been revised. New investigations have showed the process of nationalization as partially successful and the acquisition of a Spanish national identity compatible with the creation of regional identities. According to this 'revisionist' view, Spain would not be an exception among other European countries in terms of nation-building but a 'normal' country with the same peculiarities, achievements and shortcomings as any other.[11]

Throughout the nineteenth century the Spanish economy was transformed, a capitalist system firmly consolidated and a powerful bourgeoisie emerged.[12] Nevertheless, the transition from an agrarian society to a capitalist one was gradual and territorially uneven. Industrialization took place slowly in Catalonia and rapidly in Biscay and Asturias in the last decades of the century – all of which were peripheral regions far from the geographical centre of political power (Madrid). As a result, the creation of a 'national market', a by-product of the industrial revolution, was incomplete until the last quarter of the century and internal customs and taxation privileges remained in use until 1876 in the Basque provinces and Navarre. Moreover, Spain lacked an integrated system of social communications, which made the spread of modern values and the transmission of a common national identity more difficult. Regional and local identities, which had developed during the *ancien régime*, remained important throughout the century.[13] The improvement in the structure of communications that would have made possible the transmission of ideas and standardization of a 'national culture' had to wait until the turn of the century.

The liberal revolutions, however, led to profound social and political transformations during the nineteenth century. One of the main outcomes of the revolutions was the creation of the liberal state, a pillar in the development of capitalism and a shaper of a national culture at the same time.[14] On the one hand, the liberal state nationalized basic wealth (lands, mines and railways) and immediately afterwards privatized it, creating a class of property owners. Hence, it was through the state that the speculative wealth of early capitalism was forged and the new economic development legally adapted to serve the interests of the ruling classes. Additionally, liberals promoted the idea of a bourgeois citizenry via new state agencies, such as the military, the education system, the judicial system and the civil administration, which led to the consolidation of a civic political nationalism among the middle classes.[15]

Nevertheless, the liberal state was chronically in debt during the nineteenth century. This precluded the formation of powerful state agencies and therefore allowed the subsistence of old forms of legitimacies and local identities. The national education system, for example, was not created until 1857 and suffered an endemic shortage of resources. This explains the high level of illiteracy in Spain compared to other Western European states (59 per cent of the population were illiterate in 1900) and the persistence of regional languages throughout the nineteenth century. In addition, the influence of the Catholic Church in determining the contents of state education hindered the promotion of civic values associated with the idea of the nation as the ultimate source of state legitimacy.[16]

The army did not obtain better results than the education system as a state agency of nationalization. The Spanish military was not national, in the revolutionary sense of the 'nation in arms', but deeply divided between the privileged and lower classes. An exception-riddled conscription system, in which the upper and middle classes paid members of the lower classes 'to substitute' for them in compulsory enlistment, could not promote the idea of national integration. Conversely, monetary exemption showed the lower classes that service to the fatherland was not an honour but a burden and ultimately alienated them from this type of patriotic integration.[17] Moreover, the absence of a foreign threat after the Napoleonic wars and the fact that Spain was not involved in any major international war between 1814 and 1898 prevented massive numbers of people from being called to arms and being thereby instilled with patriotic fervour. Nonetheless, in the second half of the century, diverse colonial adventures were partially supported by the lower classes, and liberals and traditionalists united in their support of the Moroccan campaign of 1859–1861 in the name of national grandeur. In 1898, the outbreak of the Spanish-American war was greeted with popular jingoism by thousands in the streets, which demonstrates that a national identity had been acquired by many in the lower classes.

Finally, the centralist administrative system defended first by the moderates and later by the conservatives proved difficult to implement. The division of the country into forty-nine provinces and the unification of local governments in 1833, the creation of the Civil Governors as the state's representatives in every province in 1844, the formation of the Civil Guard to ensure the monopoly of violence the same year and the compilations of the Penal Code (1848) and Civil Code (1889) gradually set the administrative and legal bases of the modern Spanish state. Nonetheless, centralism took a long time to overcome the secular fragmentation of Spain's territory, and the unity of the state remained highly artificial until well into the nineteenth century. The political and economic problems that the liberal state faced led to a progressive but inefficient building of the modern administration and the province remained the centre of political and social life. In fact, the state throughout the nineteenth century was characterized by a profound contrast between legal centralism and real localism.[18]

At the political level, there can be few doubts that the civil wars between liberals and Carlists did little for the propagation of a uniform idea of Spain. However, while liberals and traditionalists defended antagonistic views, what was at stake was not the existence of the Spanish nation, something that both sides never questioned, but the political organization of the state. In fact, the Carlist wars had a significant mobilizing effect among the popular classes.[19] For years, thousands of Spaniards were called to arms to fight in the name of the nation (whether liberal or traditionalist) against the 'enemy within'. Yet it was the very oligarchic nature of the liberal system which mostly precluded a more effective nationalization of the masses. Moderate and conservative liberals framed elitist political systems, in which electoral participation was kept to a minimum – or it was openly fraudulent when the franchise was enlarged. A system like the Restoration, based on the manipulation of the electoral machine from Madrid but giving local bosses (*caciques*) a great deal of autonomy in regional matters, could hardly have encouraged popular identification with the official idea of the nation-state. On the contrary, liberal governments, usually oligarchies of landowners and enriched bourgeoisie, were reluctant to encourage patriotic mobilizations and, in fact, attempted to demobilize the masses. Nor was the bourgeoisie of the industrialized periphery willing to challenge the state by mobilizing the lower classes. Always dependent on the state for the protection of their economic interests, the peripheral bourgeoisie had close links with the ruling elite in Madrid and shared a common culture.[20] Therefore, the oligarchic liberal state had a twofold effect in terms of nationalization. First, the lack of political representation led to a widespread political apathy among the masses, which could hardly identify with the official concept of nation promoted by the elites. Second, the oligarchic political practices deepened the gap between what was perceived to be the 'legal country', as represented by the liberal constitutions, and the 'real country', represented by the people.

At the cultural level, the process of symbolization used by groups to construct their national identities demonstrates in the Spanish case, first, the different political conceptions of the nation and, second, the separation between state elites and the masses. In opposition to the symbols of the *ancien régime*, liberals introduced the most visible symbols of the nation, the flag and the anthem. In 1843, the national flag was adopted but the national anthem would only be introduced in 1908. Moreover, republicans challenged these symbols. They changed the flag and banned the 'royalist' anthem when in government, leading to a long-standing conflict only resolved in the late 1970s. This competing symbolism was in line with the lack of consensus on national myths and 'Golden Ages'. As the century progressed, democrats and republicans emphasized the civic and secular symbols of the nation, while, more successfully, conservatives and traditionalists adopted the Catholic symbolic universe to represent the national identity.[21]

Regarding the role of cultural processes in the construction of national identity, the liberal state promoted its vision of Spain in various fields, with the 'national' prizes on historic paintings and patriotic writings being two good examples of this. As in other Western European countries, in the last decades of the century the Spanish state structured public life around national symbols. Ceremonies and rituals, such as the cult of the 'patriotic martyrs', became a fundamental part of the official representation of the nation-state. However, more often than not the popular classes remained absent from these civic state ceremonies. More importantly, this detachment from the 'official nation' sometimes turned into hostility, and the masses developed popular counter-rituals. Alternative anthems, such as the International and the liberal *Himno de Riego*, and popular culture, exemplified in bullfighting, religious parades and *zarzuelas*, challenged the symbols imposed from above.[22]

The gap between the elites and the popular classes in the symbolic and ceremonial construction of the nation shows the difficulties that Spanish liberals faced in the nationalization of the masses from above. However, this should not lead us to conclude that the process of nationalization as a whole was a failure. The invention of alternative popular ceremonials and symbolism, the popular support for war in 1895–1898, the multiple expressions of Spanish nationalism in languages other than Castilian in Catalan, Galician and Basque newspapers, and the debate between liberals and traditionalists on the structure of the nation-state are all evidence of the existence of relatively solid Spanish national identities among the population. In fact, these cases of Spanish popular identities illustrate that other mechanisms of nationalization different than the state's, such as the press and the Church, had made an impact on the creation of a national community throughout the nineteenth century.

Additionally, one should take into consideration that the problems the Spanish liberal state faced were not exceptional in Europe. The conflict between local-provincial powers versus national representatives was common all around the continent as the liberal state developed; monetary exemptions of the military service lasted until the 1880s in France; education systems were unable to impose the official language in many French,

Italian and German regions and vernacular dialects were widely used until the First World War; nor were regional political movements seeking home rule or independence unusual in the United Kingdom, Italy, Germany or France at the turn of the twentieth century.[23]

The Spanish case in the nineteenth century shows the development of a national political language and a national political culture, but not the reality of a modern nationalist mass movement.[24] Yet things changed dramatically at the turn of the century. The acceleration of the socio-economic transformations and the 'politicization' of broad sectors of society hitherto uninvolved, deepened into the process of nationalization in the first two decades of the twentieth century. As a result, many in the middle and lower classes became much more receptive to nationalist messages. At the same time, the loss of the empire in the Caribbean and the Pacific in 1898 led to a profound reformulation of Spanish nationalism by intellectuals and politicians, a 'regeneration' of patriotic postulates that were eventually integrated as the ideological bases of Primo's Dictatorship.

From military disaster to military rule (1898–1923)

During the month of April 1898, jingoism was strongly felt throughout most of the Spanish society. As the war with the United States approached, newspapers speculated on the possibility of a rapid Spanish victory, the urban masses patriotically gathered to support the struggle and political parties united in their defence of the military.[25] By early May, the Spanish fleet lay at the bottom of the sea and Spain had lost the remains of her once great empire to the USA. The 'Disaster' of 1898, as it came to be known, signals a turning point in the development of modern Spanish nationalism. As in the Italian case after the defeat at the hands of the Ethiopians at Adowa (1896), the loss led to a crisis of national identity. An entire generation of intellectuals, the so-called 'Generation of 1898', devoted its work to solve the 'problem of Spain'. Political groups presented diverse alternatives to 'regenerate' the 'sick' nation. Disaffection with the nation-state became paramount. The lower classes radicalized and demanded deep social and political changes, while Catalan regionalism and Basque nationalism increased their social support.

The idea of national regeneration was certainly not invented at the turn of the century, but during the 1890s, and especially after the military defeat in Cuba and the Philippines, cultural elites steadily propagated the need for 'national rebirth'. During the twenty-five years that followed the loss of the empire, the Generation of 1898, which included figures such as Miguel de Unamuno, Joaquín Costa, Azorín, Ramiro de Maeztu,

Pío Baroja and Ángel Ganivet, and later the Generation of 1914, led by the philosopher José Ortega y Gasset, sought to identify the essence of the Spanish national character. Their goal was to explain contemporary reality through an understanding of the national character and ultimately provide practical solutions for Spanish regeneration. Despite the diversity of analyses, it is possible to identify some common traits in the regenerationist discourse. First, it conceived the nation as an organic whole that had to be understood as an evolutionary process. This view combined romantic German historicism and new currents of vitalism, but it was also steeped in Social Darwinist postulates and geographical determinism, so much in vogue in *fin-de-siècle* Europe.[26]

Second, regenerationist discourse highlighted the centrality of Castile in the historical formation of the nation and Castilian as the national language; and yet it also advocated the regeneration of the municipalities and local life as the starting point of national reconstruction. On the one hand, these postulates challenged the Restoration centralist system, which was considered inefficient and guilty of destroying 'popular national life'. On the other, regenerationists criticized the emerging Catalan and Basque nationalism as artificial, bourgeois and backward looking. They denounced the peripheral middle classes that were joining regionalist movements as selfish and suicidal, but held that the oligarchic system of the Restoration was ultimately responsible for the emergence of the 'separatist' ideas.[27] In doing so, the regenerationists contributed to the growth of a new Spanish nationalism, as well as to the nascent dialectic between Spanish and peripheral nationalism, which was to dominate the twentieth century.

In the political arena, the regenerationist movement proposed practical reforms to achieve 'Europeanization', that is, the modernization of the country. Its leading figure, Joaquín Costa, demanded the end of the oligarchic political system and advocated a state-led agrarian reform as the best way in which to modernize the country. The movement first crystallized soon after the 'Disaster' in the creation of the *Unión Nacional*, an association which gathered together small farmers and merchants of Castile and Aragon, led by Joaquín Costa, and representatives of the chambers of commerce from all over Spain, led by Basilio Paraíso. However, this middle-class alliance, with contradictory economic and ideological interests, was unable to form a political party to challenge the establishment, and the movement rapidly faded away in the early 1900s. Increasingly disappointed by the lack of success of the regenerationist movement, Costa turned towards the republicans and called for a radical change. It was then that he appealed to a hazily defined providential figure, an 'iron surgeon', who would lead the national revolution and operate on the 'sick body' of Spain. Costa's notion of the 'iron surgeon' was in fact related to the ideas of nineteenth-century praetorian liberalism and sought a leading figure that could overcome the ruling oligarchies to bring a real democracy to Spain.[28] Nevertheless, two decades later, Miguel Primo de Rivera would seize power claiming to be the very 'iron surgeon' Costa had called for.

A second new version of Spanish nationalism, and another immediate ideological precedent of the Dictatorship of Primo de Rivera, came out of the military barracks at the turn of the century. Military nationalism aimed to transform the nation-state and combined the requirement of modernization with conservative postulates. After 1898, professional offi- cers openly advocated modernizing the nation via an authoritarian state. In their view, Spain needed a strong economy, a regimented society, and an up-to-date army ready for new imperialist expansions to solve the post-colonial crisis. To achieve these aims, the military demanded internal state reforms, including gearing industry towards arms production, a better education system, an honest public administration and the restructuring of the relationship between the state and the Catholic Church.[29] For the military, these transformations could not be carried out by the inefficient two-party system of the Restoration. They would rather require a strong gov- ernment led by a general and not subordinated to parliamentary control.

Whilst military nationalism shared some features with regenerationism and the call for a temporary dictatorship could somehow resemble the figure of the 'iron surgeon', the truth is that the professional officers had little sympathy for the movement led by Paraíso and Costa. The military press steadily attacked the *Unión Nacional*, which it saw as an egoist petit- bourgeois movement, and defended a vague mixture of nascent corpo- ratism and populism. The army not only felt it was the guarantor of the nation-state but, moreover, saw itself as the interpreter of the popular will.[30] In a corrupt political system in which male universal suffrage was little more than a charade, army officers often presented themselves as the 'real' voice of the masses. However, this populism should not lead us to consider the military as the champions of democratic reforms. Almost invariably, the army sided with the Restoration civilian elites and was steadily used for internal repression. In reality, there was nothing demo- cratic in this populist rhetoric. Scorn for the working classes was manifest in the military press and most officials feared the inclusion of the masses in the political arena. When using the populist discourse, the army was indeed appealing to certain sectors of the population, mostly the middle classes, or, to put it in military terms, 'the healthy segments' of society. Moreover, this new military nationalism shared many of the myths of the conservative-traditionalist canon of the second half of the nineteenth century. It saw in the martial spirit of the Reconquest, the colonization of America, the fight against Protestants and the 'War of Independence' the real 'soul' of the nation.[31]

Ideologically, military nationalism gained momentum after the war due to the growing strength of Catalan regionalism and, to a lesser extent, Basque nationalism, as well as the latent anti-militarism of the working class. In defining itself as the repository of the quintessential qualities of the fatherland, the army considered criticism of the military as an attack on the patria and saw Catalan regionalism and Basque nationalism as mere treason to the nation. According to this logic, political violence to punish enemies of national unity became a patriotic duty.[32] In 1902, on three different occasions, officers attacked Catalan and Basque nationalist demonstrators. On the evening of 25 November 1905, after a series of satirical cartoons mocking the army appeared in the journal *Cu-Cut*, junior officers assaulted the editorial offices of the publication and then moved on to destroy the plant of the Catalanist newspaper *La Veu de Catalunya*. The reactions to the assault showed how deep anti-Catalanist sentiments were in many sectors of the establishment. The action was applauded almost unanimously in garrisons throughout Spain, crowds of officers gathered at stations to greet military delegates sent to Catalonia, while junior officers in Madrid and Barcelona prepared an ultimatum for the King requiring action against the Catalanists and the closure of the Cortes. The officers also formed commissions and demanded all crimes against the army, the nation and the state to be tried by military tribunals. As had been the norm in the past, the government took no action against the aggressors. On the contrary, on 29 November 1905 it declared martial law in Barcelona, enforced the closure of newspapers and arrested Catalanist sympathizers. In March 1906, the bill for the 'Repression of Crimes Against the Fatherland and the Army' (popularly known as the 'Law of Jurisdictions') was passed in Parliament. Although the new law retained offences against the nation and the state under civilian jurisdiction, it allowed military jurisdiction over verbal and written offences against the army and, therefore, showed the military that political violence and insubordination paid off in the short term.

If the Law of Jurisdictions confirmed the military belief that the army was the only genuine guardian of the fatherland and made 'official' the military idea of Spain, the consequences in the long term proved to be disastrous. Republicans, the left wing of the Liberal Party, socialists and Carlists opposed the law and its repeal became central to the political debate. In Catalonia, *Solidaritat Catalana* gathered Carlists, Republicans and Catalanists in a political alliance whose main goals were the abolition of the Law of Jurisdictions and the creation of Catalan regional institutions. The outcome of the action–reaction spiral sparked off by the *Cu-Cut* affair seems clear: the military gained even more control of the state apparatus and regionalism gained more social support.

The subsequent crises of Spanish society only widened the gap between the military and the popular classes. When, in 1909, an anti-war demonstration sparked off the revolutionary events of the 'Tragic Week' in Barcelona, another episode of the action–reaction spiral was set in motion. The working-class challenge to the imperial adventure 'confirmed' to the military that leftist ideologies operated against national grandeur. In turn, the brutal repression ordered by the Maura government and executed by the army logically amplified the bitterness and mistrust of the working class towards the military. During the period 1917–1920 this very same pattern was to be repeated on a regular basis. What began as a military revolt to defend the army's privileges in 1917, with the formation of the juntas of junior officers, ended up as harsh military repression of the working class, military control of public services and continual declarations of martial law in the following three years. These actions only radicalized popular anti-militarism, while contributing to the strengthening of a conservative military mentality. Moreover, after the Spanish military suffered a shocking defeat in Morocco, the so-called 'Disaster of Annual'

Figure 1 Spanish colonial troops pose for the camera with the heads of Rifean rebels. The brutality of the war in the Spanish protectorate in Africa alienated the popular classes from the military.

in 1921, and the abolition of the juntas in 1922, the army adopted a unified stand in the face of social tensions and peripheral nationalism, which was to crystallize in Primo's coup in September 1923.[33] It is hardly surprising that the day after the united demonstration of Catalan, Basque and Galician nationalists in Barcelona on 11 September 1923, the military press complained of the 'separatist riffraff' and demanded the strict enforcement of the laws of crimes against the fatherland. 'If impunity continued, good Spaniards should intervene to correct such grievances', the military threatened.[34] The following day, the Captain General of Catalonia staged a coup. In his manifesto, Primo justified his action claiming the nation had to be saved from the 'shameless separatist propaganda' and from the 'impunity of communist propaganda'. The military press unanimously welcomed the coup.[35]

A third key element in the reformulation of Spanish nationalism during the first quarter of the twentieth century was the emergence and consolidation in the political arena of a new radical right. Either from inside the system, as in the case of Maurists, Social Catholics and the monarchist leagues of Barcelona and Bilbao, or in direct opposition to the Restoration, as for the Carlists and Catholic Integrists, these groups proposed diverse alternatives to the political structure in an attempt to 'regenerate' the nation from an authoritarian perspective. In doing so, they further developed the nineteenth-century traditionalist canon of Spain and anticipated many of the ideas and rhetoric that the Dictatorship would eventually adopt. Not surprisingly, most of the civilian political personnel of Primo's regime would come from these authoritarian groups. Furthermore, in many ways, these groups represented the first real attempt from the right to gain popular support outside the oligarchic circles of the Restoration. This new approach to the masses was based on a genuine effort to produce a social mobilization – via political parties, Catholic trade unions, religious pilgrimages and militias – which paved the way for the model of 'national mobilization' Primo later tried under the *Unión Patriótica* and the *Somatén Nacional*.

To be sure, it was Maurism, the movement formed around the conservative leader Antonio Maura, that represented the first real attempt to organize a modern political party and regenerate the country 'from above'. In a speech in Parliament in 1899, Maura had already warned of the need to go through a 'revolution from above', in order to avoid a revolution 'made in the streets'.[36] From then on, Maura's discourse would be one of national regeneration and active counterrevolution. Deeply influenced by the thought of his friend Charles Maurras, Maura's idea of Spain was essentially based on the traditionalist canon, and monarchy and Catholicism were much emphasized as the keystones of the nation. To preclude revolution from below, the Maurist movement took to the streets. The aim was to mobilize the so-called 'neutral mass', and to create an educated 'citizenry' to change the system from within. In other words, Maurism intended to attract the middle classes hitherto not involved in the oligarchic system to transform the Restoration and ultimately combat the left. Achieving these goals involved the creation of modern propaganda machinery, the organization of mass rallies, the formation of a Maurist Youth and the creation of Maurist Centres all around Spain, something until then unknown to the monarchist parties. With a propaganda machine ready, a nationalist rhetoric and a paternalistic approach to the 'social question', Maurism felt confident to fight the working-class parties on their home ground. Since early 1915, Maurists opened 'social centres' in working-class neighbourhoods to compete with socialist, anarchist and republican popular houses. The aim was to 'educate' the lower classes in patriotic, Catholic, corporative and monarchist values and separate the proletariat from the left-wing parties.[37]

The fact that the first Spanish attempts to form fascist-type groups emerged around Maurists should not come as a surprise. Since the years of the First World War, an important sector of Maurism, and particularly the Maurist Youth, was convinced that parliamentary politics had failed and advocated a strong government to save the nation. For many Maurists the only way to stop the left was by physical confrontation, either via bourgeois militias or military-led repression. As early as March 1919, the Maurist daily *La Acción* had called for a military dictatorship.[38] When Mussolini gained power in Italy in October 1922, *La Acción* enthusiastically welcomed fascism as the solution to sweep away the political parties, and called Spaniards to follow the Italian example and form a national legion. A few months later, in December 1922, the Maurist Joaquín Santos Ecay, the director of *La Acción*, Manuel Delgado Barreto, and the president of the National Employers' Confederation, Tomás Benot, attempted to form the first fascist organization around the newspaper *La Camisa Negra*. In the summer of 1923, another pro-fascist organization, *La Traza*, was founded by a group of army officers in Barcelona. The new party blamed politicians for the loss of the colonies, the Moroccan disaster of 1921, and the *caciques'* destruction of the 'popular will' which was leading the fatherland to internal disintegration. In their foundational manifesto, *La Traza* called for a 'sacred union of Spaniards', beyond their 'monarchic or republican, aristocratic or democratic' ideas, to save the nation and suggested violence against the internal enemies of the fatherland was a valid option to redeem Spain.[39] Although the lives of both

La Camisa Negra and *La Traza* were ephemeral, their appearance proves that the ground was fertile for the growth of authoritarian nationalist alternatives to the Restoration. If they did not develop further it was because the military dictatorship, an option much wanted by the Maurists, albeit not by Maura himself, was to integrate all these extreme-right groups into the regime.

The growth of Spanish nationalism can also be detected in the formation of new coalitions of members of the two main parties to confront peripheral nationalism in Catalonia and the Basque Country. In Catalonia, the offensive was led by the former liberal Alfonso Sala, who founded *Unión Monárquica Nacional* (UMN) in 1919. The coalition of liberals and conservatives attracted some important members of Catalan high society specifically aiming to combat the *Lliga Regionalista*. This reaction of the monarchic parties was not accidental. The international recognition of the right of self-determination of national minorities after the Great War fuelled the emergence of more radical Catalanist opinions which pushed for full 'home rule'. In 1919, the moderate *Lliga* also launched a campaign to gain political autonomy for Catalonia. Against home rule, the UMN proposed monarchism, corporatism and regionalism – the latter understood in the Maurist sense of local and regional regeneration of the whole of Spain. In January 1919, conservatives, liberals and *mauristas* gathered in the Maurist Circle of Bilbao and formed the *Liga de Acción Monárquica* to fight 'separatism'. In the same years, the Bilbao daily *El Pueblo Vasco* gathered an important number of intellectuals, who first formulated an ultra-nationalist notion of Spain. Among these writers and politicians were Ramiro de Maeztu, Victor Pradera, José Calvo Sotelo, Eduardo Aunós, Rafael Sánchez Mazas, and the Count of Rodezno.[40] All of them were later to collaborate, in one way or the other, with Primo de Rivera. Although neither regional nationalism nor the labour movement was as strong as in Catalonia, the logic behind the *Liga de Acción Monárquica* was the same as in the UMN: a dual defensive reaction of Spanish conservative nationalism to fight the challenges from below and the periphery. The immediate outcome was nothing but the consolidation of Spanish nationalism in Barcelona and Bilbao, with the monarchist parties increasing their votes in both cities.

While Maurism and the unions of dynastic parties were born in the big cities, another conservative movement proposing national regeneration that was to have a key influence in the ideological and political arrangement of Primo's Dictatorship found its strength in the towns and villages of Old Castile and the northern provinces. Since the publication in 1891 of Leo XIII's *Rerum Novarum*, the interest of the Catholic hierarchy in the social situation of the lower classes had increased. The intense diffusion of Social Catholic doctrines in the press, congresses and collective pilgrimages was complemented in *fin-de-siècle* Spain with the opening of Catholic centres and, eventually, with the creation of Catholic trade unions in order to deal with the 'social question'. As left-wing ideas spread throughout rural Spain, the Catholic Church launched a multiple-front offensive seeking a complete 're-clericalization of society'.[41]

This process of 're-clericalization of society' grew intensively first in 1898 and then in 1909, as a reaction to the anti-clericalism showed by the popular classes and liberal intellectuals after the loss of the colonies and during the 'Tragic Week'. It was precisely in 1909 when the Jesuit Ángel Ayala tried to create a homogeneous Catholic movement, founding the National Catholic Association of Propagandists (*Asociación Católica Nacional de Propagandistas*, ACNP). The Propagandists' views were heavily indebted to the historic romanticism and neo-Thomist thought that had framed the nineteenth-century traditionalist canon of Spain. Following the ideas of Cánovas and Menéndez Pelayo, Ángel Herrera, the Propagandists' leader, considered nations to be the work of God in History. In his view, Spain was a 'moral unity' historically framed by the monarchy and the Church under providential supervision. Equally, Herrera considered liberal democracy not to suit Spain; first, because sovereignty was believed to lie ultimately in God, and, second, due to the fact that Spain's social and territorial disparities were thought to be too big for implementing a real universal suffrage without dangers. As an alternative, the Propagandists defended an 'organic democracy' based on the family, municipalities and corporations that would eventually rejuvenate 'the people's sap'.[42]

From the beginning, the ACNP realized the importance of propaganda to obtain Catholics' social and doctrinal cohesion. The famous 'Propaganda Campaigns' orchestrated by the ACNP mouthpiece, *El Debate*, sought to indoctrinate and mobilize followers in a militant Social Catholicism in an unprecedented manner. In addition, Social Catholics created trade unions and Centres of Social Defence to compete with the left, yet with very limited success.[43] In fact, it was in the rural areas of Old Castile, Navarre and Aragon where Catholic propaganda paid off. The diverse agrarian unions created during the first years of the Great War finally came together in 1917 and formed the National Catholic Agrarian Confederation (*Confederación Nacional Católica Agraria*, CNCA). A genuine interclass organization, the CNCA was made up of smallholders and directed by big landowners and focused on halting the advance of leftist ideas in the countryside.[44] It was no coincidence that one of the first groups to promote the creation of the *primorriverista Unión Patriótica* in 1924 emerged from this social basis of Castilian militant Catholics.

Changes also occurred in those reactionary groups that openly opposed the Restoration political establishment. After 1898, Carlists and Catholic Integrists tried to retain their customary influence in areas of Navarre, the Basque Country and Catalonia. However, political unity amongst these groups was never achieved during the Restoration. Quite the contrary: in 1919 a major split in the Carlists' ranks occurred, when the main ideologue of the party, Juan Vázquez de Mella, walked out to form the Traditionalist Party. Despite the schism, or perhaps because of it, ideologues such as Vázquez de Mella, Salvador Minguijón and Victor Pradera sought to revitalize traditionalist doctrine during the first decades of the twentieth century, by incorporating ideas from thinkers outside Spanish traditionalism such as Charles Maurras and Joaquín Costa. This new traditionalism focused on social questions in an attempt to gain mass political support and simultaneously sought to attract the most conservative political and ecclesiastical forces of the Alfonsine regime. Thus traditionalists intensified their propaganda campaigns, participated in mass pilgrimages and even opened social centres for workers in Barcelona and Bilbao.[45]

At the turn of the century, traditionalists accentuated the patriotic tones of their political discourse in response to the emergence of Basque nationalism and Catalan regionalism. These movements competed with traditionalism for a similar political market and seriously damaged Carlist popular support in Catalonia and the Basque provinces.[46] As mentioned above, traditionalists fiercely defended the *fueros* and proposed a decentralized Spain based on medieval laws. However, it is also important to notice that this conception of the nation, for all its emphasis on regional liberties, did not preclude an imperial idea of Spain in the traditionalist discourse. After all, the Carlists argued, it had been during the sixteenth century when Spain had created her world empire and maintained an internal division of kingdoms at the same time. Since the 1890s, all traditionalist factions ardently supported the Spanish struggle in the colonies. The military humiliation of 1898 was no discouragement: just three months after the defeat in Cuba, the Catholic Integrist daily *El Siglo Futuro* demanded the creation of a new Spanish colony in Morocco.[47] Soon after the intervention in Northern Africa was accomplished, Vázquez de Mella required in 1911 the revocation of the international agreements with France and Great Britain in order to strengthen the Spanish position in the Moroccan protectorate. According to this logic, if Spain was to have a 'moral empire' over the Hispanic American countries as Mella wished, she needed a more powerful expansion in Morocco.[48] Territorial gains were thus linked to 'spiritual expansion' in the imperial destiny traditionalists foresaw for Spain. The beginning of the First World War did nothing to placate Mella's imperial desires. In his book *El ideal de España* (1915), Mella explicitly declared himself imperialist and insisted on the need to claim Spanish total sovereignty over the Straits of Gibraltar, the federation with Portugal (the Spain *irredenta*) and a loose union with the Spanish American republics which would contemplate a common foreign policy under Spanish direction.[49]

This Pan-*Hispanismo*, which Mella confessed should imitate aggressive Pan-Germanism, was not without roots in the Spanish right. *Hispanismo*, the belief that Spaniards and Spanish Americans are members of the same 'race', had been an essential element in the discourse of Spanish politicians since the late nineteenth century.[50] Both the right and the left had used the idea of a transatlantic spiritual community as an external projection of the Spanish nation. On the right, Menéndez Pelayo had framed the intellectual bases of *Hispanismo* during the 1890s, stressing the Catholic, linguistic and cultural ties between Spain and its former colonies. After the loss of Cuba and Puerto Rico, this conservative *Hispanismo* gained a new impulse and a wider audience with the writings of Julián Juderías and José María Salaverría, who emphasized the Spanish concept of mission in America. The most popular work of these writers was Juderías' *La Leyenda Negra*, a book acclaimed by both press and public. A disciple of Menéndez Pelayo, Juderías denounced foreign powers for inventing the 'Black Legend' to diminish Spanish influence in the world and complained of the good reception this interpretation of history had had amongst Spaniards themselves.[51]

This new drive towards conservative *Hispanismo* has to be understood, first of all, as an optimistic nationalist response against the pessimism that invaded regenerationist writers after 1898. A good example of this patriotic optimism can be found in the writings of Salaverría, which angrily attacked the negative image of Spain portrayed by the artists of the Generation of 1898 and those foreigners that had invented the Black Legend. To overcome this 'masochism' that in Salaverría's view many Spaniards were suffering, the Basque journalist proposed the creation of 'a new Spaniard' proud of the nation's imperial history, advocated a rapprochement with the Spanish American countries and supported the occupation of the Rif.[52] Secondly, the imperial rhetoric and the promotion of *Hispanismo* have to be considered as a reaction against peripheral nationalism. Conservative newspapers like *ABC*, *El Debate* and *La Vanguardia* developed a deep anti-peripheral nationalist discourse in which the imperial past played the positive pole versus the 'mutilated' Spain wanted by

Catalan and Basque nationalists. The more peripheral nationalism grew at the beginning of the twentieth century, the more Spanish nationalism found in *Hispanismo* the sense of unity of the 'Spanish race', which implied the negation of Catalan and Basque nationalists' claims.[53]

There can be no doubt that in the twenty-five years that followed the 'Disaster' of 1898, a new authoritarian right emerged in the political arena turning nationalism into a key element of its discourse and modernizing the political attitudes of the conservatives. In this process, the traditionalist canon of Spain continued to develop. It invigorated its Catholic, imperial, corporative and anti-democratic character and incorporated new features such as radical militarism and anti-peripheral nationalism. As in other European countries, the new right showed a genuine will to gain mass support but in Spain, despite all its organizational and propagandist efforts, it failed both to reform the Restoration system and to attract great popular backing. By 1923 the authoritarian route of the military dictatorship was welcomed by all the new right groups. They hoped the army would impose on the masses their authoritarian view of Spain and implement their political agendas. It was something of an acknowledgement of their own failure to rally mass support.

A new Spanish nationalism in a state of siege

The emergence of the new right and the incorporation of nationalism as one way of coping politically with mass mobilization was the reflection of a changing society. During the first two decades of the twentieth century social and economic transformations accelerated and the state was partially modernized. These changes were to have a direct impact on the process of nation-building from the state, to the extent that during this period the complete nationalization of the Spanish political and cultural life was accomplished.[54] In other words, these were the years when the nation, and not the region or the town, became dominant in the field of social and political preoccupations.

To begin with, the loss of the colonies had the effect of increasing the integration of the national market. The Catalan textile industry lost its profitable market in Cuba and soon sought to gain new customers inside Spain. The political pressures of the Catalan bourgeoisie in Madrid proved fruitful and Spain significantly raised its already high tariffs to protect its products, which in turn led to the growth of the national markets. Secondly, during the two decades that followed 1898, the system of national education developed, urbanization proceeded and the transport system was enlarged, increasing the mobility of the population within Spain. On top of this, illiteracy was severely reduced, although it still remained high by Western European standards, and a mass press expanded creating a national market and invigorating the idea of an imagined national community.

Some of the state institutions also improved their performance as agents in the process of nation-building. Newly regulated, the public administration grew significantly in the first two decades of the twentieth century and state officers, such as magistrates and functionaries, became more influential in provincial towns and villages. More to the point, the liberal state attempted to develop a real national education system, which would include the entire population. Led by proposals of educational and social regeneration, the Ministry of Public Instruction was created in 1900, and diverse official institutions, such as the *Escuela de Estudios Superiores de Magisterio* (1909), the *Centro de Estudios Históricos* (1910) and the *Instituto-Escuela* (1918), followed. In addition, a massive corpus of legislation regulated state educational intervention, which led to serious improvements, especially in primary education, and confirmed public instruction as the agent of controlled social modernization.[55]

This state intervention has to be understood not only as an attempt to improve the appalling illiteracy rates, but also as a conscious means of nationalizing the masses in bourgeois values. As a Royal Decree plainly put it in October 1911, the curricula for adult education sought to put 'even more emphasis [than in primary education] in the formation of Fatherland loving citizens [. . .] respectful of the Law, Property, and other citizens'.[56] It is worth observing here that in this role of nationalization via education, both Conservative and Liberal governments played a key part. For all their rhetoric on the right of the Church to educate without state interference, the Conservatives (under Maura) promoted the role of state-controlled education and imposed compulsory universal primary schooling in 1909. Moreover, they were fully aware of the need to 'produce' a new patriotic youth that would 'place love for the Fatherland beyond all interest and conveniences'.[57] To achieve a complete 'national pedagogy', the Maurist Minister of Education César Silió argued, it was necessary to fight all those 'humanitarian, pacifist, anti-militarist, and anti-patriotic' doctrines taught in schools. He claimed these ideas were merely a 'hypocritical cover' of the left that sought to 'destroy those armed organizations that impeded the triumph of revolution'.[58] Nationalization went hand in hand with counterrevolution. No wonder that during Maurist rule several governmental initiatives aimed to transmit nationalist values. In September 1921, for instance, Silió created a patriotic prize awarded to the children's book that most inspired love for the nation. The following month, a Royal Order stated that there must be a portrait of Alfonso

XIII, 'as the head of the power that represented the unity of the Fatherland', in a visible place in all public schools.[59]

Not all state agencies were to improve their role in the process of mass nationalization. The army proved unable to be a competent institution in this respect in the first decades of the twentieth century. As shown above, the mounting military intervention in politics and the steady use of the army in social repression did nothing but increase popular anti-militarism throughout the period 1898–1923. Neither did the continuity of the unfair conscription system improve matters. In spite of the legislation reducing monetary redemptions introduced by Prime Minister Eduardo Dato in 1911, the system remained basically unchanged until 1921, and so did the understandable alienation of the popular classes from the army. Furthermore, in the countryside, the lower-classes' contempt for the armed forces was emphasized by the actions of the Civil Guard, a militarized force created to defend proprietors' interests in rural areas.[60]

At the political level, the dynastic parties did little to generate a cohesive national identity. For all the rhetoric of 'revolution from above' and national regeneration that followed the 'Disaster', electoral falsification and patronage continued to be the rule, thus hampering popular identification with the political system. Moreover, as the economy and society modernized, the system proved too rigid to absorb political opposition. The best alternative that the Restoration politicians found to confront political challenges was to increase the already intense military intervention in social repression, which in turn led to a higher popular alienation from the political system. Crucially, the steady growth of a socialist and anarchist proletariat, republican-leaning middle classes and Catalan regionalists meant not only an increasing challenge to the political system but also the social expansion of alternative identities to the official idea of Spain promoted by the Restoration elites.

Yet the dynastic parties seem to have realized the importance of the symbolic order in the formation of popular national identity. During the decades that preceded Primo's Dictatorship, the creation of national symbols was completed. It was then that Maura governments promoted the *Marcha Real* to the rank of national anthem (1908) and the national flag was made compulsory in every public building (1908). Again under Maura in 1918, 12 October, the 'Day of the Race' (*Día de la Raza*), was officially declared a national holiday in commemoration of the 'Discovery of America' by Columbus. The promotion of the 'Day of the Race' to the rank of official national holiday precisely in 1918 has to be understood not only as a step further in the endorsement of *Hispanismo* by the state, but also as the attempt to promote political patriotism and nationalist exaltation in the context of the dramatic institutional crisis that Spain was suffering since 1917.[61] In other words, stirring nationalist feelings among the population was thought to be the internal panacea for a seriously sick political system.

As in France and Germany, the 'monumentalist fever' of the 1880s and 1890s was to rise in Spain from the turn of century onwards. It was then that a group of artists connected to the Royal Academy of San Fernando built the monuments celebrating the nation's dead heroes and portraying the crown as the symbolic personification of the fatherland, the best examples of which were the sculpture of Eloy Gonzalo García, the 'hero of Cascorro' (Madrid, 1902), and the monumental complex to Alfonso XII in El Retiro park (Madrid, 1902). By an official directive, the same artists were active in the provinces, where all sorts of 'national' fighters were commemorated, from the Celt-Iberian resistance against the Romans (Numancia, 1905), through the sixteenth-century imperial commander-in-chief El Gran Capitán (Córdoba, 1909), to the heroine of the 'War of Independence' Agustina de Aragón (Zaragoza, 1908). All of them were manifestations of the process of creating from above a historical national identity that was gaining momentum precisely after the loss of the last colonies. These monuments, together with the ever-increasing construction of 'national' museums, libraries, theatres and archives, created 'sacred places' in which the national history and culture were venerated. After the turn of the century, the whole process of 'inventing traditions' was set in full motion in Spain. By 1923, an official image of the nation, as perceived by the state elites, had been consolidated.[62]

It is worth emphasizing here that the creation of a national 'civic religion' from above, with its symbols, holidays and shrines, usually emerged with associations to Catholic symbols, rites and traditions. As mentioned above, religion was a pivotal element in the traditionalist canon of the nation and even the moderate liberals maintained a strong identification between Catholicism and Spain. The 1876 constitution declared Catholicism to be the official religion of Spain and Cánovas soon accommodated the Church within the Restoration establishment, which meant ecclesiastical representation at almost every single public event. Thus it was no coincidence that one of the most notorious public ceremonies during the reign of Alfonso XIII was the King's consecration of the patria to the *Sagrado Corazón de Jesús*, in the opening of a huge monument devoted to its cult in El Cerro de los Ángeles (Madrid, 1902). Neither was it by chance that some memorials commemorating the 'War of Independence' were considered monuments 'to the martyrs of Religion and the Fatherland' at the same time, such as the one inaugurated in Zaragoza in 1904.[63]

This overlapping of the national and Catholic symbolism became even more obvious with the creation of the *Fiesta de la Raza*, for 12 October coincided with the popular religious celebration of the Virgin Pilar, which had already gained a strong nationalist flavour throughout the nineteenth century. The establishment of the Restoration seems to have realized that representing and celebrating the nation intermingled with religion in a country overwhelmingly Catholic was a good way to obtain popular support for the official patriotic ideal, without having to pay the toll of a real democratization of the political system.

The two decades that followed the 'Disaster' of 1898 definitively changed Spanish nationalism in terms of discourse and social scope. Ideologically, both the traditionalist and the liberal canons were reformulated. The former became increasingly martial, clerical, Pan-Hispanic and anti-liberal, and developed a deep hostility towards peripheral nationalism and the organized working class. Political parties, intellectuals, the armed forces, conservative newspapers, and a plethora of organizations generally related to the Church constructed a new Spanish nationalism in a siege situation. The fact that these groups were unable to come together into a single party should not lead us to assume the absence of a Spanish political nationalism in the years that preceded Primo's Dictatorship.[64] Indeed, most of the ideas that would eventually constitute the official ultra-nationalist discourse of the *primorriverista* regime were first formulated during the last years of the Restoration.

The endurance and centrality of Catholicism as a key factor in the traditionalist concept of nation and an element of social and political mobilization during the nineteenth and twentieth centuries debunks the assumption that Catholicism was a handicap for the development of a modern nationalism.[65] All the groups of the new right emphasized Catholicism as the constituent element of Spanish nationality and gained popular support in those rural areas in which the social influence of the Church was strongest. Furthermore, in the process of mass nationalization, the state overlapped civic and religious symbols, holidays and ceremonies to create collective memories and loyalties, with the active collaboration of a Catholic Church integrated into the establishment. Catholicism, far from being incompatible with the development of a modern nationalism, was rather an appropriate ideological, discursive and symbolic element for the creation of a national identity and the mobilization of social support.

In the field of nation-building, the first decades of the twentieth century signalled an important development in the nationalization of Spaniards. Socio-economic transformations and a partial modernization of the state were essential in the process of mass nationalization, in which Spain began to catch up with other European countries. It was somehow too late. At the turn of the century, alternative national and class identities were already challenging the official idea of Spain. Hence, the more repressive and counterrevolutionary the establishment became in the following years, the less attached the popular classes and middle-class regionalists felt towards the nation-state. The gap between the 'official' and the 'real' Spain was at its greatest when the military took power in September 1923.

The Dictatorship of Primo de Rivera inaugurated a new chapter in the development of Spanish nationalism. The heady ideological legacy of the regenerationists, military nationalism and the new right was then used to formulate an authoritarian discourse that openly challenged the liberal canon of Spain. Imposing this new canon on the masses required the modernization of the state, so that the perceived nationalizing deficiencies of the past could be rectified. Doctrinal elaboration and the creation of a new state were to go hand in hand in the *primorriverista* 'regeneration' of Spain.

2
The Military Directory (1923–1925): Discourse, Propaganda and Repression

> Our greatest eagerness is that the Spanish sentiment crystallizes in Catalonia for its own good
>
> (Miguel Primo de Rivera)[1]

On 11 September 1923, Catalan, Basque and Galician nationalists gathered in Barcelona to commemorate Catalonia's national day and demanded home rule for their regions. During the course of the demonstration some chanted slogans against Spain and in favour of the Rifean rebels in Africa, which led to violent clashes with Spanish nationalists and police forces. The street battle ended with thirty people injured. After the events, the military officers of the Barcelona garrison were fuming. For most of them this was the last straw of an escalating provocative offensive by separatists determined to destroy the Spanish nation. Noticing the high level of indignation of his colleagues, Captain General Primo de Rivera, who had been plotting an insurrection against the constitutional government for months, decided to bring forward the date of the coup – originally scheduled for 15 September. On the night of 12–13 September Primo declared a state of war in Catalonia, told the King about the insurrection, asked other captain generals for support and launched his manifesto. In Madrid, a group of generals that had also been plotting against the government formed a provisional junta. On 14 September, Alfonso XIII returned from his holiday in San Sebastian, declared his support for the insurrection, dismissed the constitutional government and invited Primo to come to the Spanish capital. The following morning General Primo de Rivera, Second Marquess of Estella, arrived in Madrid. After a brief meeting, the King named him head of a Military Directory with executive and legislative powers and dissolved both congress and senate. The coup had succeeded.

Very few shed tears for the collapse of the Restoration. To be sure, most of those benefiting from the political system, the elites of the Conservative and the Liberal parties, opposed the Dictatorship. But the very oligarchic nature of the political system meant the Liberal and the Conservative parties had virtually no rank and file to mobilize in defence of the constitutional regime. Social Catholics, Carlists, Catholic Integrists, Mauristas, and the Catalan regionalists of the *Lliga* all welcomed the coup. Even liberal intellectuals and newspapers, like *El Sol*, declared their support for the 'regenerationist dictatorship', on the understanding that Primo was to leave power in three months' time, as he had initially promised. Employers' associations, professionals' organizations, the Catholic Church and the different sections of the armed forces also showed their backing of Primo's insurrection. The fact that the peseta and the Spanish companies went up in the stock market immediately after the coup is telling of the confidence of the upper and middle classes in the new regime. Within the labour movement the response was mixed. The Anarchist trade unions and the tiny Communist party (*Partido Comunista de España*, PCE) called for a revolutionary strike and created a 'Council against the War and the Dictatorship'; but their actions were rapidly repressed and had virtually no impact. The Socialist party (*Partido Socialista Obrero Español*, PSOE) opted for not joining the Anarchist-Communist protest and decided to wait and see what the new situation would bring. From October 1923 the Socialist trade union (*Unión General de Trabajadores*, UGT) began to collaborate with the Dictatorship, while the PSOE remained aloof.

From the very first moment Primo seized power, the dictator was fully aware of the need to maintain a steady communication with public opinion. If the regime was to survive without a parliament it would need some sort of support from the masses. This backing was sought via political propaganda and popular mobilization following Mussolini's example in Italy.[2] In the field of propaganda, the Marquess of Estella initially sought to transmit his ideas and governing plans through press conferences, articles he wrote for friendly newspapers and 'official notes' (*notas oficiosas*). Given as often as twice per week, these press communiqués were declared of mandatory inclusion in all newspapers and represented the monologue that the dictator would maintain with the public for the entire Dictatorship.

As the regime was consolidated and Primo made it clear that he was to stay in power after the first three months of the Dictatorship had passed, the propaganda machinery improved. The dictator's speeches and notes were collected in diverse books and leaflets, the *Oficina de Información y Censura* was created to co-ordinate the regime line information both in Spain and abroad. The government also paid foreign newspapers to ensure the Dictatorship was portrayed in a positive light in the international press.[3] More importantly, the government showed itself especially keen on using state resources to promote the official message and seized control of over sixty regional newspapers. On 19 October 1925, *La Nación*, the regime's daily mouthpiece, was launched after a huge subscription campaign conducted by the Civil Governors in all the provinces and orchestrated by the Interior Minister (*Subsecretario de Gobernación*), General Severiano Martínez Anido.[4] The journalist chosen by Primo to direct the newspaper was Manuel Delgado Barreto, former editor of the Maurist daily *La Acción* and one of the founders of the fascist publication *Camisa Negra*. The following year, the journal of the regime's political party, *Unión Patriótica*, made its first appearance as a bi-monthly publication. Both publications soon claimed to have a circulation of 55 000 and 15 000 copies respectively.[5]

If the regime was anxious to provide itself with a propaganda apparatus hitherto unseen in Spain, Primo showed himself even more zealous when it came to silencing potential political critics. After the coup, the Military Directory made an extraordinary effort to preclude any sort of criticism from the press or, in fact, elsewhere. Martial law was declared in the whole country and was in force for eighteen months. High-ranking military officers replaced all Civil Governors and were instructed to punish 'with the most severe measures' all those questioning the Directory 'in the press or in conversations'.[6] Fully aware of the formative political role of the press, Primo declared that freedom of speech was a decadent right and that the media had to be controlled to avoid the people getting 'harmful ideas'.[7] In his view, the role of the media had to be the promotion of patriotic ideas, and any newspaper publishing otherwise should be banned.[8]

With the 1876 constitution in suspension since 13 September 1923, the Marquess of Estella established a prior censorship for all publications and, from January 1924 on, the Military Directory implemented a telephone and telegraphic censorship. The novelty of this censorship was its unprecedented scope and duration. Censorship had been often imposed during the Restoration whenever the government declared a state of war, but with Primo it reached a permanent status. The dictator personally created a censorship cabinet with the specific aim of banning 'every single rebel and opposition manifestation'.[9] Strongly centralized and responsible only to Primo, the cabinet was endowed with exceptional powers. It could cut paragraphs from articles, introduce official comments and corrections in editorials, ban entire pieces, impose economic sanctions and close down publications. It had authority over all public manifestations, including those made by the King and the dictator himself. The censorship cabinet also functioned as a press office, reviewing Primo's official notes before they were handed to the press and advising the President of the Military Directory on how to publicize political issues.

Censorship became the negative complement of the propaganda machine. Extended throughout the whole country and indiscriminately used by the government in *diputaciones* (provincial councils) and municipalities, the regime provided itself with an essential device to control public discourse and, therefore, to manipulate public opinion. The concentration of power in the figure of Primo de Rivera allowed him to put in place the machinery necessary to reduce political debate to a minimum. Thus he moved towards the governmental monopolization of public political discourse.

The secular nation

One of the most significant changes introduced by the Dictatorship was to bring the nation to the centre of the political discourse. From the manifesto of 13 September until the last day of the regime, Primo used a patriotic language in which the salvation and the regeneration of the nation became both the political aim and the justification of the Dictatorship.

The idea of the Spanish nation that the Marquess of Estella promoted heavily relied on the traditionalist canon. The dictator defined the nation as a 'supreme spiritual entity' forged by religion and history.[10] In his view of the historical formation of Spain, the different 'nationalities' of the Iberian Peninsula had unified into a single nation during the Middle Ages and crystallized in a 'sacred union' during the reign of the Catholic kings and the conquest of America.[11] By the turn of the sixteenth century, a 'providential unity' had been achieved via military struggles and 'civilizing' missions in the New World. Nevertheless, Primo's conception of the fatherland also integrated principles from the liberal vision of Spain. He considered the nation as composed of a community of citizens with equal rights and duties and the state was understood as the sovereign representation of the nation.[12] Indeed, during the first two years of the regime, Primo capitalized upon the secular ideological legacy of regenerationism, Maurism and, above all, military nationalism. The myths of the 'iron surgeon', the 'regeneration of the nation' and the Spanish empire became the essential points in the official discourse. In turn, these themes were used to justify the military Dictatorship and the destruction of the Restoration political class.

The discourse of national salvation delivered by the Military Directory was based on the organic conception of Spain popularized by the regenerationists. In taking power, the military believed they were saving a moribund Spain while they arrogated to themselves the interpretation of the will of the 'real' nation represented by the people. The manifesto and the subsequent declarations of the Marquess of Estella also showed that Primo considered himself Costa's 'iron surgeon'. During the initial stages of the Dictatorship, Primo declared his rule as a 'brief parenthesis' in the constitutional order to operate on the 'sick body of the nation'. The cure required extreme measures but would eventually extirpate the 'cancer' represented by the oligarchies. Once the surgical work was done, the argument followed, the gap between the 'real Spain' and the 'official Spain' denounced by the regenerationists would cease to exist.

The regenerationist discourse adopted by the Military Directory employed a profuse scientific vocabulary. Flamboyant medical metaphors illustrated an official rhetoric in which old political elites were represented as 'worms eating the nation', Catalan separatists portrayed as 'sick people' who needed to be cured, and Spaniards' psychology considered 'lethargic' (*abúlica*).[13] In adopting a regenerationist discourse, the Military Directory sought the backing of many different sectors of Spanish society. During the final years of the Restoration, regenerationist topics and vocabulary had penetrated deep into the Spanish consciousness, most notably among the middle classes, and the popularization of these ideas as expressed in Primo's manifesto had a large potential audience.[14] The fact that Primo at first found a firm support not only from all groups of the new right but also from important sectors of the conservative and liberal press shows the extent to which the myth of the iron surgeon had infiltrated Spanish society in the years prior to 1923.[15] It also indicates that the strategy of incorporating the regenerationist discourse initially paid off in terms of political support.

The revitalization of the fatherland demanded two essential and complementary achievements: the destruction of the ruling political class and the creation of a new type of 'patriotic citizenry'. Several policies were soon put into practice towards these ends. The destruction of the old oligarchies had begun with the coup itself and the substitution of Civil Governors by Military Governors, which deprived the *caciquil* network of the essential provincial connection with Madrid. During the first days of the Dictatorship, the directory issued new anti-*caciquil* legislation designed to undermine further the politicians' power base and to repair the public administration. The Royal Decrees of 18 September and 1 October 1923 reorganized the central administration following the criteria of efficiency, simplification and economic austerity so important to the military mentality. These decrees established the immediate removal of those functionaries who simultaneously held two posts and contemplated strong sanctions for any unjustified absences from work. Although these measures did not wipe out *caciquismo*, there can be little doubt that they were a propaganda success for the government. The wave of denunciations against politicians and municipal officials from the public and the good reception this legislation found in the press show how many sectors of society were delighted to see the old political elite dismissed and sometimes jailed.[16]

The creation of a new type of patriotic citizen was certainly a more ambitious task within the goal of national regeneration. Here Primo's ideas relied heavily on the Maurist concept of citizenry, as an interclass conservative conglomerate tantamount to the 'real Spain'. The idea of nation behind this concept of citizen was essentially civic. The fatherland, as one of the apologists of the regime put it, was 'composed by equal Spanish citizens with the same rights and duties'.[17] Primo was certainly more interested in obligations than in rights, and when describing his idea of citizenry he linked it to the 'fulfilment of four duties', namely military service, paying taxes, publicly supporting the regime, and working.[18]

The second main influence in the formation of the *primorriverista* concept of citizen came from the army barracks. As we saw in Chapter 1, military nationalist literature had popularized a series of authoritarian, irrational and militarist ideas among the officers in the years prior to 1923. The *primorriveristas* seemed happy to incorporate these ideas into the regime's discourse. Notorious among the ideas of the *primorriverista* military was the need to shape a 'New Man', a new Spaniard, in the form of the 'Citizen-Soldier'. The concept of Citizen-Soldier can be traced back to the writings of liberal officers in the 1890s.[19] However, thirty years on the idea had been transformed from a democratic educational ideal based on the French Revolution and the writings of Tocqueville into a romantic nationalist concept in which the goal was the formation of a 'permanent soldier', as part of the organic nation, acting in civil society.[20] This is not to suggest that the *primorriveristas'* view of the Citizen-Soldier was completely stripped of liberal ideas. The French Revolution's concept of the army as the 'nation in arms' and the idea of citizens' rights and duties were still present in the *primorriverista* literature of the 1920s. And yet the importance of romantic and irrational ideas was paramount in a discourse that constantly emphasized historic military deeds, religious vocabulary and patriotic symbolism over Enlightenment views. In fact, this concept of the Citizen-Soldier bore a close resemblance to the fascist *cittadini soldati*, which also took the French revolutionary myth of moral regeneration of the masses and transformed it into a policy of state-led authoritarian indoctrination of the entire population. As in the Spanish case, the ultimate goal for Mussolini was the creation of a new man, an *uomo nuovo*.[21]

The idea behind the creation of a new citizen was to co-opt the lower classes via nationalist indoctrination. As early as 1916, Primo wrote that the Great War would lead to 'key moral transformations' and called for propagating patriotic and military postulates not only in schools but also among adults in working-class areas.[22] In the period 1917–1923, the socio-political tensions in Spain and the post-Second World War revolutionary upheavals across Europe only hardened Primo's belief in the need to use nationalism as an antidote for revolution. Once in power, the formation of a new politically mobilized and militarized citizen became a priority. It was evident to the dictator that the emergence of patriotic citizens needed all the help possible from the state. The creation of the *delegados gubernativos*, the *Somatén Nacional* and the *Unión Patriótica* responded to different necessities, but they all had in common a role as 'educators' in nationalist values. The 'governmental delegates', military officers assigned to all judicial districts (*partidos judiciales*) in the country to 'supervise' local life, aimed at the destruction of the *caciquil* provincial network. But the Military Directory also wanted the *delegados* to create 'a new citizenry in towns and villages'.[23] This led to the organization of patriotic mass rallies and military parades in support of the regime together with the promotion of governmental campaigns on morals and patriotic duties. For this educational mission, the *delegados* were instructed to organize patriotic lectures, which should promote the virtues of the 'Spanish race' and emphasize the duties of defending the fatherland, respecting authority and paying taxes.[24]

The *delegados* were also regimented to organize the local *Somatén* in their districts, under the supervision of the captain general of the region. The extension of the Catalan institution to the whole country four days after the coup was an initial defensive measure to endow the regime with a civilian militia capable of backing the military government in case it came under pressure. Combined with the idea of mobilizing the population to maintain social order, the Military Directory conceived the *Somatén* as an organization devoted 'to strengthen the spirit of citizenry'.[25] As the Marquess of Estella stated, the *Somatén* was a 'school of citizenry' that was propagating the ideas of patriotic sacrifices and duties all around Spain.[26] The dictator also had great pedagogical plans for the UP. The members of the official party were encouraged to aid the Military Directory in 'shaping the soul of the Spanish youth' with nationalist values and in 1925 the Youth Sections of the UP were formed with that particular aim.[27] Moreover, showing his belief that even the poorest classes should be educated on nationalist principles, the dictator demanded that the party affiliates participate in the government's campaign for the eradication of illiteracy by creating an educational network in urban areas and the countryside. The network should reach every single family and its members would teach not only reading and writing skills but also patriotic values.[28]

An integral part of the nationalist discourse promoted by the *delegados*, the *Somatén* and the UP was the imperial myth. As explained in the previous chapter, the harsh contrast between Spain's imperial past and the 'Disaster' of 1898 had haunted the nationalist right during the first two decades of the twentieth century. It was no coincidence that Primo mentioned in his manifesto 'the picture of misfortunes and immorality which began in 1898 and threaten Spain with an early, tragic and dishonourable end'. For the dictator, who had served in Cuba and the Philippines in the 1890s, the loss of the empire was due to the incompetence of civilian rule and parliamentary politics. What followed the 'Disaster' was just a deepening of the progress leading towards national disintegration that the army had to put an end to in 1923. In other words, it was a distorted interpretation of the loss of the empire which nourished the ideological justification of authoritarian rule.[29]

The use of the imperial myth as discursive tool to justify the Dictatorship should not come as a surprise since the idea of empire lay at the very core of the military's concept of Spain. As explained by Primo, the nation's historical identity had been forged in the battlefields during the Reconquest. The empire in America was seen as the extension of the Spanish military spirit to the New World. For the army, the empire of the sixteenth and seventeenth centuries represented the peak of national grandeur, when Spaniards had successfully defended European Christianity against the Ottomans and expanded civilization to the Americas. Spain was then both the sentinel of Europe and the first civilizing nation in history.[30] It was this imperial rhetoric of Spain as protector of civilization that the Military Directory used to justify the persistence of the colonial adventure in Northern Africa. It is true that when Primo seized power he was well known for his position in favour of abandoning the Moroccan protectorate. In the years before 1923, he had stated repeatedly that the future of Spain did not lie in Africa, and proposed to swap Gibraltar for Ceuta with the British.[31] And yet, soon after seizing power, Primo realized that the survival of his regime was inevitably linked to finding a solution to the Moroccan problem. The intensification of the Rifean offensive in 1924 and the pressures from the Spanish officers in Morocco, the so-called 'Africanists', convinced the dictator that a withdrawal from the protectorate would have very serious political costs at home. In the summer of

1925, after securing French military aid, the Marquess of Estella opted for a complete military invasion of the protectorate.

It was no coincidence that in the months that preceded the main Spanish offensive over the Rifean rebels, the landing in the Alhucemas Bay on 5 September 1925, Primo rehashed the old imperial rhetoric. In early July, an official communiqué warned that 'a wormhole in the Rif would be a grave illness for Western peace and civilization'. Here, Primo argued that Abd-el-Krim, the Rifean leader, and 'his unborn kingdom could be the axes of a social-religious movement with a decisive influence in the West', since Morocco was becoming the place in where 'all the rebels of the universe [. . .] look for a field to cultivate their morbid microbes'.[32] The following month, when explaining why he had switched his policy on the Moroccan question, Primo alleged that the Communists had inflamed the rebellion and were about to create an Islamic-Bolshevik republic, which posed a real danger for Spanish national security.[33]

In portraying such a picture of the Rifean tribes Primo was following a long-standing Spanish tradition of depicting Moors as barbaric sub-humans, a view shared by middle and lower classes alike.[34] Nineteenth-century Spanish culture was imbued with myths about Moroccans, who represented the archetypal Other of Spanish national identity. At the turn of the century a layer of pseudo-scientific rhetoric and a veneer of civilizing zeal were added to the traditional romantic vision of Moroccans fostering the process of 'orientalization' of Africans.[35] By the 1920s, the *primorriveristas* added a new dimension to this process and presented the Moor as Communist – a feature that increased the alien nature of the external enemy and potential threat to Western civilization. A month after the landing of Alhucemas Primo's second in command, Martínez Anido, insisted on the supposed Communist nature of the African tribes and declared that Europe and America should be grateful to Spain for saving the civilized world from the Islamic-Bolshevist menace. Martínez Anido, who in the summer of 1923 had proposed a massive blitz of the rebel villages and corps with toxic and incendiary bombs, was also keen to proclaim the benefits of Western civilization and emphasized 'the numerous gains the Spanish protectorate [would] bring to the indigenous peoples'.[36] In promoting the colonial adventure in these terms the government presented a modern reinterpretation of imperial Spain, in which Rifeans became the substitutes for the American Indians and Islamic-Bolsheviks for the Ottoman menace. The novelty of the discourse lay in the introduction of the Communist threat and the biological vocabulary, but the main ideas of Spain as the sentinel of the West and a civilizer remained at the core of the imperial myth.

The practical use of imperial discourse was the justification for an extremely unpopular war in Spain. The Military Directory wasted no time in capitalizing on the victory. Although the war in Morocco was far from being over, a Royal Decree of 6 October 1925 described the landing in Alhucemas as 'the most arduous enterprise ever to be carried out by a colonial army' and awarded Primo the highest distinction of the Spanish military, the Gran Cruz Laureada de San Fernando.[37] If before the invasion of Alhucemas, Primo had been linked to Mussolini, Mustafa Kemal and even Lenin for his revolutionary zeal and his role as 'saviour of the fatherland', in the autumn of 1925 the *primorriverista* press compared the Marquess of Estella's military talents to those of Napoleon's.[38] The dictator himself considered it was a good moment for patriotic exaltation. When returning from Africa he delayed his arrival in Madrid in order to visit some towns in Andalusia and participate in public celebrations organized in his honour. Once in the capital, the dictator was awarded the title of 'Adoptive Son' by the mayors of the province of Madrid. Military parades were celebrated all around Spain to commemorate the conquest and the repatriated troops received a heroes' welcome in a tour organized by the regime in early October 1925. The final destination of the

Figure 2   Colonial troops parading in the streets of Madrid in October 1925. The Dictatorship was eager to capitalize on its victory in Alhucemas Bay and organized patriotic celebrations all around Spain in the autumn of 1925.

tour was Madrid, where the troops marched through the crowded streets of the capital in a parade presided over by the King and military, civil and religious authorities.[39] Eager to mobilize the population, the regime ordered the *delegados* to organize 'patriotic acts' in their districts in memory of those who had fallen for the patria. The reports of the *delegados* and the Civil Governors confirm that dozens of these 'patriotic acts' were successfully organized by the military. Some towns and villages even renamed their streets and plazas with the name of the dictator or the anniversary of the military coup as a part of the celebration.[40]

The sacred nation

Primo's regime pushed the identification of the nation with religion further than any other previous government. In the *primorriveristas'* view, Catholicism was perceived as an essential element in the historical formation of Spain and Spaniards were seen as essentially Catholics.[41] This religious concept of the nation was reflected in the prolific use of a Catholic vocabulary integrated into the *primorriverista* patriotic discourse. The dictator's speeches and notes were soaked in a religious rhetoric, in which patriotism was considered a 'faith', its propagation defined as 'preaching' and the members of the official party urged to become 'apostles' of Spanish nationalism.[42] For the Marquess of Estella, adoring the patria was 'sacrosanct', the national union 'holy', and talking against the fatherland 'a civic sin'.[43] His own role as the 'saviour' of Spain was repeatedly presented as God's will and Primo himself declared that Providence had chosen him to save the nation.[44] Put in another way, the civic myth of the 'iron surgeon' was sanctified as a divine figure by the regime's propaganda.

One of the biggest promoters of the religious-military concept of Spain was Alfonso XIII. The monarch, who had been educated under the tutelage of a traditionalist priest, made his ultramontane views very clear when visiting Italy in November 1923. At the Vatican, the King affirmed that Spain had been and still was 'the soldier of religion' and offered the Pope the utmost assistance should he declare a new crusade.[45] In return, Alfonso XIII expressed the hope that the Pope would use his influence to foster patriotic unity among the different regions and peoples of Spain. The idea was simple: nationalism and Catholicism were highly compatible and the promotion of the former had to be concomitant to the strengthening of the latter. The Vatican should promote the cult of the nation among its Spanish flock and the newly established military government would support Catholicism at home and abroad.

Such clericalist speaking truly shocked liberal newspapers, but the conservative press and the Catholic hierarchy warmly welcomed the speech. Rafael Sánchez Mazas, then the *ABC* correspondent in Rome and eventually one of the founders of the fascist party *Falange Española*, wrote that the 'petition for a Papal contribution to the union of all Spanish Catholics in faith and patriotism – both signs of the most elevated citizenry – constituted one of the essential points of what could be called our policy in the Vatican'.[46] The pro-fascist journalist urged the episcopate to assist the Spanish Dictatorship and, quoting Mussolini, demanded a new state legislation to 'harmonize civic and religious duties'. The Catholic hierarchy was also delighted. From the first, it had supported Primo and instructed parishioners to fulfil their duties as 'Christian citizens' praying for the patria, the King and the dictator.[47] After the royal visit to Italy, the Spanish prelates ordered the King's speech to be read in all the churches across the country. Even the Vatican seemed to have felt happy with the promotion of a sacred Spain. The Pope publicly blessed the 'Spanish nation' on various occasions and the nuncio in Madrid consecrated Alfonso XIII as the new 'Catholic King', while praising the Lord for the Christian victory of the Spanish army in Africa.

The use of the Catholic Church to indoctrinate the population with nationalist dogmas was one of the central strategies of Primo throughout the entire Dictatorship. The Marquess of Estella wanted the priests to get involved in the regeneration of the nation and demanded active ecclesiastical co-operation with UP members in their 'educational' campaigns.[48] The idea, the dictator confessed in a letter to his friend Admiral Magaz, was to use the Church politically and socially to propagate the unity of the fatherland and to combat Catalanism.[49] At first, the strategy seems to have worked and the Catholic hierarchy openly co-operated with the regime. For instance, when in late 1924 the government launched a propaganda campaign against its critics in exile, the dictator was pleased to find the Church gave its full support and mobilized its flock to demonstrate in opposition to some 'wrongly called Spaniards abroad'.[50] It was precisely the Church's support for the Spanish 'civilizing mission' in Morocco which pushed even further the identification of Catholicism with the nation. During Primo's and Alfonso XIII's official visits to Spanish towns, masses for those fallen in Africa or to commemorate Spanish victory over the Rifean rebels became a central part of the nationalist rallies and military parades. The consecration of the national flag and the blessing of the troops became paramount in these nationalist rituals, in which thousands of ordinary citizens took part.[51] The process of the 'sacralization of the nation' thus went beyond political speeches and was performed as a Christian ritual.

The religious character of nationalist ceremonies was not limited to the visits of the dictator and the King. One of the major contributions of the Dictatorship to the expansion of patriotic ceremonies was their propagation in towns and villages all around Spain. Together with the ceremonies for those fallen in Africa, the Fiesta of the Sanctification of the *Somatén* Flag was the most widely celebrated. Co-ordinated by Martínez Anido from the Interior Ministry and organized by provincial military authorities, the celebration usually followed a similar pattern everywhere. It began with a military parade by the members of the army and the local *Somatén* and it was followed by an open-air military mass (*misa de campaña*). Once the mass was over, the ecclesiastical authorities blessed the *Somatén* and the Spanish flags and delivered short speeches supporting the war in Africa and the Dictatorship at home. Then military authorities reproduced the official *primorriverista* discourse of blood, heroism and patriotic sacrifice in the African fields, while emphasizing the role divine intervention played in 'national deeds' from Covadonga during the Reconquest to the landing of Alhucemas. Frequently, the ceremony concluded with the official unveiling of a plaque devoted to the Spanish army or Primo de Rivera.[52]

Whether in huge urban ceremonies or in modest villages the Military Directory promoted a new type of nationalist discourse and ritual interweaving of religious and secular elements. At the discursive level, the Dictatorship interlaced scientific vocabulary with religious rhetoric and carried out a process of sacralization of the secular myths of the 'iron surgeon' and the 'regeneration of the nation' by linking them to divine intervention. The nation was endorsed with the Christian symbolism of death and resurrection, and the mystical connotations of blood and sacrifice of those fallen in Africa became part of the public 'communion' of the dictator with his people. Like fascist Italy, all these elements became essential ingredients for a new 'patriotic religion', which placed the nation on the main altar.[53] Unlike Mussolini, Primo's 'patriotic religion' had the initial blessings and active participation of the Catholic Church.

The state as protector of the nation

The Dictatorship amounted to a fundamental breach with the Restoration system in terms of the role assigned to the state. The military identified the state with the nation and stressed the function of the former in defending the latter. As Primo blatantly put it, the 'state and its laws' were the representation of the nation and the authorities had the duty to punish every single attack on the unity of the fatherland.[54] Moreover, the idea of constructing a modern, efficient and authoritarian state as a tool to regenerate the nation was in the very nature of military nationalism. The implications of this concern towards the state were soon felt after Primo seized power. Although Primo did not proclaim his new vision of a strongly centralized authoritarian state until 1926, the truth is that its construction had already begun during the Military Directory. With regard to the territorial division of Spain, Primo came to power as a defender of regional administrative autonomy. In the early hours of 14 September 1923, the Captain General of Catalonia drew up his first programme which included a new administrative division of Spain. Much in the same manner that Maurism had proposed, Primo advocated the creation of regional departments with administrative functions in the whole country. This new state division should lead to the emergence of 'strong regions' but, Primo warned, never 'to the loosening, or even the questioning, of patriotic ties'.[55] The initial option was the creation of regional departments seeking not only to crush the provincial networks of the *caciques*, but also to give equal status of administrative autonomy to all regions in Spain. Primo's initial regionalism was not so much concerned with regional liberties but with unification of regional legislation and minimization of Catalan particularities within the state structure. He clearly resented the 'special character' the *Mancomunitat* (the administrative union of the four Catalan provinces in 1914) had gained.[56] During his first months in power, the Marquess considered different options for a territorial reorganization, including the formation of ten or twelve regional administrations matching the military regions.[57] It is telling that among the plans were proposals for dividing Catalonia by creating a Valencien region including Tarragona and an Aragonese region with Lérida inside its borders.[58]

Yet the dictator soon abandoned these plans for regional division altogether and begun his restructuring of the state at the municipal level. Maurists and progressive regenerationists had consistently denounced *caciquil* control of town halls as the key problem that hampered national regeneration from the bottom-up. Primo was determined to remove that burden. A Royal Decree of 30 September 1923 dissolved all town councils and put them under military control. The decree also reserved to the government the right to choose the mayor of those towns with more than 100 000 inhabitants. Immediately after, the Dictatorship encouraged members of the public to anonymously denounce *caciques* to the military authorities, something that proved immensely popular.[59] During the following months, the wave of anonymous accusations was of such magnitude that the army found it difficult to cope with. In January, Martínez Anido wrote to all Civil Governors and delegates urging them to curb the number of detentions, for he feared that many of those arrested would be eventually released by the judges and this could damage the public's support for the regime.[60]

The creation of a new Municipal Statute was commanded to the young Maurist José Calvo Sotelo, then Director General of Administration, who formed a work team with Social Catholics, such as José María Gil Robles and the Count of Vallellano. After some weeks of deliberations and the direct 'advice' of Martínez Anido, the Military Directory approved the statute on 8 March 1924. The new law reflected an organic conception of Spain in which the municipality was described as a 'complete human society' that in turn formed 'natural base' of the state.[61] By stating that one-third of the town council members had to be elected by corporations, the Municipal Statute also introduced for the first time since the *ancien régime* the principle of corporate representation. This aimed to filter the 'natural' character of the locality and ultimately reaffirmed the organic dimension of the nation.[62]

Primo considered the municipality as the fatherland's 'primary cell' on which vigour partially depended the 'health of the national body'.[63] The province came next in the *primorriverista* endeavour to regenerate the nation. The second step towards the transformation of the liberal state was taken with the promulgation of the Provincial Statute on 21 March 1925. Calvo Sotelo and his team were again responsible for the work. As in the case of the Municipal Statute, they introduced corporative representation and reinforced the power of the state. The statute emphasized the province as a historical reality and the perfect link between the municipality and the state. Considered the natural bases of the state, the municipalities were represented at the provincial level by the *diputaciones*, which in turn were responsible to, and in fact controlled by, the Civil Governors. Since the Civil Governors were directly appointed in the Interior Ministry in Madrid, this state structure gave an indisputable power to the central government. The authoritarian political practices of the regime only confirmed the centralist character of the statute: the Civil Governors formed, dissolved and renewed both *diputaciones* and town councils as they pleased during the whole Dictatorship.[64]

This territorial and administrative conception of Spain had obvious ideological and political implications. In presenting the province as the direct link with the state, the statute eliminated the region as an intermediate bond. In fact, the new legislation specifically forbade the creation of any sort of association among provinces and, consequently, the *Mancomunitat* was abolished the same day the Provincial Statute was implemented. Primo's conversion to 'provincialism' was only a means of discarding his initial regionalism and creating a centralized state. In an official note coinciding with the promulgation of the Provincial Statute, the dictator explained his abandonment of 'historical regionalism'. The Marquess of Estella acknowledged that in 1923 he had believed that regional decentralization was a good way of 'strengthening the ties of national union in Spain', but the functioning of the *Mancomunitat* had forced him to change his mind. He argued that the Catalan institution had promoted anti-Spanish sentiments and exalted Catalanist feelings, which in turn were spreading pro-independence ambitions among the population. According to this logic, the creation of a regional adminis-trative div-ision of the state would lead to the glorification of regional particularities and, therefore, 'contribute to ruin the great work of the national unity'.[65] As Primo crudely put it in a letter to the former leader of the *Lliga Regionalista* Francesc Cambó, the masses' conceptions were 'simplistic' and could not understand subtle differentiations between the promotion of love for the region and the fostering of love for the nation.[66] Thus the idea of region, Primo insisted throughout 1925, had to be silenced for a quarter of a century so that the Catalanist problem would disappear.[67]

In portraying regionalism as the path to separatism, the regime opted for the identification of Spain with centralization as defended by military nationalism and, hence, the old Maurist and traditionalist idea of a regional Spain compatible with a great nation was jettisoned. When in the summer of 1926 the dictator announced his vision of a new state structure, the implications of the hierarchical, organic and anti-regionalist concept of the nation-state elaborated during the Military Directory became evident. In a new manifesto to the nation, Primo described the 'family, with its ancient virtues and its modern concept of citizenry', as 'the cell of the municipality'. The latter in turn constituted the basic unit of the nation and the province became 'the nucleus' of the patria. On top of them, 'the main vertebra in charge of directing the whole system' was the state.[68] It is worth observing that this concept of the nation as a hierarchical sequence of family, municipality, province and state not only put an end to whatever hopes of 'regionalization' the Spanish nationalist right may have had, but clearly anticipated the unitarian views defended by *Falange* in the 1930s and implemented by Franco for forty years.

In the short term, Primo's anti-regionalist drive was politically explo-sive. It constituted a frontal ideological attack on many groups which had originally supported the Dictatorship. Regional decentralization had been on the agenda of almost every single right-wing political group in the years prior to 1923. As explained in Chapter 1, Carlists, Maurists, Social Catholics and *lliguistas* demanded diverse forms of regional devolution. Furthermore, in the first two decades of the twentieth century, regionalist movements had emerged all over Spain, gaining a wide audience as a reaction to the pro-Catalan autonomy campaign launched by the *Lliga* in 1917. These movements presented the region as the essence of the Spanish nation and proclaimed the need to politically strengthen the former as a necessary step in the 'healthy regeneration' of the latter.[69] By presenting regionalism as the road to national dissolution Primo was not just challenging the ideological postulates of regionalists but also potentially undermining the social bases of his own regime.

The political backlash did not take long to materialize. Already in 1924, Vázquez de Mella had complained about the centralism of Primo and publicly advocated the political rights of the regions.[70] On 1 April 1925, Don Jaime, the Carlist pretender, addressed a manifesto to the Spanish people denouncing the Military Directory's centralist policies. Among his main grievances, Don Jaime listed Primo's attack against 'regionalist aspirations [and] very especially, against the feelings of Catalonia'.[71] The initial political truce between the Dictatorship and the Carlists was finally over. As a result the Military Directory forbade all Carlist propaganda and increased the pressure on traditionalist militants, arresting dozens of them and closing down Carlist centres around the country.[72]

Social Catholics found themselves in a difficult position. When founding the first UP sections in Valladolid in December 1923 they had made clear their regionalist aspirations.[73] However, when Primo changed his mind about regionalism, some cracks emerged among Social Catholics with regard to their support for the Dictatorship. In Zaragoza, for instance, the formation of the UP was delayed for some months due to the obstructions posed by the Social Catholics of the *Unión Regionalista Aragonesa*, extremely reluctant to support what increasingly seemed a centralist dictatorship.[74] In the following months, as the regime intensified its attacks on regionalism, Social Catholics remained silent on the issue. This was part of the political price Social Catholics had to pay for their co-operation with the Dictatorship.

Yet the most important *primorriverista* loss in terms of political support was the Catalan regionalist movement. The *Lliga* had welcomed the coup and during the first months of the Military Directory co-operated with the regime in Catalonia.[75] However, in January 1924, after a series of meetings with the dictator in Barcelona, the leaders of the *Lliga* realized Primo was not going to increase Catalan home rule.[76] On the contrary, he handpicked Alfonso Sala, a man from the Spanish nationalist *Unión Monárquica Nacional* to direct the *Mancomunitat* seeking to curb the influence the *Lliga* had in the regional institution. The following year the *Mancomunitat* was dissolved. The *Lliga* had not only failed to improve the level of Catalan autonomy but had lost the regional institution which it had controlled since its foundation in 1914. This could only alienate the regionalist faction of the Catalan bourgeoisie from a dictatorship it had been so eager to support. More dramatically, by 1925 the *lliguistas*, like all Catalan regionalists and peripheral nationalists, were officially labelled 'dissolving forces' working against the national unity. In the eyes of the *primorriveristas*, they had become the 'enemy within'.

The enemy within

Peripheral nationalism constituted the negative pole in the *primorriverista* conception of Spain. The army perceived Catalan, Basque and Galician nationalists as the 'internal enemy' aiming to destroy the sacred union of Spain. Only five days after the coup, the government promulgated the so-called 'Royal Decree against separatism', which aimed to employ an 'urgent and severe remedy' against the regional nationalist 'virus'.[77] In the preamble, the decree described the actions and propaganda of separatists as one of the biggest problems of the patria and a challenge to the 'state and people's security'. Article 1 put under military jurisdiction all crimes against the unity of the fatherland, whether verbal or written. Article 2 detailed a series of prison sentences for those propagating separatist doctrines in school and political meetings, and regulated death penalties for insurgent uprisings. In other words, less than a week after seizing power, Primo had modified the 'Law of Jurisdictions' and, as demanded by the army in 1906, crimes against the nation were finally under military jurisdiction. In this, the idea of the army as the protector of the nation reached full legal status.

The 'Decree against separatism' not only targeted those groups claiming independence for Catalonia, the Basque Country and Galicia. It also began a process of 'Spanishization' (that is, of nationalization in Spanish values or *españolización*) of Catalan, Basque and Galician provinces via cultural and linguistic assimilation. The decree made Spanish 'the official language of the state', compulsory in all public ceremonies of national and international character, and declared it obligatory to keep the records of all provincial and municipal institutions in Castilian. Also concerned with symbolism and ceremonies, the new legislation forbade the display of regional and local flags on all public buildings and vessels, while making compulsory the exhibition of the Spanish banner. Moreover, the display of regional flags considered 'anti-Spanish', namely the Catalan, Basque and Galician ensigns, was outlawed, both at public meetings and on private properties. The idea behind this legislation was not only to deprive peripheral nationalists and regionalists of their symbolism and propaganda. In effect, it granted a symbolic monopoly to Spanish nationalism in the public sphere, much in the same manner Mussolini had done by imposing the Italian national flag in all provincial and communal public offices.[78]

Of all the Spanish regions with alternative nationalist movements, Catalonia was by far the regime's main concern. For the *primorriveristas* Catalonia was sick with separatism and syndicalism and it needed to be cured.[79] As the self-styled iron surgeon put it, the regime's 'greatest eagerness [was] that the Spanish sentiment crystallize[d] in Catalonia for its own good'.[80] In order to fulfil this task the *primorriveristas* tried a combination of legislation, repression and nationalizing policies. It is revealing that just forty-eight hours after the coup, General Carlos Losada, Civil Governor of Barcelona, had already issued an edict ordering the display of the Spanish flag in communal public buildings and forbidding all regional and local ensigns.[81] On 19 September 1923, Emilio Barrera, the new Captain General of Catalonia, issued yet another edict reminding the public that Spain was under martial law, which meant all crimes against national security were under military jurisdiction. Among the crimes against the fatherland, the proclamation included oral or written attacks on Spain, its flag, anthem and any other national emblem, as well as mockery or disobedience of army officers and *somatenistas*.[82] Additionally, police officers visited bars, cafés and theatres informing managers and the public that singing *Els Segadors*, the Catalan anthem, was forbidden.[83] In the following months, Losada and Barrera launched an indiscriminate repressive campaign against all those they considered to be Catalanists. Scores of cultural associations were closed down, public officers accused of being Catalanists were dismissed or jailed, and municipalities, the *Mancomunitat* and the education system were purged by the military.

Despite its support for the coup, the Catalan Church was considered a propagator of Catalan nationalist ideas and therefore targeted by the *primorriveristas*. After returning from his visit to Italy in December 1923, the dictator warned that all those priests propagating ideas against the principles of authority and patriotism would pay a 'high price' as they did under the fascist government. The state, Primo threatened, would not show any weakness in dealing with these aspects.[84] General Barrera, a close friend of the dictator, developed the official discourse in Catalonia.

He publicly warned clerics that propagating Catalanist ideas constituted a 'very big sin' and called upon parishioners to manifest their contempt for those 'traitors to Spain', who 'worked against the Fatherland from the pulpit'.[85] In fact, actions preceded Barrera's words. On 21 September 1923, the *Pomells de Joventut*, Catholic youth groups of regionalist ideology controlled by the Church, were dissolved all around Catalonia. During the first weeks that followed the coup, many regionalist priests were jailed and, by the end of 1923, the Dictatorship closed down the Catholic Academy of Sabadell. In 1924, *primorriverista* actions against the Church continued apace: in February, the Capuchins of Barcelona were fined 500 pesetas for letting children hear mass with a white hood, symbol of the *Pomells de Joventut*; in June, Father Carreras, from the Catholic Academy of Sabadell, was sent into exile; in July, Father Fuster was arrested in Gerona and fined 500 pesetas for 'exceeding his religious duties'; the same month, the procession (*romería*) to Montserrat, the shrine of Catalanism, was forbidden by the *primorriveristas*.[86] During the following years, the Dictatorship kept up the pressure on ecclesiastical institutions and personnel, as priests continued to be arrested and exiled, ecclesiastical publications censored, processions forbidden, Catholic associations closed and teachers purged for teaching in Catalan.[87]

The repression of Catalan priests demonstrates that the regime was determined to use the state apparatus to curb the social influence of all those it deemed 'enemies of the fatherland'; even if this meant imprisonment and exile of clerics and potentially alienating the Catholic Church's support for the Military Directory. As shown above, the *primorriveristas* developed a sacred concept of nation and welcomed the help of the Church in propagating patriotic ideas, but when the nation was perceived to be under threat from members of the clergy, then confrontation and repression became acceptable. For the *primorriveristas*, the nation was the main deity and the state the supreme political institution. The Church could co-operate in the process of nationalization but always under the leadership and ultimate control of the state.

The supremacy of the state can also be detected in the 'Decree against separatism' and the polemic that followed. The political reactions to the legislation were illustrative of the dialectic between Spanish and peripheral nationalisms. Spanish nationalist groups applauded the law. *El Ejército Español* considered it showed Primo's talent as a state leader and predicted that the decree would lead to the end of the *Mancomunitat*, as 'a state within the state'.[88] Some sectors of the Catalan bourgeoisie became alarmed. On 30 November 1923, the President of the *Sociedad Económica Barcelonesa de Amigos del País* Francisco Puig i Alfonso and

Catalan entrepreneurs wrote a letter to the King demanding the abolition of the decree. Puig argued that Catalan was as Spanish a tongue as Castilian and reminded Alfonso XIII of the futility of imposing some languages and prohibiting others.[89] The dictator took the matter personally and answered Puig with a public letter six days later. In his response, Primo strongly denied that the state was persecuting the Catalan language. Moreover, he accused Catalan regionalists of discriminating against Castilian in Catalonia, especially since 1898 when 'the nonsense of preaching that the Catalans had a different character than the rest of the Spaniards worsened'.[90] It was the duty of the state, the dictator argued, to protect the 'common language' and to ensure that Castilian was known by all citizens. The state, the letter continued, had also the obligation of defending the symbolic representation of the nation and the indoctrination of its inhabitants. Hence, it must ban all symbols and education hostile to Spain as a way to protect the unity of the fatherland.

The promotion of Castilian as the only official tongue of the state illustrates the central role language had in Primo's conception of Spain. In April 1924, following the publication of a letter in which Madrid intellectuals expressed their support for the Catalan language, the Marquess of Estella was to insist on the 'sovereignty of the state' to defend Castilian language from been discriminated against by Catalan institutions.[91] For the dictator, the duty of the 'national leaders' was to make the Spanish race more homogeneous and expand the 'central language'. Regional traditions should be confined to 'museums and archives' insofar as they were a 'burden in the great unifying work of the Catholic Kings'.[92] Primo was resolved to fulfil his 'mission' and nationalize those areas of Catalonia, the Basque Country and Galicia where Castilian was not the first language. Shortly after the promulgation of the 'Decree against separatism', the Military Directory transmitted a royal order imposing compulsory education in Castilian without exceptions in the whole of Spain and forbidding Catalanist schools and textbooks.[93] In October 1925, and again in June 1926, royal orders appeared with sanctions against teachers who propagated 'anti-social and anti-Spanish doctrines in the classrooms' and taught in a language other than Castilian.[94] The idea behind these laws was that the promotion of regional languages led to the expansion of peripheral nationalism in an indirect way. Hence, the state had to promote education in Castilian only, so that peripheral nationalists would lose the potential support of new generations. The reaction from peripheral nationalists and regionalists was hardly surprising. They took refuge in cultural activities and concentrated their efforts on the promotion of the regional languages. The teaching in

Catalan, Basque and Galician became the main political demand made by the nationalist movements, which found in their opposition to Primo's educational policies a common cause.[95]

The limits of the negative discourse

When in December 1925 Primo formed the Civil Directory, a new government in which civilians replaced military officers in the cabinet, the ideological bases of National-Catholicism had been laid.[96] During his first two years in power, the dictator drew selectively from the principles of regenerationism, Maurism, Social Catholicism, and military nationalism to formulate a synthesizing discourse, which turned increasingly authoritarian and centralist. In the contents of official discourse, the patria gained an unprecedented religious connotation not only at a conceptual level but also in the fields of rhetoric, public ceremonies and symbolism. This identification between fatherland and Catholicism has to be understood as part of a process of the sacralization of the nation, in which secular myths and celebrations acquired religious connotations. In an attempt to mobilize the masses on its behalf, the regime sought to monopolize patriotism and took the first steps towards the creation of a 'religion of the fatherland'.

This was not, as has sometimes has been suggested, a liberal discourse nor was the Military Directory a liberal conservative dictatorship.[97] True, the *primorriverista* discourse incorporated some elements from nineteenth-century liberalism, such as the term 'citizen' or regenerationist rhetoric. And yet Primo took the most anti-democratic idea of the regenerationists (the 'iron surgeon') and transformed the concept of citizen into a militarized patriot similar to the fascist *cittadini soldati*. In addition to this, Primo's anti-liberal record was impressive. He suspended the 1876 constitution *sine die*; closed down Parliament; declared it to be the duty of the state to politically indoctrinate citizens; banned political opposition; censored all criticism of the regime (it is worth remembering here that censorship was introduced in 1926 in Italy); unleashed an unprecedented and arbitrary repression which saw the imprisonment of hundreds of political opponents; left the authority of the judiciary in limbo due to the continuous personal interventions of the dictator and his political servants; and purged the civil service, the municipal administration and the education system.

By December 1925, industrialists, landowners, employers, different sectors of the army, the hierarchy of the Catholic Church, the Social Catholics and the Maurists still fully supported the Dictatorship. Yet Primo's discourse and policies had alienated some of the political groups that initially backed the coup. Carlist and Catholic Integrists opposed the regime's centralist policies. Intellectuals and the liberal press resented the regime's repressive measures and the perpetuation of a dictatorship which had originally claimed to be a three-month parenthesis in Spain's constitutional life. As for the working class, those groups which in September 1923 had remained passive after the coup, by May 1925 were demanding the return to the constitutional system.[98] But the biggest damage in terms of the regime's popularity was felt in Catalonia where the *primorriverista* anti-Catalanist campaign was having counterproductive effects. As early as 1924, Calvo Sotelo observed that the situation in Catalonia was worse than ever. Not only was 'separatism' on the increase but many social sectors which previously had shown contempt for the pro-independence movement were now sympathetic to Catalan nationalism. Repressive policies, Calvo Sotelo warned, were useless against 'the problem of collective psychology and popular feelings'.[99]

Like many other nationalist discourses, the *primorriverista* rhetoric was intentionally vague and ill-defined, seeking to reach a wide audience familiar with a series of popularized topics.[100] This populist strategy, based on Primo's belief that the masses' understanding was essentially simplistic, was framed as a 'negative discourse' seeking to integrate different political groups in opposition to common enemies (*caciques*, peripheral nationalists, Anarchists, Rifean rebels and so on). By insisting on the various dangers threatening the fatherland, whether internal or external, Primo sought to legitimize the exceptional and illegal nature of his regime, while at the same time transforming the state structure via municipal and provincial reforms. Nevertheless, during the Military Directory the Marquess of Estella maintained that the country would eventually return in one way or another to the constitutional system of 1876 – even if the creation of the state-controlled UP, the new municipal and provincial statutes and the destruction of the dynastic parties indicated otherwise. The formation of the Civil Directory meant that the regime had to develop further its ideological bases. The creation of a new state required a further ideological development of the Dictatorship.

3
The Civil Directory (1926–1930): National-Catholicism and the New State

Against Bolshevism, the Dictatorship! Against subversion, the bayonets!

(Ramiro de Maeztu)[1]

When in December 1925 Primo de Rivera formed the Civil Directory a definitive step towards the perpetuation of the Dictatorship was taken. The dictator, who had announced in early November his will to change the constitutional framework and replace parliamentary democracy with a unicameral system based on corporative suffrage, openly oriented his regime towards an authoritarian model. The transition to civilian rule was accompanied by an attempt to reinforce the role of the UP and to endow the official party with a well-defined political doctrine. After a period of recruitment and organization, explained one of the Dictatorship's propagandists, the time had come 'to elaborate an ideology just as Gentile did in Italy years after Mussolini had seized power'.[2] Thus, the emergence into the political arena of a group of UP ideologues in 1926 was related to the Dictatorship's needs to provide the regime with a solid doctrinal base and to gain mass support for the official party.

José María Pemán, José Pemartín and Ramiro de Maeztu were the three main writers to develop the ideological tenets of the regime, both in the pages of *La Nación*, the regime's official newspaper, and in their own books. Pemán and Pemartín were newcomers to politics and played an outstanding role in the Dictatorship's organization and propaganda. They became what could be called the 'organic intellectuals' of the regime and eventually would hold key positions in Franco's government in the late 1930s and early 1940s.[3] By contrast, Maeztu, a well-known journalist and intellectual, already had a well-established political career by the mid-1920s. He was a member of the Generation of 1898, defended socialist views in his youth, and had turned into an authoritarian conservative during the years of the Great War.[4] During the Second Republic, all three, Pemán, Pemartín and Maeztu, were to be leading members of the extreme-right monarchist party *Renovación Española* and became regular contributors to *Acción Española*, the journal that was to play a key role in establishing the ideological bases of Francoism.

Admittedly, Primo's ideologues did not represent the vanguard of European conservative thought in the 1920s. The central importance of late nineteenth- and early twentieth-century traditionalism heavily conditioned their concept of the Spanish nation and the political postulates derived from it. The ideas of Menéndez Pelayo, Vázquez de Mella, Juan Donoso Cortés and Jaime Balmes are constantly found in the writings of UP essayists. Nonetheless, it is possible to differentiate a second main current of influence in the *primorriveristas'* thought, which endowed the regime's discourse with a touch of modernity. This trend came from the European radical right, including Italian fascism, the monarchist *Action Française*, Portuguese *Integralismo*, and the emerging currents of irrationalist and vitalist philosophers, such as Oswald Spengler, Hippolyte Taine, Henri Bergson and, above all, José Ortega y Gasset.

Both ideological streams were going to show a constant dialectic between the will to preserve 'traditional' values and the need to formulate a modern authoritarian doctrine according to what the UP essayists thought was the new European *Zeitgeist*, the spirit of the age.[5] Both currents were also going to endow the official discourse with an idiosyncratic language. On the one hand, the *primorriverista* was a 'baroque discourse', passionate and powerful, seeking to reach the whole of society and modify actions and attitudes of every individual. This discourse was based on the so-called three 'Ps of baroquism': poetry, purity and patria.[6] The *primorriverista* rhetoric showed a poetic style in the sentimentalism and the hyperbole of the lyrics of texts, in which Catholic concepts of salvation, purity and redemption conveyed a sense of exclusivity and unity in the idea of the Spanish nation. This baroque discourse, in turn, appeared frequently blended with a medical vocabulary used to explain the 'illness' of Spain and the way to 'regenerate' the fatherland. This was a scientific rhetoric directly bequeathed from Social Darwinist thought, which had often been used by both the European right and the regenerationists in Spain and later incorporated by Primo to the Dictatorship's official discourse during the Military Directory. In the period 1926–1930, Primo de Rivera's political lieutenants presented in their message an amalgamation of sacred and scientific 'truths', very similar to that found in the writings of Charles Maurras.[7] As in the French integral nationalism, this combination of religious and pseudo-scientific principles made the existence of contradictions in the *primorriverista* ideology unavoidable and endowed the official discourse with a dogmatic connotation which left little, if any, room for political discussion.

Discrediting liberalism was the major contribution of the regime's ideologues to Spanish right-wing thought. Philosophically, Primo's propagandists argued that the twentieth century had brought to an end 'rationalism, individualism, and all those universalistic perceptions of human equality' that had guided liberal political postulates in the nineteenth century.[8] Pemartín, who had been a pupil of the vitalist philosopher Henri Bergson in Paris, considered that Kantian rationalism and liberal individualism symbolized the past, the era that had ended. The new stream in philosophy was in his view represented by Oswald Spengler, José Ortega y Gasset and, of course, Bergson, whose works showed that the world was entering into 'the field of intuition, action, and vitalism'.[9] Maeztu was on a par with this philosophical approach. He considered valour and discipline as fundamental values in the modern man and, based on Nietzsche's ideas, advocated complementing 'rationalist activities' with 'sentimental and intuitive ones'.[10]

This philosophical critique of rationalism had a clear political goal. It aimed at creating a new ideology, whose first principle was 'a great and universal negation; the negation of nineteenth-century general and abstract political forms: Universal suffrage, Parliamentarism.'[11] Maeztu saw contemporary French and German philosophy was leading to new political doctrines. In *La Nación*, he wrote: '[a] new philosophy requires the renovation of political ideas. Liberalism is leaving. Collectivism is accompanying it. Something different is beginning to take shape.'[12] The Basque intellectual identified fascism, the works of Charles Maurras, Henri Massis, Antonio Sardinha (the father of Portuguese *Integralismo*), Enrico Corradini and, not very modestly, his own writings as the vanguard of 1920s European political thought.[13]

Liberalism was not only a senile creed; it also opened the gates to the establishment of a communist society, according to the National-Catholic theorists. In their bipolar conception of the world, liberal democracy aligned with socialism, communism and anarchism. Maeztu held liberalism 'responsible' for the rise of class struggle (and 'separatism' in the Spanish case), because, in the name of individual liberty, it had tolerated the destruction of the national 'social unity'. This, he predicted, would eventually 'lead to social revolution and civil war' in Spain.[14] Pemartín pushed the argument further and tried to prove that liberal democracy 'logically' and 'inevitably' led to communism, via universal suffrage. The

Andalusian philosopher sustained that after the French Revolution established the 'dogmas' of the Rights of Man and universal franchise the people was empowered to overthrow 'traditional, historical, social, and economic values, which were qualitative' by definition.[15] If free elections were to be held in Spain, the triumph of the left ultimately would impose a communist regime. After all, the Russian Revolution was just a 'direct descendant' of the French one.[16]

The sacred concept of the nation and the myth of anti-Spain

Primo's ideologues propagated an organic concept of the nation based on the traditionalist theory of society and proclaimed Catholicism to be intrinsic to the Spanish soul or 'race'. According to Pemán, who acknowledged that Vázquez de Mella had inspired his model, the nation was 'the live organism formed by men when they gather in society'.[17] The creation of the nation was considered the last step in a historical process of cohesion in which 'natural societies', like the family, the municipality, and the region had evolved and congregated to bring into being the fatherland.[18] From its very conception the National-Catholic idea of nation was endowed with an organic character and directly confronted nineteenth-century liberal individualism, which, in Pemán's view, represented society as a 'shapeless aggregation of individuals'.[19]

UP ideologues' interpretation of the Spanish nation was heavily influenced by the Catholic traditionalist historiography of the second half of the nineteenth century. They found the specific character in the formation of nations in the key role played by religion in European history. Pemartín argued that the nation was 'a creation of Christianity' and the Ancient world had not witnessed them because it 'lacked the moral unity of beliefs that would have allowed their emergence'.[20] Nations, he explained, needed a spiritual element above 'all the geographical, ethnic, philosophical, and historical factors [. . .] to be unified'.[21] Historically Spain had been the best example of that creative influence and Catholicism was portrayed as the core of the nation and the element that defined Spanish identity. The reign of the Catholic kings at the end of the fifteenth century was identified as the era in which religion had completed the formation of the Spanish nation.[22] The discovery and colonization of the Americas, the European territories of the Habsburgs and the battle of Lepanto against the Ottomans were portrayed as the supreme expression of the Spanish *Volkgeist*, as opposed to the Reformation, the Enlightenment and liberal revolutions, all of them considered intrinsically anti-Catholic and, therefore, anti-Spanish.[23]

Traditionalist interpretations were complemented with vitalist views of history. Primo's ideologues were deeply influenced by Oswald Spengler's understanding of history as a continium of vital cycles of creativity and decline. The German philosopher had argued in *The Decline of the West* that these historical cycles had a series of constants that could be drawn out of analogies of the diverse historical periods. Depending on these constants, the argument went, one could ultimately elucidate the rise and fall of civilizations.[24] Pemartín applied this irrational interpretation of history to the Spanish case, only to 'prove' that those periods of national grandeur were due to the pre-eminence of national essences, while the decadence of Spain was blamed on the introduction of 'foreign ideas', such as liberalism.[25] Moreover, Spengler saw the crisis of liberalism after the First World War as a turning point for Western civilization. He explained Western decadence by stressing the lack of aristocratic and heroic values in the liberal system and foresaw a new era of strong political leaders as the only solution to save Europe from barbarism. This was music to the ears of the *primorriveristas*, who repeatedly argued that the Dictatorship was the only way to stop Bolshevism from taking over Spain.

The UP essayists added to this view the definition of a Spanish spiritual character put forward by the Generation of 1898 in the previous decades. They mainly relied on Ángel Ganivet's *Idearium Español* to define a particular Spanish collective psychology. The *primorriveristas* shared Ganivet's determinist assertion of the existence of a 'territorial spirit', a consequence of the peninsular geography of Spain and its history, which endowed Spaniards with an 'independent character' and differentiated them from the rest of Europe.[26] This pseudo-scientific concept of 'territorial spirit', based on the works of Henry Buckle and Hippolyte Taine, emphasized the relationship between national character and environment and had been influential in France at the turn of the century. Ganivet considered Spanish character as a martial, stoical, intuitive, bellicose and spiritual one, but also depicted the Spaniards' psychology as 'lethargic' (*abúlica*).[27] Pemán and Pemartín went a step beyond Ganivet's geographical determinism. They portrayed Spanish psychology as 'particularist', a feature that acted in opposition to national consolidation. Hence, they inferred that liberalism and democracy were unsuitable to the Spanish character and argued the necessity for a strong government, a dictatorship, and for the regeneration of the nation.[28]

It is easy to discern here the importance of Social Darwinist thought in Primo's ideologues. Linked to the use of a religious rhetoric, the application of pseudo-scientific analysis and psycho-medical language to describe the nation as a living organism shows that there was a need to present the concept of Spain on natural science and deterministic grounds. As mentioned above, in doing so the UP luminaries endowed their discourse with a 'scientific-religious' dogmatism, similar to that found in their much-admired Charles Maurras. The political implications of the discourse were also akin. Like the French monarchist, using providential, idealist and vitalist interpretations of history, Primo's leading ideologues framed an organic concept of the fatherland in which the 'people' played no significant role in the formation and development of the nation. Unlike the liberal canon of the fatherland, Spaniards became a passive object on whom the 'national essences' were projected throughout history. Individuals were shown as merely part of an integral organic whole guided by superior and divine historical forces. As was the case in Gentile's fascist political philosophy, and earlier in the writings of Maurice Barrès, the Primo luminaries' approach to the nation led to the absolute subordination of the individual to the collective spiritual body.[29] Like French integral nationalism and Italian fascism, National-Catholicism attacked the idea of a plural society as a handicap to the spiritual union of the nation.

The connotations of the official concept of the nation as a living organism have to be understood within UP ideologues' tendency to present all political struggles as bipolar fights. In their view, the 1920s were witnessing 'the great world revolution' against liberalism and communism led by the principles of 'nation' and 'order'.[30] Fascist Italy, Spain under the UP, and Germany with the emergence of nationalist groups were different manifestations of the same phenomenon of formation of 'national blocs against communism'.[31] In the new contest the world was divided into 'national alliances and soviet alliances'.[32] The duality of the 1920s was clearly underlined by Maeztu: 'Civilization on the one hand; Bolshevism on the other. This is the issue of the present time.'[33] In the future, Pemán foresaw, the masses would be either 'Christian or Anarchic', different liberal political nuances were out of the question, and it was time to choose 'between Jesus and Barabbas'.[34]

This dualistic vision of the world political situation had its domestic version in the myth of the two Spains. The UP essayists defended the existence of a 'real Spain', represented by the Catholic working masses, opposed to the 'Anti-Spain', a miscellany of liberals, socialists, republicans, communists, anarchists, regionalists and Catalan and Basque nationalists, who continuously threatened the essences of the nation. To be sure, the myth of the 'two Spains' was not invented by the Dictatorship's ideologues, yet the *primorriverista* treatment of the concept integrated its different versions, transforming and renovating the myth into its modern form. The UP ideologues' main contribution to the theory of the 'two Spains' was to blend the traditionalist and the regenerationist currents, albeit in a very approximate manner. The *primorriveristas* represented the 'real' Spain as traditional and modern at the same time, whilst Anti-Spain became both the 'heterodox' and 'foreign' ideologies and the 'decrepit' and oligarchic Restoration system. On the one hand, the 'real Spain' was the 'historic Spain' that was defined by religious and monarchical values, as in the case of the nineteenth-century reactionaries. On the other, the 'real Spain' was the 'vital Spain', depicted as the great masses of working, modern Spaniards who made the country progress. Vital Spain was the 'vast majority of the common people' who had stayed away from the old political system.[35] Consequently, the 'real Spain' acquired a modern, regenerationist, inter-class connotation. The *primorriverista* discourse gained clear populist tones seeking support from those middle and lower-middle classes which had felt alienated from the oligarchic Restoration system.

The UP essayists blurred the ideological distinctions among liberals, republicans, socialists, communists, anarchists and peripheral nationalists and portrayed all political adversaries as a united whole: the Anti-Spain. This mythological figure was not only opposed to the 'national essences' and worked to destroy the fatherland, but was also described in pathological terms. From Pemartín's viewpoint those supporting democratic and left-wing ideas were 'hallucinated dogmatics', 'mentally sick people, [who] had no cure'.[36] To Maeztu, who also liked to use the 'cancer' metaphor to refer to the 'enemies of the fatherland', socialists had 'turbulent and confused minds which prefer passion to truth and step by step were incubating a profound hatred against intelligence'.[37] This characterization of the 'internal enemy' in such terms was mainly a process of dehumanization of the political opponents. In doing so, the official discourse aimed to legitimate coercion and violence against all those opposed to the Dictatorship. Maeztu put it in a crude and blatant way: the nature of Bolshevism was nothing but 'the revolt of the sub-human being against civilization'.[38] It made no sense to negotiate with Bolsheviks because their 'resentful and sick souls' would not understand the reality of the world. The solutions were plain: 'Against Bolshevism, the Dictatorship! Against subversion, the bayonets!'[39]

A similar approach was taken when dealing with regionalists and peripheral nationalists. Repression from the state and a centralist organization of the country were the two main measures proposed by the ideologues to combat the 'separatist problem'. As Primo himself proclaimed, the state had 'the duty to confront anyone harming the unity of the fatherland' and no middle ways would be used to ensure the 'oneness of the nation'.[40] As the *primorriverista* intelligentsia (a term that I use in a descriptive sense rather than as a qualitative evaluation) acknowledged, the regime had to base its policies on a 'forthright and prompt repression of all separatism and disrespect for the common Fatherland'.[41] This repressive measure had to be complemented with 'the development of an intensive provincial policy', as opposed to a regional one.[42]

The regime's repressive reaction was the quintessential one of a dominant nation-state when facing the emergence of a different nationalism within its boundaries. In these cases nationalist agitators of a non-independent country are accused of inventing artificial problems. At the same time, the region of the nationalist agitators is punished with sanctions. In turn, the punishment consolidates those alleged artificial problems and reinforces the very nationalist phenomenon whose mere existence was denied by the authorities.[43] In fact, this was exactly the case in Catalonia and to a lesser extent the Basque provinces, where *primorriverista* repression led to the reinforcement of nationalist tendencies and the consolidation of a popular nationalist left in Catalonia. Moreover, the repression aligned Spanish Republicans, socialists and Catalan nationalists in their fight for a democratic republic.[44] The association between the left and Catalan nationalism that the *primorriverista* ideologues denounced was in fact the outcome of the dictatorial policies.

The myth of Anti-Spain was often presented together with the idea of a universal plot against Spain. Behind the internal and external opponents to the Dictatorship, the official press insisted, there were obscure forces conspiring against the fatherland. The Soviet government was ultimately held responsible for the actions of anti-Spaniards of all types.[45] The social protests of the years 1917–1920, Rifean resistance, peripheral nationalists and anarchist actions . . . virtually every movement of opposition was regarded as controlled in the shadows by Moscow, in what has to be considered as the institutionalization of the 'Bolshevik threat' by the *primorriverista* regime.[46] As in French integral nationalism, the resort to a Masonic-Marxist-democratic plot was wrapped in providential vocabulary, seeking to portray an apocalyptic picture of the world.[47] Providing this threatening vision of the global political situation aimed at creating a sensation of insecurity in the audience. At the same time, this discourse allowed the representation of the Dictatorship as the only possible solution for Spain. Just as Mussolini had done in Italy before seizing power in 1922, the *primorriverista* discourse portrayed all political parties as incompetent, unable to stop the labour movement and responsible for the social unrest; whilst the UP was meant to aggregate the 'real' national forces and prevent the rise of the left.

The regime's employment of the mythological figure of Anti-Spain and its parallel legend of the Masonic-Communist international plot clearly sought to integrate the audience into a nationalist political community and to mobilize support for the Dictatorship. But the *primorriveristas* faced a serious paradox that certainly diminished the impact of the utilization of the myth of Anti-Spain on the audience. The institutionalization of the 'Bolshevist threat' could have potentially appealed to a large section of the middle and upper classes, which had been terrified by the social unrest that preceded the Dictatorship. However, the official discourse steadily emphasized that the main achievement of the new regime had precisely been to end that social unrest and to deliver 'order' and discipline to the country. The 'success' of the Dictatorship in dismantling and repressing organized labour seems to have convinced the bourgeoisie that the military were the proper instrument to control the working class and that the crisis of the years 1917–1923 was finally over. Under the Dictatorship, the bourgeoisie did not feel the country was suffering a socio-political crisis and, therefore, the appeal of the myths of Anti-Spain and the Masonic-Marxist-democratic conspiracy was severely reduced and their ability to politically mobilize sectors of the middle and upper classes decreased. The lack of perception of a political crisis and the economic boom of the 1920s would partially explain the failure of the myth of Anti-Spain in gathering together larger sectors of the population around the UP, as opposed to the power of mobilization the same myth would eventually have during the Second Republic and the Civil War.

The regeneration of the nation and the creation of the new state

The idea of regeneration acted in the discourse of the regime's ideologues as the positive pole of the Anti-Spain. An ideal-typical common denominator which lay at the core of fascist ideology, the rebirth of the nation was the main tenet in the Dictatorship's propaganda. Pegging the ideas of Costa, Ganivet, Ricardo Macías Picavea and Ortega to their discourse, the *primorriveristas* presented the regenerationists as the intellectual forerunners of the UP.[48] This representation of regenerationist ideas was a biased, selective and simplistic one. It intentionally overlooked a general advocacy for a genuine democracy in the regenerationists' writings and twisted all their postulates on national regeneration towards anti-liberal and authoritarian solutions. For example, while Ganivet had disapproved of dictatorship as the means to carry out the regeneration of Spain, the

UP theorists argued the *abulia* of Spaniards' psychology and the 'mental damage' done by the liberal politics could only be entirely removed by a government of coercion, force and order, that is, by a dictatorship.[49]

Aware of the need to propose new national goals to Spanish society as a way to strengthen patriotic sentiments the *primorriverista* intelligentsia proposed various routes. As far as the concept of regeneration is concerned, it is possible to differentiate two main themes on which the official discourse framed the idea of a new nation: *Hispanismo* and Spanish Morocco. Neither of them was in fact brand new as topics of Spanish nationalism, but certainly both of them were to acquire a renovated strength during the Dictatorship. More importantly, they were conceived as a means to nationalize society on the principles of National-Catholicism. Pemán did not hide his intentions when he declared that the governmental aim of these 'collective enterprises' was to 'give a sense of unity to the nation' and to strengthen 'the affirmation of our [Spanish] personality – one and powerful – in the international arena.' Moreover, these 'national aspirations' were being promoted to 'shock the totality of society and beget the necessary social consciousness'.[50]

Pemán also understood the domestic utility of the Hispanic-American ideal. He portrayed Mussolini's territorial demands towards France, Austria and Greece as an attempt to buttress Italian nationalism within Italy. Spain needed to follow the fascist example and promote 'a policy of national affirmation, of Spanish cohesion and unity', in order to create an 'imperial consciousness'.[51] *Hispanismo*, Pemán claimed, had to be at the core of this new imperial consciousness and work to inculcate Spaniards' nationalist goals. It also represented the antithesis of peripheral nationalism and regionalism. The 'rebirth of the imperial consciousness', Pemán insisted, 'is in itself the very negation of all movements of [national] dissociation'.[52]

The second of the 'great collective enterprises' the ideologues proposed to the Spanish people was the colonial adventure in Africa. Like Pan-Hispanism, it had a clear neo-imperial connotation. In many respects, the UP luminaries simply followed the line the dictator and Martínez Anido had established during the Military Directory: Spain was fighting against barbarism and Bolshevism in the name of Western civilization.[53] The same Manichean rationale that we have seen in the ideologues' attack against peripheral nationalism can be appreciated here. It also had a domestic political objective, for it sought to endow Spanish identity with a strong counterrevolutionary flavour that would cement unity among Spaniards on religious bases. Maeztu, for instance, confessed his dream was to see his 'Fatherland becoming the vanguard of the Counterrevolution, as it was of the Counterreformation in the sixteenth century.'[54]

To accomplish the regeneration of the nation, the UP ideologues reckoned that what was needed was not just a strong dogmatic system but also mighty state institutions. Patriotism was a powerful sentiment 'to stir the human being' and had to be encouraged. But patriotism would not last unless it was 'tied to a system of ideas by individuals and to an order of institutions and laws by society'.[55] The *primorriverista* intelligentsia regarded the importance of both the elaboration of a nationalist doctrine and the state agencies as two complementary elements for promotion of nationalist feelings.

The first effective step towards a new authoritarian state was the creation of the National Assembly (*Asamblea Nacional Consultiva*), the government-controlled chamber which substituted the constitutional *Cortes*. Following the advice given to him by Mussolini, Primo sought the formation of some sort of parliament in order to gain international legitimacy for his regime.[56] The dictator had advanced the idea of a new unicameral assembly as early as November 1925.[57] In July 1926, the UP National Congress took the decision to create a new corporative parliament that would represent the 'natural' entities of the nation: family, municipality and province. On 4 September 1926, the UP Central Committee asked the government to organize a plebiscite in order for the Spanish people to give a vote of confidence to Primo and to express its desire to have a national assembly. The dictator immediately called the plebiscite for 11, 12 and 13 September and declared all men and women over 18 would be allowed to participate, that is, to sign in favour of the government and the formation of a national assembly. After a week of intense propaganda and orchestrated mobilization by military officers, civil governors, public servants, *somatenistas* and UP rank and file, the plebiscite took place with no guarantees whatsoever. UP members and *primorriverista* town councillors set and controlled all polls. Not surprisingly, Primo won the plebiscite: the government collected 7 478 502 affirmative signatures, an estimated 57.04 per cent of the men and women with the right to sign.[58]

The project of the National Assembly, however, soon encountered problems. Different sectors of the right feared they would lose out in the new authoritarian model Primo was trying to create. Their fears were understandable, for the official propaganda warned the National Assembly should be based on corporative representation and would mean the final and definite dissolution of political parties.[59] The goal of the new chamber was to integrate all social classes, via 'corporative and class suffrage', and reach 'efficient solutions' for the problems of the nation, especially in social and economic matters.[60] Initially, the King also opposed the Assembly for he realized it meant the institutionalization of the Dictatorship

Figure 3   The statue of Eloy Gonzalo, the Spanish national hero of the colonial wars in Cuba, in the Plaza de Cascorro in Madrid. The statue is covered with *primorriverista* propaganda asking for the yes vote in the 1926 plebiscite.

and increasing Primo's power vis-à-vis the monarch. Signing the decree for the formation of the National Assembly effectively meant burning all bridges for an eventual return to the Restoration, a system in which the King was the supreme arbiter of the political situation. But Alfonso XIII also understood that Primo's support was still considerable. Despite his reticence and under pressure from the dictator, he finally signed the decree convoking the National Assembly in September 1927.[61]

This conception of the National Assembly was conditioned by the influence of both traditionalist corporativism and Italian fascism.[62] The government controlled the entire process of selection of the 400 members of the Assembly from the Ministry of Interior. Civil governors and mayors were instructed by Martínez Anido on whom to select representing the provinces and the municipalities. Most of its members were chosen representing the state administration or the UP (including Pemartín, Pemán and Maeztu), while a minority represented professional groups such as lawyers and academics. The government always kept a complete control over its own congress. The *Asamblea Nacional Consultiva*, the first corporative chamber in post-war Europe, was divided into eighteen sections, each of them formed by eleven members. The President of the

Assembly, in agreement with the government, chose the members of each section and proposed the topics to be analysed – generally related to economic and technical matters. Once the section had discussed the issues assigned it produced a consultative report for the executive. The government could then take the report into consideration or ignore it. The National Assembly had no power whatsoever to question the actions of the executive. It was just a puppet of Primo designed to integrate different political currents under the institutional umbrella of the Dictatorship.

Notwithstanding the participation of Social Catholics and some conservative politicians of the Restoration regime in the National Assembly, the new chamber utterly alienated liberals, who complained that its corporative nature was a direct attack on the most elemental democratic principles. The radical political implications of the creation of the National Assembly were clearly perceived by *El Sol*. In early October 1927, the liberal daily highlighted the fact that not even in Italy had parliament and universal suffrage been abolished. Spain was the only European country where parliamentary institutions had been replaced.[63] The socialists also refused to join the *primorriverista* charade. Members of both the PSOE and the UGT rejected the invitation to become Assembly members. Rather than integrating the different strands of support for the Dictatorship the creation of the *Asamblea Nacional* exacerbated the difference between political groups.

Even those who accepted the dictator's invitation soon realized that Primo did not want the National Assembly to discuss any sort of policy, but rather to rubberstamp his decisions. In January 1928, Víctor Pradera, the main ideologue of the traditionalists after the death of Vázquez de Mella, accused Primo's centralist policies of having a negative effect. In a debate at the National Assembly, Pradera told the dictator his repressive approach to the regional question was in fact fostering peripheral nationalism and advocated the political representation of the regions. Primo's reply was categorical. First, the Marquess of Estella firmly denied the accusations. Then, he blamed the 'weak governments' of the past for the emergence of Catalan nationalism and confirmed state repression as the main policy to suppress peripheral nationalism. Finally, he forbade any further discussion of the regionalist question in the National Assembly in the future and announced that 'the Government, responsible for the Nation's Power, feeling itself assisted by the unanimity of the national thought, will ban all discussion on regionalism in the press, books, and cultural centres.'[64]

The following step in the construction of the *primorriverista* state was endowing the system with a new supreme law and the First Section of the

National Assembly was commissioned with the drafting of a new constitution. The dictator constituted the section which was formed by important figures of different conservative groups, such the traditionalist Pradera, the Maurists Antonio Goicoechea and Gabriel Maura, the conservative Juan de la Cierva and a majority of UP members: José de Yanguas Messía, Carlos García Oviedo, Pemán and Maeztu. Once again, Primo sought integration of right-wing currents under UP supremacy. However, it did not take long until the first clashes emerged in the First Section. When the former members of the Conservative Party demanded a return to the 1876 constitution, only adding some amendments, the *primorriveristas* opposed them and defended a radical rupture with the Restoration system.[65] Maeztu proposed the substitution of universal ballot for a corporative suffrage and the restriction of the 'right of citizenship' to those who supported the government.[66] Pemán publicly insisted on the need to reject the 1876 constitution and create 'a new modern and effective organization' of the state, which should encourage the executive power and concentrate on the economic issues of the nation. It was time 'to go from the individualist state to the social state'.[67]

When the final draft was completed in July 1929, no one was pleased with the result. Liberals, conservatives, republicans and socialists came together to publicly reject the constitutional draft. Alfonso XIII also disliked the text and, in private, reiterated his desire to return to the 1876 constitutional model. More importantly, the dictator showed serious reticence over adopting the text, for he considered the new constitution gave too much power to the King.[68] The Dictatorship had reached a cul-de-sac and the plans to implement the new authoritarian constitution were abandoned in the autumn of 1929. The efforts of the First Section had been in vain but the experience was eventually seen under a positive light by the *upetistas*. In the 1930s, the most radical *primorriveristas* were to regard the constitutional draft as the 'germ' of the new 'doctrinal movement' they were setting up against the democratic Second Republic.[69]

The creation of a corporative system to regulate national production and eliminate class struggle was doubtless one of the main contributions of the Dictatorship to the formation of a new state. The corporative reform was masterminded by the Minister of Labour, Eduardo Aunós, who framed the system combining doctrines of fascism, Georges Sorel's syndicalism, and late nineteenth-century Social Catholicism.[70] Aunós wanted the new system to be the backbone of a modern technocratic corporative state.[71] Fascinated with the Italian example after his meeting with the fascist leader Giuseppe Bottai in Rome in 1924, the Spanish Minister of Labour created a state-controlled corporative organization. The *primorriverista* system was divided into 27 corporations and controlled by 27 corporative councils (*consejos de corporación*), which covered all sectors of the economy. Aunós also formed arbitration committees (*comités paritarios*) to resolve disputes between employers and workers. Crucially, the corporations were conceived not only to solve labour conflicts but also to inculcate in both 'workers and employers a great patriotic feeling',[72] that is, to indoctrinate the population in nationalist values. It was, after all, a system embedded in organicist theories of German nationalism, closer to the models of the European radical right than to Social Catholicism.[73]

Such a fascist leaning in the structure of the state proved highly controversial. The system was soon severely criticized by many industrialists, landowners and Social Catholics, who considered it led to a huge state interventionism.[74] They also resented the involvement of the socialist UGT in the corporative model, which in many cases meant the exclusion of the Catholic trade unions from the *comités paritarios*. It was precisely at this point that the new corporative system became a challenge to ecclesiastic interests, since the non-incorporation of Catholic trade unions into the *comités paritarios* seriously hampered the Church's attempts to expand its social influence and to defeat the forces of secularization. The Catholic daily, *El Debate*, criticized Aunós' system as centralist and denounced the state manipulation of the *consejos* and *comités*.[75] Social Catholics especially lamented the formation of *comités* in the countryside (for they thought it would pave the way for a socialist takeover) and managed to paralyse the implementation of the *primorriverista* agrarian legislation.[76] The opposition of the Social Catholics was especially damaging for the Dictatorship. They represented one of the main bases of social support for the regime and feeling betrayed by the government led many of them to abandon the UP from 1928 onwards.

Aunós' model was designed to co-opt the moderate sectors of the labour movement into a system that attempted to indoctrinate workers in patriotic values. Yet the political price paid by the Dictatorship was enormous. The UGT accepted the invitation to participate in the arbitration committees, but it did not renounce industrial action. As social conflict grew in the years 1928 and 1929, so did the government's repressive measures against the labour movement. In the last years of the Dictatorship, the *primorriveristas* closed down 93 UGT local branches, which seriously antagonized the socialists and thus hampered the effective functioning of the arbitration committees.[77] The corporative system also alienated employers, who thought the arbitration committees benefited workers. This meant that large sectors of the upper and middle classes, which had supported the regime precisely on the basis of crushing the working class, felt betrayed when the corporative system was created.[78] On top of this, when in 1926 the Chancellor of the Exchequer, Calvo Sotelo, announced a tax reform aiming at collecting more revenue from benefits of the landed upper and middle classes (whose benefits were in most cases simply not declared to the Inland Revenue), the most important professional associations of landowners, farmers, industrialists and employers reacted in anger and eventually forced Primo to withdraw the plan. Things took a turn for the worse. In 1928 Primo made public his intention to implement a land reform which seriously alarmed the rural oligarchy. The following year the financial policy of Calvo Sotelo collapsed and the peseta plummeted in the stock exchange. Landowners and industrialists began to reconsider their support for a dictator who they now deemed was turning against them.[79] In the autumn of 1929, as the economic crisis deepened, the employers demanded the dissolution of the arbitrary committees but Primo refused to give in.

The construction of the new state ended up alienating all those groups that initially supported Primo. The National Assembly, the constitutional project and the corporative model antagonized employers, landowners, Social Catholics, the Church, liberals, republicans, socialists and the King. By early 1930, the regime was in a terminal crisis. On 4 January 1930, Calvo Sotelo resigned, admitting his economic policies had failed. Three weeks later, it was Primo himself who was forced to go.

National-Catholicism, fascism and the *primorriverista* heritage

What is the place of the Primo de Rivera regime among the European dictatorships of the interwar period? A political science comparison may tell us that the *primorriverista* regime was more similar to Pilsudski's dictatorship in Poland than to Mussolini's in Italy. Military-controlled governments and the creation of an official party as a mechanism of social control are common elements in the 1920s Greek, Polish and Spanish dictatorships.[80] But from a historical perspective, the truth of the matter is that in terms of ideology and political goals the UP luminaries looked to Rome for inspiration, not Warsaw. Primo's propaganda machinery steadily presented the Spanish and the Italian dictatorships as equivalent historical movements. It claimed both regimes had defeated Bolshevism and regenerated their nations in a similar authoritarian manner. It also forecast that the UP would follow the Italian example in the mobilization of the masses.[81] The UP theorists contributed to the promotion of this parallelism and stressed in the press the ideological similarities between the two dictatorships.[82] However, such an apologetic view of fascism did not mean a mimetic assimilation of Italian doctrine but rather a selective incorporation of some principles and ideas. Thus the conception of the UP as anti-party, the *Führerprinzip*, the corporative system, the state intervention to overcome class struggle, and the need to mobilize the masses, were ideas similar to (when not directly taken from) fascist postulates; whilst some other aspects, such as the non-confessional character of the fascist state or the clashes between the Italian government and the Vatican, led the UP essayists to censure Mussolini's standpoints.

The UP essayists' occasional criticism of the Italian dictatorship has been considered as evidence of the ideological differences between National-Catholicism and fascism.[83] Pemán's negative characterization of the fascist state as 'agnostic' and Pemartín's disapproval of the 'divergences' between the Italian government and the Church are usually portrayed as examples of this ideological discrepancy.[84] This view, however, overlooks the steady defence Primo's ideologues made of fascism as a modern political doctrine and fails to recognize that the aim of the Spanish thinkers was to present fascism as compatible with Catholic political doctrines. It was not by chance that, when in November 1928 the Catholic daily *El Debate* launched a campaign criticizing the increasing power achieved by the state in Italy and the fascists' quarrel with the Vatican, Pemartín responded virulently from the pages of *La Nación* defending Mussolini's regime.[85] He argued that Mussolini's postulates were attuned with the Vatican doctrine (especially Leo XIII's anti-liberal theses) and suggested the 'Roman Question' would be solved simply by locating 'fervent Catholics in the Fascist high ranks'.[86] It was a matter of people not of doctrine.

This attempt to incorporate fascist postulates into a hard core of authoritarian conservatism was by no means exceptional in the European right. Conservative regimes all around the continent began in the 1920s to borrow selectively from the Italian example – a tendency only to be increased in the 1930s with the Nazis in power.[87] This process of ideological *fascistization* and the political alliances among fascists and conservatives in many European countries have made the task of differentiating between fascism, the radical right and other forms of conservatism all the more difficult for historians. Nevertheless, for analytical purposes it is possible to differentiate at least two strands of a new right-wing thought in the interwar period: a radical right, as represented in the main by fascism, and a conservative right, which included constitutional conservatism but also various currents of conservative authoritarianism.[88]

Among the different groups of the radical right there were, surely, ideological differences. Fascism represented, at least on paper, a form of revolutionary ultra-nationalism for national rebirth that was based on a vitalist philosophy. Fascists considered their respective nations as being in a state of decadence due to the effect of liberal and democratic institutions and sought to create an authoritarian system led by a new ruling elite that would bind society together within a new social order.[89] Mussolini's party and regime were, of course, the touchstone of fascism in the 1920s. Other groups in the radical right which emerged as a reaction to the socio-political changes of the first quarter of the twentieth century were also extremely nationalist and opposed liberalism and democracy but their political views relied more on traditional religion than Italian fascism. *Action Française*, for example, was virulently anti-Marxist, violent and defended a hierarchical social order; yet the ideas of mobilizing the masses and transforming class structures were not as discursively prominent as in the fascist case.[90]

If we are to locate UP ideology within the European framework of the new right of the 1920s, National-Catholicism would represent a significantly *fascisticized* Spanish variant of the radical right, which went beyond the postulates of both liberal conservatism and reactionary traditionalism and bid for an authoritarian and centralist state. True, National-Catholicism incorporated ideas and policies from the Italian regime. Yet the discourse of Primo's ideologues cannot be considered fascist *sensu stricto*. Their core postulates resembled much more those of *L'Action Française*, both in their use of Catholicism as an ideological tool to promote a hierarchical social order and in their limited will to change social structures.

It is in the conception of the nation and the political principles derived from it where we can find the key differences and similarities between National-Catholicism and fascism. As shown above, at the core of the UP discourse lay the organic concept of the nation in which Catholicism is identified as the essence of Spain. Based on a providential and vitalist interpretation of history, the nation is endowed with a sacred quality in its inception and Catholic religion defended as the Spanish *Volkgeist*. As in any other nationalism defined by ethnic factors following the German romantic tradition, including Italian fascism, the nation is portrayed as a living organism to which individuals and territories are completely subordinate. As opposed to the 'civic' model of nation defended by liberals, Spanish National-Catholic identity is not linked to any sort of political rights or liberties, but rather by a spiritual character: religion. However, while in the fascist example the concept of fatherland originates from a secular concept of nation, and later incorporates Catholic rhetoric and rituals, in the case of National-Catholicism the very concept of nation was endowed with an essential Catholic connotation. As opposed to the fascists, the *primorriveristas* directly incorporated religious ideas, myths and rituals into their nationalist discourse.

Yet the trees of difference should not preclude us from seeing the forest of similarities. Mussolini and Primo's regimes emerged from analogous socio-political crises in the aftermath of the First World War.[91] This had an impact on the ideological similarities of both dictatorships. Nationalism and counterrevolution became the main tenets of both regimes because they were considered the most appropriate ways to overcome the leftist challenge. The idea of the nation as the supreme sacred value, the use of the state as a means to indoctrinate and control the whole of society, the attempt, at least on paper, to overcome class struggle via 'national solidarity' were all common elements in fascist and National-Catholic ideology. Primo and Mussolini realized the profound transformations brought about by the Great War and considered new challenges required new measures, such as rebuilding the nation-state and incorporating the masses into the political system via anti-democratic mobilization. As a result, both dictatorships produced a twin populist and Manichean discourse of national rebirth and fighting the anti-nation – a black and white picture that could simplistically explain a rapidly changing Europe.

The political discourse bound to this concept of the nation was violently authoritarian and it established a double ideological rupture with conservative and traditionalist doctrines in Spain. First, the ideologues of Primo de Rivera went beyond Maurist postulates by defending an absolute rejection of liberal political principles, including universal suffrage, the constitution of 1876, parliamentarism and political parties. Here, the influence of the new European radical right became paramount. In this sense, it is difficult to accept the view that 'the ideologues of the regime belonged to a not radically anti-parliamentary traditional right' and their postulates were far from fascist ideology.[92]

Second, National-Catholic discourse clearly detached itself from traditionalism in several main issues. Here, the assumption that Primo's theoreticians were unable to go beyond the traditionalist political discourse seems highly questionable.[93] The defence of a centralist state, the fascist influence in the formation of a single party and the conception of the corporative organization in which the state was to play a dominant role are all examples of issues that differentiated the *primorriveristas'* position from both Social Catholics and traditionalists, and indeed led to the political confrontation of the latter with the Dictatorship. Moreover, the invocation of tradition and national glories among Primo's political collaborators did not mean an attempt to return to an idealized past, as was the case with the Carlists. Rather, the *primorriveristas* wanted to build a new political regime in keeping with modern times, while preserving what they deemed to be national essences.

The significance of National-Catholicism as an ideology has also to be considered in the light of its own historical development and the highly influential role it was going to play during the Second Republic and Francoism. Soon after the fall of Primo in January 1930, ex-ministers and ideologues of the regime gathered together to form the *Unión Monárquica Nacional* (UMN). In April 1930, Maeztu, the Count of Guadalhorce, Calvo Sotelo, Pemán, Pemartín, Vicente Gay, Delgado Barreto, and the son of the dictator, José Antonio, founded the new party in an attempt to replace the UP. The political discourse of the UMN did not vary substantially from the one of the UP, reproducing its apocalyptic vision of Spain if democracy was to succeed. During 1930 and early 1931, the main propagandists of the UMN campaigned around Spain, praising 'sacred violence' to retake power and accusing both liberal and conservative monarchist parties of being willing to return to the 'decadent' parliamentary system.[94] In turn, the dynastic right openly condemned the UMN's ideological radicalism and ostracized the *primorriveristas* because of their belligerent model of action.[95] The abrupt breach with the formulae of the dynastic right that began during the Civil Directory continued after the fall of Primo's regime.

The coming of the Second Republic on 14 April 1931 did nothing but accelerate the ideological radicalism of the *primorriverista* intelligentsia. In December that year, the Alfonsine Monarchists, as the former *primorriveristas* came to be known, published the first issue of *Acción Española*, a political journal created to develop a theory of counterrevolution able to endow civil-military insurrections against the Republic with a doctrinal base.[96] During the following years those who gathered around *Acción Española*, and its political party, *Renovación Española*, steadily propagated the beliefs that they had first anticipated during the Dictatorship. True, opposition to a democratic state gave the *primorriveristas'* discourse a more traditionalist flavour. And yet the main principles of *Hispanismo*, militarism, the myth of Anti-Spain, the incorporation of fascist ideas and the sacred concept of the nation remained at the core of 1930s National-Catholicism.[97]

The *primorriverista* influence on authoritarian thought in the 1930s went well beyond the members of *Renovación Española*, since it also provided the doctrinal bases of what has been considered the 'real' Spanish fascism of *Falange* and the *Juntas Ofensivas Nacional Sindicalistas* (JONS). The Spanish fascists, led by José Antonio Primo de Rivera, inherited the concept of Catholicism as 'co-substantial' with the nation to frame a discourse in which the unity of Spain, the imperial dreams, the condemnation of Enlightenment thought and the exaltation of Mussolini became paramount in the same manner the UP propagandists had done the previous decade.[98] This ideological bond has to be understood in two ways. First, it is important to bear in mind that the characteristics of fascism in every country partially derived from the specific national traditions in terms of conservative and patriotic rhetoric.[99] In this case, the doctrine of Primo's ideologues was the final contribution to the Spanish nationalist tradition and certainly paved the way for the *Falange*. Second, the political, economic, and even family links that the *falangistas* had with figures of *Renovación Española* facilitated not only the funding of *Falange* and the JONS but also the process of mutual ideological reception.[100] Thus the advent of Spanish fascism did not occur suddenly in the 1930s, but rather represented a process of ideological crystallization of *primorriverista* nationalism from the previous decade onwards.[101]

The Civil War was the final step in the ideological development of the Alfonsine Monarchists. It was during these years when they openly advocated the merging of Nazism and Italian fascism with traditionalist postulates to formulate a 'Christian Totalitarianism', as the bases of the 'National-Catholic state' – the Spanish variant of the regimes of Hitler and Mussolini.[102] This ideological task had an extension at the political level. Pemartín and Pemán actively intervened in the creation of the *Falange Española Tradicionalista y de las Juntas Ofensivas Nacional Sindicalistas* (FET y de las JONS), the single political organization that fused *Falange*, the Carlists, and the rest of the rightist groups under Franco's leadership in April 1937.[103]

The former UP ideologues also took a leading role as propagandists of Franco's nationalists. Soon integrated in his provisional government, they defended the army as the redeemer of the nation and emphasized the struggle against Anti-Spain in religious and pathological terms to justify the uprising against the democratic Republic and the subsequent repression of Republicans.[104] The same totalitarian rationale that the *primorriveristas* had employed ten years ago was then applied in the process of dehumanization of the 'internal enemy'. Pemán's famous work, *The Poem of the Beast and the Angel* (1938), in which supreme Good has to fight a 'crusade' against Evil, was only one of the numerous writings exhorting this course of action.[105] In the late 1930s and early 1940s, however, the destruction of the 'internal enemy' was no longer a political metaphor; it became the actual physical extermination of political opponents.

Franco, who himself subscribed to *Acción Española* during the years of the Second Republic, sought a kind of national regeneration, based on the Catholic idea of redemption and a bastardized version of regenerationism, which was nothing but a duplicate of that elaborated by Primo's intelligentsia.[106] The same 'baroque' rhetoric of Patria, Purity and Poetry was used *ad nauseam* to gain control of society after the war.[107] Indeed, the entire Francoist corporate state was constructed on these ideological bases in which nationalist postulates, violence and economics were inter-related to frame a totalitarian Spain that, as in the cases of Italy and Germany, was able to protect existing traditions, while adapting them to modern times.

4
School of Patriots: the Army's Indoctrination of Soldiers

> Gentlemen, have you ever considered that over the next ten years approximately one million Spaniards will complete military service? Just imagine . . . One million Spaniards! Imagine that those men when they leave the barracks for the last time take away embedded in their brains the idea of the fatherland. [Because] the fatherland is a common good that has been willed to us and we must transmit it entirely to our successors.
>
> (Emilio de Rueda)[1]

The role of the army as an agency of nationalization is often highlighted as essential to the process of nation-building. By its very nature, the army of the modern state has become an institution devoted to fostering the feeling of national unity among the masses. Daily life in the armed forces requires soldiers to expand local attachments and to consent to, if not accept, the ideology of the state. Nineteenth- and early twentieth-century systematic conscription provided European states with the possibility of teaching the language of the dominant culture and indoctrinating a vast part of the population in patriotic values. With its rituals, ceremonies and regimental schools, the army grew to be a 'school of the fatherland' in which all social classes were integrated and national allegiance was forged.

And yet historical analyses have proved that the army as a nationalizing state agency was not without its problems. At the turn of the twentieth century, the process of nationalization of the masses within European armies was hampered by several factors. First, military service meant the temporary loss of crucial manpower for many families and, therefore, a severe economic disruption. In addition, a system of monetary exemptions allowed the upper classes to pay in order to get their sons exempted from military service. Understandably, the lower classes saw military service more as a burden for the poor than a universal duty to protect national interests. In France, for instance, anti-militarism was prominent in rural areas and rates of draft evasion and desertion remained high throughout the entire nineteenth century.[2] In Italy, the ruling class did not show sufficient zeal in spreading liberal values via military service, nor did the attempts of the liberal state to create a systematic plan to increase national identity among the recruits, find any success. Before the First World War, indoctrination into the army remained weak and even the effort to create a soldier's handbook to promote national consciousness failed.[3]

The situation was very similar in Spain. As we saw in Chapter 1, the frequent use of the army in social repression, the Moroccan War and the maintenance of monetary exemptions perpetuated the popular classes' alienation from the army. This can be clearly detected in the popular press and culture, where dozens of books, theatre plays and songs denounced a conscription system that benefited the rich. At the other end of the social ladder, the upper classes and the bourgeoisie showed little interest in contributing in person to the military. The widespread use of monetary exemptions by these sectors of the population clearly hampered inter-class integration into the national ideal. Moreover, the state faced serious problems in incorporating recruits into the national army at the turn of the century. Figures of draft evaders and those declared unfit or exempted were extremely high from the time of the colonial wars in Cuba and the Philippines, and remained so during the first two decades of the century.[4] Notwithstanding the introduction of new legislation reducing monetary exemptions in 1911 and 1912, official figures of the period 1914–1923 show that 46 per cent of potential recruits never joined the army, because they were declared exempt, physically unfit or they simply deserted.[5]

This failure contrasted with the military officers' idea of an army-led national regeneration that firmly took root in the barracks during the twenty-five years that preceded the Dictatorship. For decades Spanish officers were educated in the belief that national regeneration was only possible if they were able to inculcate strong patriotic feelings among the population and, therefore, to 'make' better Spaniards that would, in turn, improve the fate of the fatherland. As political tensions increased in Spain, so did the number of officers that advocated a dual role of the army as nationalizing agency and social pacifier – in fact two sides of the same coin. Echoing the regenerationist discourse, officers insisted on a better distribution of wealth combined with nationalist education as the best manner to transform society from above.[6] In all cases, the nationalization of the masses aimed to stop the growth of socialist and anarchist ideas.

Notwithstanding the political differences among officers, it is possible to detect two major common points in post-1898 military literature.[7] First, officers considered their educational task as sacred and presented themselves as 'apostles' of the nation. Primo de Rivera, himself, gave voice to this belief in 1916, when he wrote that the 'ideal of the Fatherland' must be 'sermonized and popularized religiously'.[8] Symptomatic of this nationalist discourse soaked in religious terms was the main role military educators accorded to the flag and the anthem as sacred representations of the fatherland. Well aware of the emotional power of symbols, army textbooks paid special attention to the holy meaning of the national emblem. The military presented the oath of allegiance as a religious ceremony and associated national symbols with the family, ancestors and national heroes, in an attempt to inspire loyalty to the patria by appealing to emotive feelings.[9] The very insistence on promoting national symbols in the army also suggests that military educators were conscious of the minimal impact patriotic emblems had on the population before recruitment.

Secondly, military literary production and the press clearly show that during the Restoration army officers were fully aware of the shortcomings of the military as an agency of nationalization. The main burden was clearly monetary exemptions and the lack of a truly universal conscription. Demands for the reform of military recruitment were common among the officer corps and did nothing but increase after 1898.[10] In addition to universal conscription, officers stressed the need for a different kind of military instruction. Teaching in military academies and barracks was seen as ineffective, monotonous and lacking in physical education. Instructors proposed to turn the emphasis from technical into moral education and the improvement of the physical education system, as the way to form healthy and well-indoctrinated patriots.[11]

By 1923, army officers had been educated for more than two decades in the idea that the military was not succeeding in nationalizing the masses. It is within this context of state failure to turn the army into an institution that encompassed all classes and promoted patriotic feelings among them, that the *primorriverista* use of the military as an agency of nationalization has to be understood. For an institution that had taken over the state proclaiming that the nation was on the verge of disintegration, the employment of military service to strengthen patriotic values amongst young Spaniards was not surprising. Once in power, Primo carried out a reform of army structures, the military education system and the recruitment scheme in an effort to intensify and broaden the transmission of nationalist ideas amongst both soldiers and officers.

Shaping officers

Instruction and control of officers became of extreme importance if the regime wanted to succeed in nationalizing the population, or indeed to assure its own political survival. Although all the different factions of the Spanish army (*junteros*, Africanists, *palaciegos* and the Artillery Corps) gave Primo their support in overthrowing the Restoration regime, this was more of a ceasefire between them than a proper integration under a single figure. How the regime was able to incorporate these factions was the key to the Dictatorship's performance and, hence, Primo's endeavour to unify military doctrine under his supervision. *Primorriverista* propaganda made its way into the military clubs and garrisons via lectures and publications. The Dictatorship created the appropriate framework for the promotion of military publications, granting them official status and distribution and, from early 1926, officers were encouraged to produce patriotic works as part of the regime's campaigns of nationalization.[12] Monetary awards, official recognition and prestige seem to have been a good incentive for military authors. Literature on patriotic indoctrination flourished and an important number of new official books, addressed both to military instructors and soldiers, circulated in the barracks during the Dictatorship.

Accompanying the boom in the publication of army textbooks and pamphlets, the regime orchestrated a series of lectures and training courses for those officers who had educational responsibilities. Even civilians serving as reservists, the so-called *oficiales de complemento*, were considered 'apostles of the fatherland' and trained to promote militarist feelings 'in schools, factories, mines, workshops and the countryside'.[13] Primo himself was at the fore of the most important campaigns, such as the 1927 lecture series at the Casino de Clases in Madrid. In the opening lecture, the dictator devoted his speech to explain to non-commissioned officers (NCOs) the educational role of the army in civil society. He insisted upon the sacred duty NCOs had in propagating patriotism and military values, not only when instructing soldiers but also in their daily life dealing with civilians outside the garrison.[14] When in March 1929 the regime organized a two-week course in Toledo to teach officers how to indoctrinate civilians with patriotic ideas, the entire Dictatorship's intelligentsia was summoned. In late February, the dictator personally addressed his ideologues encouraging them to participate and, finally, Pemán, Pemartín, Aunós, Calvo Sotelo, Yanguas, and Pérez Agudo were among the lecturers in the course.[15] It is important to notice here that the impact of the lectures went far beyond those attending the meetings, since the official propaganda machinery was always keen on producing and distributing books after the events. For example, once the course in Toledo finished, the *Junta de Propaganda Patriótica* published a volume of the proceedings. The dictator wrote the preface and ordered 20 000 copies to be printed for the first edition. Out of this first edition, almost 2000 copies were sent to military schools, libraries, clubs and barracks.[16]

Primo's search for unity of doctrine and comradeship among corps was to find momentum with the creation of the General Military Academy (*Academia General Militar*, AGM) at Zaragoza. The idea of an academy in which cadets from all different corps studied for two years together had been implemented in the first General Military Academy at Toledo between 1882 and 1893. This was something the Marquess of Estella knew well, since Primo had been a cadet at Toledo. Reforms in military education and the reopening of the AGM were soon on the *primorriverista* agenda. In February 1924, Primo announced his intention of creating a new military general academy and, in September that year, a committee was formed to study the reorganization of military education. From 1924 on, the regime also sent officers abroad to investigate different educational models in military academies. Colonel José Millán Astray, the founder of the Spanish Legion, went to the French academies of Saint Cyr and Saint Maixent, whilst Lieutenant Colonel Fermín Espallargar travelled to the USA. But it was the conflict between the dictator and the Artillery Corps over the system of officers' promotions that hastened the plans for a new academy. In September 1926, the stubborn opposition of the Artillery officers to accept the new promotion system proposed by Primo, which in fact benefited the Africanist sector of the army, led to the dissolution of the Artillery Corps and the subsequent closure of the Artillery Academy at Segovia. The creation of an AGM in which all corps would study together became then an urgent necessity.

The Royal Decree of 20 February 1927 established the new AGM at Zaragoza with the specific aim of providing 'a common military spirit in all corps'.[17] The law highlighted 'moral instruction and education' of cadets as one of the main goals of the academy in order to achieve unity of military doctrine. In other words, the regime thought that a fervent moral teaching would first lead to solidarity among the officers and eventually to strong indoctrination of soldiers under the same military principles. The conditions for entering the academy did not radically differ from those established in the 1880s, nor did the subjects taught. Yet when comparing the original programme of 1882 to the one of the 1920s, it is possible to detect an increasing emphasis in those subjects designed to promote national consciousness, such as Spanish history and civil and military law.[18]

Probably the most relevant factor in understanding the sort of education Primo wanted in the army has to do with the team the dictator selected to direct the AGM. Initially, Primo considered Millán Astray for the post of director. Millán Astray had previously taught in the Infantry Academy in Toledo, where he instructed cadets in *bushido* (the samurai code). Furthermore, as chief of the Spanish Legion, Millán Astray educated his soldiers in a blend of irrational principles, military symbolism and theatrical liturgies, extremely similar to those of fascism.[19] But the many enemies Millán Astray had within the army, especially among the *junteros*, made the dictator think twice. It was then that Primo decided to give the post to another Africanist officer, Brigadier General Francisco Franco. Franco had participated in the formative phase of the new AGM too. Like Millán Astray, he had gone to the École Militaire de Saint Cyr on a study trip. In March 1927, Franco was called to be part of the committee formed to create the new academy and in January 1928 he was named director of the AGM.[20]

As a student in the Infantry Academy at Toledo Franco had achieved only very poor results but, once in Morocco, he had been quickly promoted in the officer ranks due to the fact that he was the protégé of General Sanjurjo, one of the most influential Africanists in the Spanish army.[21] The educational skills of the would-be dictator had been developed in Africa, where Franco had co-founded the Legion with Millán Astray in 1920. As the second in command of the *Tercio de Extranjeros*, he soon earned a reputation for the brutal punishment of his own men and the widespread use of terror against civilians and soldiers alike. The colonial experience was certainly incorporated into the life of the AGM, where Franco formed the teaching team with his Africanist friends. He himself wrote the 'Ten Commands of the AGM', following the Decalogue of the Legion and the eighteenth-century Military Ordinances of Charles III. In it, Franco emphasized patriotism, loyalty to the King, discipline, courage and sacrifice, as supreme moral values that had to be exteriorized in everyday life.[22] The Decalogue of the AGM perfectly illustrates Franco's mentality as a mixture of basic authoritarianism and medieval military idealism.

The education given in the AGM was pure indoctrination. It was not only that the Africanists who taught in Zaragoza exalted authoritarian and militarist principles, but also that their educational techniques led to the irrational manipulation of the cadets. Most of the Africanists had no educational training whatsoever and they merely applied in Zaragoza the brutal conductivist methods learnt in the colonies. Moreover, Franco selected teachers according to their war experience in Morocco, rather than their knowledge of the subjects they had to teach. This certainly created a pedagogic environment that, while concentrating on 'moral' and physical education, subordinated technical and theoretical instruction. No wonder that Ramón Franco accused his brother in a private letter of giving the cadets a 'troglodyte education'.[23]

It was precisely this fanatical indoctrination of cadets in authoritarian values, among other things, that led the republican Minister of War Manuel Azaña to close down the AGM in July 1931, as part of a general plan to reform the army.[24] Notwithstanding the relatively short life of the AGM, its historical legacy is significant. The 'unity of military doctrine' to consolidate the regime that Primo sought with the creation of the AGM could not be achieved, since the first promotion graduated in July 1930 once the Dictatorship had fallen. On the contrary the creation of the AGM deepened the fractures within the army during the Dictatorship. The unification of studies had been a longstanding demand of the *junteros*, who understandably enough did not like the Africanists' monopoly of the AGM. As for the Artillery Corps, always proud of their separate education as elite, the AGM only added insult to injury. After Primo's dissolution of the corps and the closure of their academy with the King's acquiescence, artillery officers turned towards republicanism.

In the long term, the consequences of the creation of the AGM were dramatic. During his years in Zaragoza, Franco cemented the group of loyal officers, who would in time rebel with him against the Second Republic in 1936. Many of the cadets educated in the AGM would eventually join the *Falange* in the 1930s and almost all of them fought under Franco in the Civil War.[25] When in 1942 the AGM was reopened, Franco reinstalled the same educational model he had created during Primo's Dictatorship and insisted that it was the duty of the army to transmit its values to the rest of society.[26] At the heart of the Francoist ideological justification for reopening the AGM lay the *primorriverista* belief that the army must shape civil society.

Shaping 'Citizen-Soldiers'

When in 1925 the Chief of the Infantry Instruction Battalion Major Emilio de Rueda addressed the reservist officers in a course, he stated that patriotic indoctrination had to be the main priority in the barracks. Since family and schooling had failed in the process of nationalization, he argued, it was down to the military to indoctrinate citizens in patriotism. The army's potential for the task was certainly appreciated:

> Gentlemen, have you ever considered that over the next ten years approximately one million Spaniards will complete military service?

> Just imagine . . One million Spaniards! Imagine that those men when they leave the barracks for the last time take away embedded in their brains the idea of the fatherland.[27]

Deploying Fichte's views on the power of patriotic ideas and the need to propagate them, Rueda concluded: '[The army must] bring to the most remote corners of the Peninsula the emotion of unity among the individuals and the bodies which constitute the nation [. . .] emotion that, with the passing of time, *produces the illusion of the anthropological unity, of the unity of origin.*'[28] Rueda's lecture perfectly illustrates the regimen's perception of military service as a tool of mass nationalization. First, the *primorriverista* army was aware of the shortcomings of the process in the past and firmly convinced of the utility of military service as a means of solving the 'patriotic deficit'. Second, they knew that national feeling could be artificially created and imposed upon the youth.

Reforms were needed if the military was to successfully transmit its values to soldiers. As shown above, one of the foremost problems of the army was that almost half of the potential conscripts never enrolled. In addition, partial exemptions continued to exist, therefore hampering inter-class integration. Soon after seizing power, Primo reformed the recruitment system. The Royal Decree of 29 March 1924 reduced the possibilities of being exempted for reason of physical or psychological deficiency and toughened the penalties for deserters.[29] It also set out to create a strong reservist corps not only for reasons of defence but to indoctrinate citizens during peacetime.

The *primorriverista* reforms were a partial success. The percentage of those potential recruits actually joining military service steadily increased during the Dictatorship. In 1923 the percentage of draftees joining the army was 56.46 per cent. By 1930, the figure had risen to 62.66 per cent.[30] The explanation for this growth lies in different factors. First, a broader conception of those fitted to join the army sent many to serve in 'auxiliary services' in the barracks. Self-mutilation of fingers and toes, a widespread practice before, might now not ensure being declared unfit. More importantly, the military control of the municipalities via *delegados* ensured the recruitment process was not manipulated by the *caciques*. Thus the possibilities of falsifying family circumstances in order to be exempted substantially decreased. In addition, since the very beginning of the regime the *delegados* made clear in public addresses that desertion was a crime of lèse-Patria. They encouraged public denunciations of deserters and their prosecution became more common.[31]

Finally, the 'pacification' of the Protectorate and the resulting decrease in the number of Spanish troops in Africa might have had an impact on those previously reluctant to die in the Moroccan war.

If figures show us the steady increase in those receiving military indoctrination, in terms of soldiers' educational quality the success of the *primorriverista* reforms is much more dubious. In the name of modernization the *primorriverista* reform reduced the length of the military service from three to two years, which obviously abridged the time for indoctrination within the barracks.[32] Not less important was Primo's decision to maintain the partial monetary exemptions. This allowed serving for just nine months for those who could afford it, paying different quantities according to their family or personal income.[33] Thus the old officers' demand of achieving a truly universal military service was never accomplished under Primo and the gap between upper and middle classes and the lower classes remained.

The Marquess of Estella tried to justify the monetary exemptions, arguing that they were based on the soldiers' cultural capacities and portrayed the pecuniary emancipation as a mere 'complementary economic measure'.[34] No one could seriously believe it. Even officers close to the dictator publicly acknowledged that the maintenance of monetary exemptions was due to the state's need of money to fund the army. As a result, Infantry Major Luis Pumarola admitted, the 'reduced service of the soldier in the barrácks' did not allow a 'scrupulous education on military morality'.[35] More criticism of the effects of both the reduction and the exemption came from inside and outside the military in the subsequent years. Gabriel Maura, son of Antonio and one of the leaders of the conservative opposition to the Dictatorship, denounced the redemptions as a 'flagrant injustice', which led to the 'unavoidable failure of the educational mission aimed at by the dictator'.[36] General Mola, eventually one of the leaders of the July 1936 revolt that led to the Spanish Civil War, summarized the officers' dissatisfaction with the measures as follows:

> with the reduction of service and the facilities given to obtain the monetary exemption, difficulties in instruction and in the number of individuals with deficient war preparation rose, so that only the miserably poor felt obliged to continue soldering full-time and to suffer the pains of the African campaign. All these measures, intended to gain support from big opinion sectors, were extremely detrimental for the Army's efficiency, without gaining, in exchange, the political support aimed for.[37]

To be sure, the regime tried to promote a new type of education along military lines. This new model aimed to politically indoctrinate soldiers while taking into consideration the reduction of service time. Already the early 1924 reforms established that all Spaniards must 'acquire a strong martial spirit' during their military service.[38] Subsequent annual programmes incorporated the official principles into the soldiers' syllabus. These included the teaching of concepts such as love for the fatherland, the King and the flag, heroism, obedience and honour.[39] Additionally, new military schools were planned in every region aiming to improve educational performance.[40]

Fully aware of the different political positions within the army, the regime laid stress on the need to achieve a 'unity of doctrine' in those principles to be taught to soldiers, which in reality meant to homogeneously reproduce the official authoritarian canon.[41] Since the beginning of the regime new teaching manuals for officers and textbooks for soldiers were published in ever increasing numbers and publications rocketed after the 1926 governmental campaign to produce 'patriotic books'.[42] These nationalist works were widely circulated in military garrisons by the Bureau of the President (*Secretaría Auxiliar de la Presidencia del Consejo de Ministros*). These writings popularized nationalist, authoritarian, irrational and interventionist ideas, which had become paramount among the officer class in the years prior to the Dictatorship. Yet the fact that these ideas had become official doctrine and were now intensively promoted among the soldiers made the transformation of the army into a vehicle of mass indoctrination all the more remarkable. This new military literature was no longer the reflection of a mounting stream of discontent within an institution at odds with the liberal state, but the official propaganda of a military dictatorship in which the army effectively controlled the state apparatus. Proposals for change now had real possibilities of being realized. As we saw in Chapter 2, *primorriverista* military literature emphasized the need to shape a 'New Man' in the form of the 'Citizen-Soldier'. The most ambitious plans envisaged this 'New Spaniard' as being educated from childhood in nationalist and militarist values in state-controlled schools, followed by pre-military academies and, finally, military service as the last step in the making of the Citizen-Soldier.[43] Once the process of indoctrination was complete, he had to act as a 'good citizen'. And this, in the words of the military writers, meant that he had to adore the leader of the nation, join the *Somatén*, participate in patriotic ceremonies, help local authorities, and politically mobilize himself for the regime.[44] Crucially, these views presented Dictatorship, army and nation as intrinsically linked, in an attempt to monopolize the idea of Spain. The army had been turned not only into a key state agency devoted to propagate patriotism, but also into an official organization seeking to attract support for the *primorriverista* regime.

In the 'patriotic' battle for the hearts and minds of young Spaniards leftist ideas became the main enemy and the conquest of the rural masses the foremost goal. The director of the Infantry Academy, José Villalba Riquelme, drew a neat line when dividing the bulk of soldiers into peasants and urban proletarians:

> the former, the most healthy and robust and with scarce education, constitute the main mass in Spain; the problem in instructing them lies in the fact that they are simplistic and lack culture, but, on the other hand, their moral and physical development is better, since they are not contaminated by the atmosphere of the factory, the mine, or the political meeting. The latter, with greater culture, and with easily learnt skills in the use of war machinery, are infected with alcohol and socialist predicaments.[45]

It is highly significant that those in charge of military education emphasized the importance of indoctrinating peasants as opposed to urban workers. The regime saw the agrarian masses as a vast non-politicized social group, which should be indoctrinated by the state before the left could gain active support from them. Even the most humble members of society were now considered important for indoctrination. In this sense, it is easy to understand the efforts made by the government to increase the number of illiterate soldiers joining the regimental schools in the barracks.[46] According to military instructors, the key was in selectively teaching soldiers and providing them with a carefully chosen range of books, so they did not follow 'negative propaganda'.[47] The goals behind this policy were twofold. First, reduction of illiteracy would mean a better-educated population and this would eventually improve national production. Second, if a certain cultural level was provided in the army according to nationalist principles, the chances of the lower classes being attracted by socialist or anarchist propaganda would be severely reduced.

An essential component in the formation of the 'New Man' was to endow Spaniards with a strong physique. Improving the strength of the 'race' had been part of military plans in the decade prior to the Dictatorship. Following Social Darwinist principles, military officers had come to the conclusion that the survival of the fittest applied to nations and races as well as to individuals and, therefore, nations needed strong men to defend the fatherland and, ultimately, to stay alive.[48] The problem enthusiasts of physical education faced was that it was in a state of total disarray in the military garrisons. José Villalba Riquelme was the most active officer seeking to improve physical education in the army. A man well aware of new European educational initiatives, Colonel Villalba created a special unit in the Infantry Academy for the teaching of physical exercise and, in 1911, he organized a tour to study the teaching of gymnastics at different military academies around the continent. The conclusions of the report produced upon his return urged for the creation of a physical education teaching college for both soldiers and civilians in Spain.[49] But despite the efforts of Villalba and his colleagues, very little was done in the years before the Dictatorship. As bitterly described in a textbook for physical education instructors published in 1923, physical education in the garrisons was absolutely overlooked and NCOs without any sort of previous training were those in charge of organizing and overseeing soldiers' physical exercise.[50]

Improvement of physical education training soon became an important goal of the Dictatorship. The regime not only upgraded the level of gymnastics in recruits' study plans but also attempted to professionally train officers and NCOs in the teaching of physical education.[51] In the quest for professional instructors, the regime transformed the Military Institute of Physical Education into the Central School of Gymnastics (*Escuela Central de Gimnasia*, CSG) in 1924. The old Institute, an organization linked to the Infantry Academy, was then turned into a semi-independent military college devoted to the training of officers and NCOs.[52] By 1927, the dictator established that only military officers with a degree in gymnastics could be in charge of physical education in the barracks. NCOs working as instructors' aides were also required to have been educated at the CSG.[53]

In 1925, Villalba considered the CSG to be the only institution capable of properly shaping gymnastics teachers and yet he acknowledged it could not 'have an important impact due to its scarce resources and economic means'.[54] The following year, a team of three members of an inter-ministerial commission visited military academies in France, Italy, Sweden and Germany, seeking to come out with the ideal educational plan for Spain.[55] Yet progress was bound to be slow. Although the CSG drafted a new statute for the physical instruction of troops unifying the 'doctrine' of the different corps in the army, by 1927 it had yet to be passed and the old 1911 Provisional Infantry Gymnastic Statute still remained in place.[56]

The number of officers joining courses at the CSG doubled during the Dictatorship, rising from 32 in 1923 to 64 in 1929.[57] But for all the

Figure 4   Soldiers exercising in public. The physical improvement of the 'Spanish race' became one of the main targets of the *primorriverista* Dictatorship.

significance that the CSG gained in *primorriverista* plans, the reality was that the number of officers and NCOs graduating from the school was simply not enough to substantially improve the instruction of physical education in the army. According to Villalba, a total of 220 officers and 200 sergeants had become teachers and instructors respectively in the period 1919–1927.[58] In other words, assuming that all graduates at the CSG were teaching physical education, by the late 1920s the Spanish army had approximately one teacher and one instructor per 1000 soldiers. In addition, the economic conditions of the garrisons remained terribly poor throughout the Dictatorship. By 1930, soldiers still lacked the most basic equipment and facilities for practising physical exercise.[59]

Together with moral indoctrination and physical education, the Dictatorship was keen to promote patriotic rituals and reinforce national symbolism in the barracks. *Primorriverista* military textbooks insisted on the importance of making the recruits feel an emotional attachment to Spanish symbolism. The regime's obsession with the 'unity of doctrine' was matched only by the *primorriverista* passion for unifying national symbols. In March 1925, the regime imposed a single military uniform for the entire army in order to increase the sense of belonging to the same patriotic institution.[60] Two years later, a Royal Decree established that the merchant ships had to sail under the same flag as the Royal Navy.[61] The red and yellow flag of the monarchy had progressively been adopted by all state agencies and the merchant navy was the last Spanish institution with other colours. With this unification the regime completed a phase which had begun in 1843 with the appropriation of the Royal Navy insignia as the national flag. It did not, however, bring an end to the conflict regarding the national flag. Republicans remained loyal to the red, yellow and violet tricolour flag, workers kept on waving their red and black insignias and peripheral nationalists preferred their own flags to the Spanish one.

In line with its efforts at doctrinal and symbolic unification, the regime also attempted to regulate military ceremonies within the barracks. The most important of all, the Oath to the Flag, was radically transformed during the Dictatorship. In early 1924, Primo decided that the national standard was not to be kept in the barracks anymore and ordered the recruits to 'take their military sacrament under the sun, together with their fellow citizens', effectively turning the Oath to the Flag into a popular ceremony.[62] The Royal Decree of 31 March 1924 was unambiguous. It ordered military authorities to organize a public commemoration of the pledge to the national flag aiming to unite soldiers and the people 'in a single will'. The government also declared the celebration a 'National Day' and established that all state buildings, schools, universities, seminars, garrisons and military and civilian boats had to display the Spanish flag to commemorate this patriotic festival. In search of a public communion between the people and the soldiers, in which the national emblem became a sacred item, the decree was self-explanatory:

> In order to endow the oath with that popular support that cannot be officially legislated and enforced, Authorities must organize the fiesta (because this day must be a celebration of the Fatherland) in a way which contributes to exalt the masses' love for the Flag, itself the representation of national honour and the emblem in which all Spanish regions merge.[63]

The regime wasted no time in implementing the new legislation. In early April 1924, the King presided over a massive ceremony in which hundreds of recruits pledged their allegiance to the national flag on the Paseo de la Castellana in Madrid.[64] Integration of the masses into military public ceremonies went a step further the following year with the creation of the Festival of Graduating Soldiers. The Military Directory, attempting to assimilate civic, military and religious rites into a nationalist ceremony, invented the ritual via royal order. The first act was to be a public mass with the presence of one infantry, one cavalry and one artillery battalion. Following the mass, the military governor had to give a speech reminding the soldiers of the significance of their vow to the patria and their duties outside the barracks. After the speech, the soldiers, wearing festive uniforms, had to march and bless the flag while the military band played martial music.[65]

In seeking to assure public success, the Festival of Graduating Soldiers was declared a public holiday. Under the military governors' command, the entire ceremony was to take place in front of civil and ecclesiastical authorities. Members of trade, industrial and agricultural associations were to be invited, together with workers' unions and any other 'local prestigious corporations'. There is little doubt that the Dictatorship attempted to turn this ceremony into an all-class integration ritual, in which the army remained the 'sacramental administrator'. It is telling that the religious character of this nationalist ceremony was emphasized with the incorporation of a Catholic mass, a very well-known ritual among Spaniards. Indeed, the military governor's speech and the soldiers' kissing of the flag were reminiscent of the priest's sermon and the congregation's communion in the Catholic mass. But it is also worth noting that here the Catholic ritual was performed in order to 'sacralize' a national item (that is, the flag) and was part of a broader patriotic ceremony. In this ceremony, the fatherland, and not the Christian God, was the supreme divinity celebrated. In the same manner that the ideologues of the regime drew selectively from Catholic doctrine in order to frame official nationalist discourse, the Dictatorship openly incorporated Catholic rituals into nation-state ceremonials. In both cases, Catholic forms were subordinated to the nation as the supreme deity.

It is difficult to evaluate the impact *primorriverista* reforms had on those young men joining the military service. The record suggests that more Spaniards participated in military service than ever before: the number of reservist officers was unparalleled, political indoctrination and propaganda in the barracks reached unprecedented levels and new patriotic rituals were invented. However, it is possible to detect certain factors which critically hampered the process of nationalization. As noted above, the preservation of monetary exemptions hindered inter-class integration into the national ideal and the reduction of military service to two years allowed less time for indoctrination. Contemporary accounts of garrison life portrayed a gloomy situation. Most of the companies lacked the number of troops required, the vast majority of the recruits graduated without having proper military instruction and many soldiers worked as officers' personal assistants.[66] According Major García Benítez, indifference and corruption pervaded life in the garrisons and soldiers soon understood that the best thing to do was not to get involved, not to enquire about anything and to automatically obey the orders given by officers.[67] The effect of this way of life was not the creation of a 'New Spaniard' but of apathetic soldiers whose only aim was to survive in the barracks for eight months waiting for permission to return home.

The transformation of the military education system was far from being completed. For all its legislation and propaganda, the regime was powerless to sufficiently increase the number of political and physical education instructors. Once again, the reason is partially to be found in a lack of funds. As General Mola observed, economic restrictions and the African campaign precluded the materialization of Primo's military reforms.[68] From 1925 on, the military budget was gradually reduced both in terms of total money received by the army and in relation to the percentage taken out of the national budget.[69] In addition, the growth in the numbers of recruits (more than 10 per cent throughout the Dictatorship) put further pressure on the military education system.[70] Ironically, Primo was somehow a victim of his own success in incorporating more recruits into the army. With a military budget constantly decreasing and the number of recruits steadily increasing, the intended conversion of the army into an indoctrinating machine proved impossible.

5
The Apostles of the Fatherland: the Army's Nationalization of Civilians

> Patriotic instruction must be directed at the masses, at the whole of society, not just at a few exceptional individuals
>
> (General Villalba)[1]

The most ambitious plans for army-led mass indoctrination took place outside the military garrisons. During the years prior to the Dictatorship the majority of military officers had come to the conclusion that the army was the only institution capable of regenerating a decadent Spanish society. For the most radical military officers, fulfilling this self-imposed task meant that the army had to leave the barracks and indoctrinate civilians in patriotic values in their own towns and villages.[2] Once in power, Primo de Rivera attempted to carry out these plans of total mass indoctrination and sent hundreds of officers out of the barracks to preach patriotism all around Spain as 'apostles of the fatherland'.

In the *primorriverista* bid for civilian mass indoctrination, the main role was played by the *delegados gubernativos*. The Military Directory established the figure of the *delegados* in October 1923 to assist the generals who were acting as new civil governors after the coup. Directly controlled by the Minister of the Interior, Martínez Anido assigned one *delegado* to each judicial district (*cabeza de partido*) in the country to 'inspect and orient' municipal life.[3] Their initial task was to gain total military control of provincial life and destroy the *caciquil* local networks. Primo was fully aware of the fact that the destruction of the old political structures had to be complemented with the making of a 'new type of citizen' at the municipal level. The delegates were ordered to organize the local *Somatén*, boy-scouts, gymnastic associations and cultural clubs for men and women. They were also responsible for organizing patriotic lectures, which should promote the virtues of the 'Spanish race' and emphasize the duty to defend the fatherland, respect authority and the head of the state, protect the environment, and pay taxes.[4] For this educational undertaking of 'strengthening the citizen's soul and body', delegates were advised to enlist the participation of local teachers, priests and doctors.[5]

The regime found no problems in gathering volunteers for the job. Most of the *delegados* were previously in the military reserves, earning 75 per cent of an active officer's salary, and becoming an 'apostle of the fatherland' meant getting full pay. By early December 1923, 523 governmental delegates were already in posts all around Spain. Out of the 523 delegates, 434 were commissioned to serve at judicial districts and 89 at provincial capitals. Popular response to the arrival of the delegates appears to have been sceptical. According to the memoirs of a former delegate, at first most of the locals in towns and villages were profoundly mistrustful of the officers, whom they saw as new *caciques* in uniform.[6] Despite the cold reception, during the first months the delegates showed a strong zeal in their repression of public administrators. Fuelled by an avalanche of anonymous denunciations made by the public, they arrested and jailed dozens of municipal councillors and *caciques*.[7] Soon the situation became chaotic. On 1 January 1924, Martínez Anido sent 'confidential instructions' to the civil governors and the *delegados* as new guidelines to inspect the municipalities. The Interior Minister requested caution when pursuing *caciques*, since an eventual judicial liberation of the alleged criminals would weaken the delegates' public image.[8] The petition was ignored and four weeks later Martínez Anido insisted on moderating the number of arrests, deportations and fines imposed by the *delegados*. Once again, the minister argued that massive confinements were worsening public support for the delegates and maintained that anonymous denunciations should lead to investigations and not to immediate detentions.[9] In the following months, Martínez Anido often insisted on minimizing captures in different letters sent to the *delegados*, clearly showing that ministerial guidelines regarding detentions were not being followed.[10]

The actions of the delegates were devastating for the old political elite. After the dissolution of municipalities, the delegates became the new local lords. They formed the new provisional town councils, imprisoned political opponents and controlled information published in local newspapers. The implementation of the new municipal statute in 1924 did not change the delegates' position. For all the instructions ordering the delegates to respect 'municipal autonomy',[11] military officers seem to have reinforced their local power after the enactment of the statute. Four months after the implementation of the law, Martínez Anido complained to the governors about the delegates abusing their authority. As described by the Interior

Minister, the delegates were involved in every single detail of municipal life, such as the designation of all public officers, including minor posts.[12] In October 1924, Calvo Sotelo wrote to Primo demanding the gradual elimination of the delegates. In his view, the delegates had already fulfilled their initial mission and were by then causing 'a huge moral damage to the regime'.[13]

Reducing indiscriminate imprisonments and respecting municipal autonomy were questions of public image. Secretly using the delegates to spy on political opponents and purging suspicious liberals from the state apparatus were very different issues. In early January 1924, the Interior Minister ordered the delegates to send him 'confidential reports' on those judges 'who weakly support governmental actions'.[14] In this manner judges would not obstruct the regime's eradication of *caciques*. Invigorated by Martínez Anido's orders not to tolerate 'whether in the press or in conversations anything that could damage the Directory's prestige', political repression touched all those opposing the regime.[15] Republicans, liberals, communists, anarchists, conservatives and Carlists were imprisoned and exiled for propagating 'anti-Spanish' ideas.[16] Civil governors soon understood the huge potential delegates had for crushing provincial political opposition. At the local level, delegates selected those civilians who were willing to collaborate with the Dictatorship. The role of these civilians was essentially to gather information on anti-*primorriveristas* and pass it to delegates, who in turn filtered the information to the governors.[17] At the top of the pyramid, Martínez Anido controlled the whole network.

The destruction of local *caciques* and repression of political opponents went hand in hand with the 'educational mission' of the delegates. Despite the reduction in the number of delegates and the different duties they were assigned throughout the Dictatorship, the regime always insisted on the task of mass indoctrination as an essential obligation.[18] As Martínez Anido explained to the delegates, nationalist teaching was an 'investment' in eventual patriots:

> The Delegates will find a wide field for their activities in cultivating the moral energies and civic virtues of our youth. The Fiesta of the Tree, the Boy Scouts, school friendly societies, the Fiesta of the Flag, etc, etc: these are some examples of patriotic goals which are completely under the delegates' jurisdiction. The educational action [. . .] exercised over the current generation of children will eventually flourish with positive impetus. For this reason, although at first sight the action seems sterile, the delegates must work on it carefully, since it always gives a mellow fruit.[19]

The regime used the same technique for nationalizing civilians that it was using for indoctrinating soldiers. A combination of theory, put forth in patriotic lectures and practice, through national rituals and gymnastics, was implemented in the same manner that military instructors 'educated' recruits. However, indoctrinating entire towns and villages required much more personnel. From the very beginning, the Interior Minister asked public school teachers, priests and civilians not linked to the old regime to co-operate in the educational campaigns directed by the delegates. The delegates were especially aware of the importance teachers' co-operation had for patriotic propaganda. In fact, one of the first things the military officers did when taking charge of their posts as delegates was to gather together all the primary school teachers (*maestros*) in the judicial district. The delegates demanded support for the regime and active co-operation from the local teachers' associations. A great number of these meetings concluded with a public declaration of allegiance to the Dictatorship. The record suggests that the system was effective. During the first months of 1924 dozens of 'patriotic lectures' to indoctrinate adults and children took place throughout Spain. More often than not, the delegates' speeches were complemented by the participation of teachers.[20]

Figure 5   The sacralization of the nation. A public military ceremony of the Oath to the Flag in which the national emblem is blessed by the ecclesiastical authorities.

Teachers were also involved in the celebration of public ceremonies. In this the delegates progressed apace. Following Martínez Anido's orders, the military officers took every single chance to mobilize the population. They organized the celebration of the Day of the Race and the Fiesta of the Sanctification of the *Somatén* Flag in towns and villages where these ceremonies had never taken place before. The anniversary of the 13 September 1923 coup and *primorriverista* military victories in Africa were also popularly celebrated under the administration of delegates. In these fiestas the delegates gathered the local authorities for the occasion, hoisted the Spanish flag and delivered patriotic speeches. In many of these ceremonies, a public mass was given. In some other cases local priests collaborated by giving homilies as a part of the ritual.[21] As in the nationalist ceremonies organized for soldiers, Catholic imagery and rhetoric were integrated into civic patriotic rituals. In all cases, the nation was considered the supreme deity.

The physical improvement of the Spanish 'race' was also one of the delegates' duties. Martínez Anido's initial orders emphasized the importance of promoting physical education among adults and children.[22] The Royal Order of 7 April 1924 announced the creation of a gymnastic record book, which the delegates should deliver to locals to keep a record of their physical exercises. However, the evidence suggests the delegates failed to promote physical education during the Military Directory. Two months after the Royal Order, some of the delegates complained to the Interior Ministry because they had yet to receive the physical education diary.[23] In fact, very few delegates mention in their reports any sort of gymnastic activities organized in their district whatsoever. With the exception of a few delegates, who instructed civilians with the military gymnastic book in municipal fields, most of the 'apostles of the fatherland' were far from prioritizing physical education among their activities.

The formation of the Civil Directory brought the intensification of the indoctrination of the masses. The Royal Decree of 29 January 1926 officially sanctioned a new campaign aiming to 'plant moral and patriotic ideas in the humble minds' of the lower rural classes.[24] It established 'the celebration of Sunday lectures for adults of both sexes in every town with less than 6000 inhabitants in the kingdom'.[25] The lectures should deal with the fulfilment of citizens' duties, Spanish and local history, and professional topics, such as agriculture or small industries. The events were to be organized by the mayor and would take place in the town hall. The legislation recommended mayors select the lecturers from amongst teachers, doctors, pharmacists, military officers and priests. Paralleling soldiers' education, the regime prioritized indoctrination of rural masses, a vast social group considered not yet 'intoxicated' by leftist ideas.

The selection of mayors as organizers of patriotic lectures enlarged the scope of those involved in mass nationalization. Nonetheless, the campaign did not signal a lesser involvement of the delegates and the civil governors in rural indoctrination. Delegates continued to organize lectures and ceremonies in towns and villages from 1926 on presidential instructions. Less than a month after the legislation on rural lectures for adults came out, the chief of the Bureau of the President Antonio Almagro Méndez wrote to Martínez Anido enquiring about the lectures. In his letter, Lieutenant Colonel Almagro reminded the Interior Minister that Primo had a special interest in the celebration of the lectures and urged Martínez Anido to encourage mayors, via governmental delegates and civil governors, to fulfil their duties.[26] Obediently, the Interior Minister sent a telegram to all civil governors the next day. He ordered them to press mayors to celebrate the lectures and demanded reports on the events.[27] Moreover, Martínez Anido sent 200 copies of Primo's book *Disertación ciudadana* to every single province the following week. The aim was clear: the dictator's work had to 'reach all towns and be the text on which Sunday lectures must be based'.[28]

Sunday lectures in small towns were conceived as a second mass. The entire adult population would gather to hear the missionaries of the fatherland, preaching the dictator's gospel. The homogenization of doctrine that the Royal Order of 29 January 1926 demanded for these lectures should be based on the national leader's thought. This model anticipated a form of mobilization and propaganda later used in fascist Italy during the 1930s. In 1932, Mussolini created the 'Sunday meetings', at which party speakers propagated fascist doctrine. The idea behind this model was very similar to that of the *primorriveristas'*. The propagandists gathered the entire adult population in every commune and preached nationalist dogma. As in the Spanish case, governmental representatives focused their weekly activities on small towns and villages. Unlike Spain, however, in Italy all those exercising the patriotic apostolate belonged to the official party.

Yet this sort of mass indoctrination proved difficult to realize. In the province of Álava, for example, the civil governor found serious problems in organizing the meetings, since most of the villages had a very small population of farmers and 'lacked suitable people for cultural tasks whatsoever'.[29] As a result, he had to recruit personnel, namely teachers, from outside the villages, and this delayed the organization of the events. In Barcelona, Primo's plans for organizing Sunday lectures in small towns had to be postponed until the summer because the delegates were participating in a very similar campaign promoted by the provincial government. In the spring of 1926, the *Diputación Provincial de Barcelona*, the provincial government of the Catalan capital, subsidized a series of 'patriotic and professional courses' held in the Popular Libraries of Pineda, Canet del Mar and Sallent.[30] Only when the courses ended, could the delegates of Arenys de Mar and Manresa organize a few the Sunday lectures during the summer.[31] Even in those provinces where the governor acted efficiently, like Santander, only 50 per cent of the municipalities had celebrated the lectures by early March 1926. The civil governor of the province optimistically reckoned that all municipalities would have had their first meeting by April.[32] Whether it was due to lack of co-ordination or human and economic resources, Sunday lectures seem to have had an irregular implementation. The Royal Decree of 28 December 1927 insisted on the necessity of stimulating the celebration of Sunday lectures in towns with less than 6000 inhabitants.[33] Two years after the creation of Sunday lectures, the regime deemed the number of events clearly insufficient.

The problems of the *primorriveristas* to mobilize the rural population for the Sunday lectures should not come as a surprise. When the Italian fascists institutionalized 'Sunday meetings' in the 1930s, they also failed to make an impact on the masses.[34] In fact, the work of the delegates as propagandists was hampered by a series of factors throughout the Dictatorship. First of all, the actions of the delegates seriously contributed to the destruction of the *caciquil* network in the countryside.[35] Still, during the Dictatorship some *caciques* remained active in the shadows opposing and obstructing the work of the delegates. According to the reports civil governors sent to Madrid in late 1927, the 'virus of the old politicians' continued to menace the regime in Orense, Biscay, Málaga, Teruel, Valencia and Granada; and as late as December 1929, the civil governments of La Rioja and Navarre informed Primo that the removal of the delegates would lead to the immediate re-emergence of *caciquismo* in their provinces.[36]

Another real danger of the actions of the delegates was that the 'apostles of the fatherland' would turn into *caciques* themselves. Placed in the position of local lords, the delegates could not always resist the temptation of using their power for their own benefit. For all the warnings Martínez Anido gave about the necessity of demonstrating unquestionable moral behaviour, accusations of corruption soon appeared. On some occasions delegates were corrupted by the old political elites, who bribed the officer in order to keep control of municipal governments. This was the case, among others, of José del Olmo Medina, a delegate in the province of Valencia, who was allegedly paid 5000 pesetas to dismantle the town council of Guadasuar in March 1928 and set up a new one in April that year with different councillors. In some other cases the delegates simply abused their positions for material gain. For example, Alberto Serrano

Montaner, delegate of the province of Granada, agreed to live in a mansion offered by the town council, and was accused of buying jewellery and tickets to bullfights with public money. Moreover, Serrano allegedly abused his position by doing business with the municipality of Motril and pressed the town council to recommend him to the government as a member of the National Assembly. Although an enquiry by the Ministry of War concluded that none of these accusations could be proved, Martínez Anido discharged him immediately. This was the general line followed by the Interior Ministry: delegates accused of corruption were dismissed without delay, even in those cases when investigators had not found them guilty.[37]

Martínez Anido followed a very similar policy in those districts where the military officers had family and friends, and the possibilities of corruption grew. In Lérida, for example, delegate José Valladaura was fired for having connections with the old political elites. Not willing to run any sort of risk, Martínez Anido decided not to keep any delegate who had influential relatives in the districts under his jurisdiction. This was the case of Fernando Suárez de Figueroa, delegate of Tortosa, who, despite having 'good conditions for the post' according to the civil governor of Gerona, was not reappointed in 1926 because his father was the director of the Bank of Spain in Tortosa and his father-in-law was a businessman connected to liberal elites. The same applied to those blamed of 'immoral behaviour', like Humberto Gil Cabrera, delegate in Lérida, anonymously accused of having a debased life and equally dismissed.[38] Martínez Anido was aware of the damage these accusations had in the eyes of the public and got rid of any questionable delegate. But for all the zeal the Interior Minister took in dismissing delegates, the proliferation of corruption and charges of immorality seriously damaged the public image of the 'apostles of the fatherland'.

The fact that the town councils had to pay the delegates' salaries and costs also played a part in alienating the population from the military officers. In December 1923, the regime established that all municipalities in the judicial districts had to contribute *pro rata* to 25 per cent of the delegates' wages. In addition, the town councils were forced to pay the delegates' travel expenses, plus 100 pesetas for stationery supplies. The head of the judicial districts also had to provide the military officers with housing, an office and an administrative assistant.[39] This was an important burden for the municipal treasuries and soon problems with the payments arose. In June 1924, Martínez Anido urged the town councils to accelerate these payments. After seven months of the creation of the delegates, some municipalities had not paid a single peseta to the officers.[40] The problem spread to the army, since the military garrisons advanced the money to the delegates before collecting it from the municipalities. In June 1926, the

Minister of War wrote to the Interior Minister complaining about the 'important and long-lasting debts' the municipalities had with the army.[41] He claimed that several municipalities were ignoring the payments, despite the military's continuous demands and the civil governors' mediation, which had 'disturbed accountability in almost every regiment'. The Minister of War attached a report from the Military Governor of the 8th Military Region, which illustrated the magnitude of the trouble. In the second semester of 1925 and only referring to advance payments, the municipalities of Galicia and León had accumulated a debt of 20 343.45 pesetas with the delegates.[42]

Support for the delegates within and outside the army gradually diminished. Initially conceived as a tool to fight *caciquismo*, by the end of the Dictatorship the governmental delegates had become an uncomfortable agency linked to political and economic scandals and a burden for the municipalities and the army itself. The early popular scepticism towards the delegates turned into disapproval before long.[43] Indiscriminate political repression, corruption and diverse cases of power abuse proved those who originally saw the delegates as 'new *caciques* in uniform' to be correct. The fact that after the fall of the Dictatorship a village welcomed republican campaigners with the banner 'Long live to the men who bring us the rule of law' is revealing.[44] The *primorriverista* disregard for legality backlashed and led many to associate the rule of law with democratic reforms and a non-arbitrary constitutional system.

Many military officers also realized the negative consequences of the delegates' experience. Officers acknowledged they were simply not prepared to carry out governmental and administrative tasks at the local level and their acts caused dismay among civilians.[45] General Mola keenly noticed that the delegates' actions increased the civilians' animosity towards the entire military.[46] An institution designed to nationalize the people with military values ended up producing the reverse effect, that is, a reinforcement of civilian values. General Dámaso Berenguer, the man Alfonso XIII chose to replace Primo as Prime Minister in January 1930, perfectly understood how related the figure of the delegates was to the *primorriverista* regime in the public's mind. Attempting to dissociate himself from the former dictator, Berenguer abolished the institution three weeks after Primo's dismissal.[47]

Pre-military education

The figure of the governmental delegate was conceived as a 'shock treatment' to regenerate local life. Initially, Primo declared the institution of the 'apostles of the fatherland' to be provisional and the gradual reduction in the number of delegates seemed to indicate that the institution would one day be finally abolished. However, nationalist indoctrination was always a factor of extreme importance in the Marquess of Estella's policies. While the delegates were carrying out their commissions, much more ambitious plans of mass indoctrination were developed. From 1925 onwards, the regime began the design of an education system that would instruct every child and youngster in nationalist values. The result was the creation of the *Servicio Nacional de Educación Física Ciudadana y Premilitar* (National Service for Physical, Citizenry and Pre-military Education, SNEFCP) – a state military organization designed to morally and physically improve the Spanish 'race'.

As in many other European countries, pre-military education was present in Spain before the First World War. This was an education given by the state-funded National Rifle Association (*Tiro Nacional de España*, TNE) and private colleges, which entitled a reduction in the time spent in military service to those who took a series of courses and gunfire practice. As with many other institutions in Spain during the Restoration, the system did not work. Fraud in obtaining the degrees to avoid some months of military service was widespread in private colleges and only the rich could benefit. More importantly, the TNE lacked the economic and human resources for setting up schools to offer pre-military education to the lower classes.[48]

Determined to overturn the inefficient conditions of pre-military education, Primo reorganized the system. According to the regime, pre-military instruction was too theoretical and very little attention was paid to physical and 'moral' education. The guiding principles of the *primorriverista* reform were 'unification of doctrine', inter-class integration and bringing schools under direct control of the state. Seeking to achieve 'unity of doctrine', the Royal Decree of 8 May 1925 established that all pre-military education teachers had to be military officers, including those instructing in private schools, and placed all schools under direct control of the Military High Command (*Estado Mayor*).[49] The pre-military education system reform also underlined the educational role of the state. The state would provide its own schools free of charge in order to make the instruction available to the lower classes.[50] The following month, a Royal Order specified the academic programme to be taught in pre-military schools. Not surprisingly, the Military Directory introduced a new study plan, which strongly emphasized the teaching of physical education and 'citizenry education' – the latter drawing heavily upon love for the fatherland, discipline, honour and loyalty, among other concepts.[51]

These measures sought to improve an inefficient system. However, Primo made very clear that the 1925 reform was being enacted on a provisional basis and promised extensive changes in two years' time.[52] What the government wanted was an entirely new educational model, not merely an upgrade of the Restoration one. At the same time as legal modifications were introduced, Primo created an inter-ministerial commission aiming at organizing a new pre-military and physical instruction in every centre of education in the country, from elementary schools to universities.[53] As we saw in Chapter 4, the commission organized fieldtrips to European military academies in 1926, seeking to come out with the ideal options for Spain. Following the report of the investigation team, the commission concluded that the improvement of the 'race' required drastic measures.[54] It drew up a plan which established compulsory gymnastics for all Spaniards of both sexes from the ages of 6 to 18. Moreover, the state would enforce mandatory patriotic gymnastics in private associations and companies. Even as part of young ladies' 'domestic teachings', physical education now became obligatory. All children and teenagers would be given a biometric card so that the government could follow their physical and moral development. Finally, the commission's plans also included a post-military education for those who had finished their military service in the garrisons but were yet to have their annual reviews. Post-military instruction was to be given by the same centres teaching pre-military education to civilians up to the age of 38.[55] The entire society would be under direct governmental scrutiny, regardless of gender or class.

Especially radical were those plans designed for female indoctrination. The view of women as the keystone of the 'Spanish race's physical regeneration' was common among *primorriveristas*. Both as girls and would-be mothers, it was argued, females had to be 'scientifically trained' to improve their bodies and adequately educate their sons.[56] Hence, the inter-ministerial commission encouraged the creation of a 'Female Association', which would foster 'intellectual, moral and citizenry education' and prepare women to fulfil 'their high social mission' – that is, being patriotic mothers.[57] The commission took further steps along these lines and sent a plan called 'Female Physical Education National Project' to the dictator. Drafted by the school inspector Cándida Cárdenas, the report considered women, 'as citizens, [have] the same obligation as men to defend their patria and contribute to its progress'.[58] Ms Cárdenas put forward a scheme of physical and political indoctrination, in which girls and youngsters would be educated from the ages of 3 to 25. This indoctrination would take place 'at home and in all private and public schools, from kindergarten to university'. Their physical development and the fulfilment of their patriotic duties would be monitored on a biometric card. Those failing to present the card would be automatically excluded not only from all state, provincial and municipal posts, but also from workshops and factories. Even marriage would be forbidden for those lacking the appropriate physical record. Mothers, Cárdenas penned, had the unavoidable duty to educate their sons in 'vigour, health and energy' and those not well-prepared were failing the nation and, therefore, should not be allowed to marry.

In general terms, Cárdenas' proposal reflected the biological ideological trends so much in vogue all around Europe in the 1920s. These pseudo-scientific theories stressed the need to redeem racial decadence and considered maternity to be a patriotic duty. Nevertheless, the implications of Cárdenas' plan were an unprecedented state intervention in controlling the lives of Spaniards at work, school and home. If the plan was to be implemented, possibilities of a clash between the state and the Catholic Church and between the government and employers seemed high. Contrary to the passive role fascism awarded women as 'reproducers of the nation', the *primorriveristas* envisaged the 'making' of the patriotic mother as a radical state-led process, which blurred public and private spheres in a way not conceived in 1920s Italy.[59]

It was not, however, until November 1928 that the dictator created the National Physical Culture Committee. Primo decided to place it under direct control of the Bureau of the President and named General Villalba director.[60] Simultaneously, an internal report of the Bureau of the President provided the guidelines on which the SNEFCP would be framed. It established the need to directly transmit the national leader's ideas to the people, assuring 'unity of doctrine' and proposed that all books, documents and lecture topics had to be selected by the Bureau of the President.[61] In January 1929, the government established the organization of citizenry education for adults and pre-military and gymnastic instruction for youngsters in all non-provincial capital judicial districts. Once again the regime prioritized the indoctrination of the rural masses over industrial workers. Those majors in a situation of 'forced availability' (*disponibles forzosos*) could apply for the post on a voluntary basis with the important incentive of regaining their full salary – as opposed to the 80 per cent of the wages paid as *disponibles forzosos*. Their duties included lecturing to adults and co-ordinating and directing patriotic physical and pre-military education in the judicial districts.[62]

The mission of these officers was very similar to that assigned to the delegates in terms of promoting physical education and organizing patriotic lectures. When in the last weeks of January 1929 Villalba developed

the programme, he chose to give the SNEFCP the same hierarchical structure of the *delegados*. Thus the SNEFCP officers were responsible to the Civil
Governors, who, in turn, were accountable to Villalba. The latter only
had Primo commanding him. Seeking to have as much impact as possible,
Villalba ordered the SNEFCP officers to require assistance from the mayors
and the UP local leaders in order to gather the masses in nationalist lectures, which would take place on Sundays and other holidays. As for pre-
military education, Villalba believed this patriotic instruction had to be
'directed at the masses, at the whole of society, not just at a few exceptional
individuals'.[63] Above military doctrine, gunmanship and gymnastics,
Villalba emphasized the importance of 'moral education', designed 'to
develop in the audience the feeling of love for the fatherland [. . .] and
everything else which tends to make them proud of being Spaniards'.[64]

The *delegados* had received much criticism due to their lack of preparation as educators of civilians. Villalba was resolved not to let this hap-
pen with the new 'apostles of the fatherland'. In February 1929, he
began to prepare a course to indoctrinate SNEFCP officers before they
were posted to their districts. This course was to be divided into political
and physical education and included lectures by regime ideologues and
classes given by the members of the CSG. Villalba personally drafted the
topics of the political lectures.[65] The selection of subjects on which the
director of the National Physical Culture Committee wanted his men indoctrinated is self-explanatory. The first lecture should focus on national
unity; the second on the doctrine of the father of Portuguese *integralismo*
Antonio Sardinha; the third on ecclesiastical doctrine, aiming to explain to
Catholics that 'submission to constituted powers' was a moral duty and
that there was no religious impediment in supporting the *primorriverista*
regime; the fourth simply sought to expound upon fascist minister Alfredo
Rocco's ideas on the corporative state. Primo was delighted with the syllabus. He personally wrote to the regime's main ideologues to demand their
participation in the event and opened the course with a short lecture.[66]

The course took place from 10 to 30 March 1929 in Toledo. The training
gathered together about fifty officers of the SNEFCP who were lectured
by the Dictatorship's intelligentsia in the military fortress of the Alcázar.
The government was so pleased with the results that it decided to publish the lectures in a book and distributed 20 000 copies among the Civil
Governors for propaganda purposes. Concurrently, captains and majors
of the CSG trained SNEFCP officers in teaching physical education.
The training here included both theory and practice and the CSG used
its most modern educational means, such as filmed documentaries on
how to teach and research devices from the physiological laboratory.[67]

The courses had a good reception amongst the conservative military press, which described the topics of the lectures as 'a real gospel of citizenry brought to the rural soul' of the nation. The Gallic *Le Journal* was a bit more analytical and portrayed the new Spanish pre-military education system as 'inspired on the French model in terms of practical training and based on Fascist principles in terms of moral education'.[68]

The course in Toledo certainly provided SNEFCP officers with a better preparation as 'apostles of the fatherland' than the delegates ever had. By June 1929 some SNEFCP officers were already working in their districts and, in July, Villalba published a Royal Order designed to cover the vacancies of SNEFCP local leaders as soon as possible.[69] Yet when the new agency was put into action, old problems arose. SNEFCP officers needed active co-operation from the municipal governments if they were to succeed in their propagandist mission. In March 1929, the Dictatorship ordered both Civil Governors and mayors to co-ordinate their efforts in helping the officers. Provincial and local authorities were instructed to provide premises for patriotic lectures, rifle ranges and gyms. In addition, they were required to publicize officially pre-military courses and adult lectures.[70] But for all governmental pressure, many mayors refused to provide the necessary facilities, arguing that there was no money in the annual municipal budget to spend on this issue. By early July the number of municipalities declining co-operation was such that Martínez Anido ordered the Civil Governors to force municipal councils to include a special item for acquiring sports premises in the following year's budget. In the interim, Civil Governors should press local associations and individuals to temporarily and freely hand over their ranges and gyms to SNEFCP officers.[71]

Increasing pressure on municipal treasuries was not the only factor leading to the failure of the SNEFCP. For all Primo's support, Villalba was unable to properly organize the SNEFCP. As late as December 1929, a Royal Order commissioned the 'definitive organization' of the SNEFCP to the National Physical Cultural Committee and provisionally suspended all further incorporation of officers into the service. When the Dictatorship fell in January 1930, the SNEFCP had only 267 officers distributed throughout Spain and, by the end of that year, 50 per cent of the Spanish judicial districts had yet to be assigned an officer.[72]

Berenguer's government reformed the *primorriverista* model of pre-military and adult education and reorganized the National Physical Culture Committee.[73] Berenguer tried to get rid of the most radical *primorriverista* innovations in his attempt to return to the old Restoration system. It is revealing that the first measures taken by the new government were scrapping 'citizen indoctrination' from the educational plans and the incorporation of schoolteachers into the pre-military programme.[74] The officers of the SNEFCP, now renamed the National Service of Physical and Pre-military Education (*Servicio Nacional de Educación Física y Premilitar*, SNEFP), were not to lecture or train anymore. They were transformed into 'inspectors' whose job it was to supervise civilian teachers.[75] In addition to political reasons, the motives behind the reform were also economic. According to Berenguer, the *primorriverista* system cost the government 950 000 pesetas per year and the state simply could not afford such expenditure on a model that was not working and depended on the altruism of municipalities and private clubs. The reformed system would just concentrate on pre-military education and incorporate civilian instructors. But the Berenguer system was also doomed to failure. In January 1931, the new dictator ordered the 327 infantry officers of the SNEFP to cease their activities. Three months later, the provisional Republican government suspended the National Physical Cultural Committee *sine die* and dissolved the SNEFP.[76]

The *primorriverista* dream of imbuing all Spaniards with nationalist and militarist values never came true. Most of the mass indoctrination plans, whether concerning children, teenagers or adults, were never realized. When attempted in their most basic form, the complexity of the task and the lack of state resources led to failure. Under-funded, short-lived, badly organized and dependent on municipal charity to function, the SNEFCP could not have a real impact on the population.

A negative nationalization

How successful might the army be considered as an agency of nationalization outside the barracks? An overall deliberation of the actions of the delegates and the SNEFCP officers indicates that the use of the army to indoctrinate the masses was a failure. True, the delegates managed to stage some nationalist ceremonies and partially mobilized the population, especially in rural areas. And yet the public image of the delegates soon deteriorated owing to indiscriminate repression, accusations of corruption and the financial strain put upon the municipal treasuries. This process was abetted by the very nature of the delegates' work, which merged the role of political commissariat with that of 'apostle of the fatherland', and thus combined repression and instruction in the same figure. When the regime created an institution specifically devoted to nationalization, the SNEFCP faced the same problems of under-funding and had no time to make an impact. Military intervention outside the barracks actually produced the reverse effect to what it sought to accomplish. As we have seen, some military officers and members of the government noticed that the work of the delegates besmirched not only the regime but also the entire army. It also led to the discrediting of the National-Catholic idea of Spain. Since the *primorriverista* officers constantly presented nation, Dictatorship and army as the very same thing, the drop in popular support for the regime led to a fall of support for the idea of Spain that the delegates were propagating. Thus the effects of the military indoctrination of civil society were what might be called a 'negative nationalization', in which increasing opposition to the state agents propagating the official canon of the nation accompanied the rejection of the very idea of nation defended by those agents. The fact that all those groups challenging the official concept of Spain, and prosecuted by the 'apostles of the fatherland' (that is, peripheral nationalists, regionalists, liberals, republicans, Carlists, anarchists, communists and socialists) re-emerged stronger than ever immediately after Primo's dictatorship shows the negative effects that military propaganda had achieved in the process of state nationalization. Moreover, conservative monarchists, Social Catholics, socialists and liberals agreed on one point immediately after the fall of Primo: the army should never again intervene in politics.[77] As an editorial of the monarchist *ABC* put it, the regime's policies had turned the army into a state institution 'incompatible with the nation'.[78] Primo's militarist policies led to a consensus on the supremacy of civil power.

This is not to say that the *primorriverista* use of the army as agency of nationalization can be overlooked. The regime's plans were unparalleled in Spanish history both in terms of scope and ambition. The Dictatorship sought inspiration in some other European countries and chiefly found it in fascist Italy. The SNEFCP was partially built on the Italian model and plans to indoctrinate women, although more radical in Spain, were based on a similar conception of mothers as 'procreators of the nation'. In some other cases, such as the Sunday lectures, the Dictatorship's policies anticipated those eventually adopted in Italy in the 1930s. The desire to shape Spaniards' minds and bodies led the government to envisage a society militarily monitored and instructed from the cradle to the age of 38. In this respect, the regime advanced towards a position of totalitarian control over Spaniards' lives.

The *primorriverista* indoctrination of officers and the direct military intervention in governing and educating the masses at all social levels also played an undeniable part in the army's politicization. The experience of hundreds of officers in local government partially explains the widespread military predisposition to intervene in politics during the 1930s.[79] It has been argued that one of the main differences between *primorriverismo* and Francoism was that in the 1920s the army regarded itself as the 'inter-preter' of the national will, whereas in the 1940s the army would consider itself the 'maker' of the national will.[80] This might have been the case of the military conspirators in September 1923. However, if we consider the *primorriverista* plans for mass indoctrination, the record suggests that the regime was willing to forge, if not the 'national will', at least the national identity of Spaniards. In fact, the idea of forging civil society on military values was kept alive by the *primorriverista* intelligentsia during the Second Republic and the Civil War. In the electoral campaign of January 1936, Calvo Sotelo, then leader of the Alfonsine Monarchists, declared military values had to shape civil society and announced the building of a 'New State' based on martial principles.[81] During the Civil War, José Pemartín also advocated a 'profound militarization of the state' that would emerge from the Nationalist side.[82] There was nothing new, then, when Francisco Franco stated in 1942 that military values should shape civil society.[83]

6
The Nationalization of Schools: Primary Education

> Schools must be nationalized. Every single one, whatever the
> type, in which children are not educated in Catholicism and
> love for Spain must and will be shut down
> (Suárez Somonte, General Director of Primary Education)[1]

Socio-economic transformations, brought about by industrialization, and political changes, linked to the emergence of the liberal state, paved the way for the creation of a modern system of public schooling in nineteenth-century and early twentieth-century Europe. The national education system was designed not only to match these social changes and to complement the needs of a literate population, but also as a way to achieve social cohesion within the national ideal. Teaching the official culture and indoctrinating the masses in patriotic values became essential in the process of nation-building, as the social cement in which allegiances to the state were formed.[2] The process of 'creating nationals' in public schools had two, intertwined, main mechanisms. First, oral and written transmission of the official language took place in schools controlled by the state, leading to cultural and linguistic homogenization of the population. Second, state control over the curriculum provided governments with an enormous power when selecting which 'histories' of the fatherland were taught, which sort of cultural values were transmitted as 'national', and which ideas and beliefs were considered part of the nation's identity.[3]

And yet historical analyses have shown that state education systems were far from being completely effective in the process of nationalization in the late nineteenth and early twentieth centuries. The lower classes seldom found sending their sons and daughters to school worthwhile, since it deprived them of an important source of manpower and disrupted family economies. In France, for instance, most children in the countryside worked in the fields nine months per year and many peasants considered educating their sons and daughters useless.[4] Nor was it that linguistic acculturation made great progress either. In many rural areas, the majority of the adults and many children were unable to speak French and continued using their local languages and dialects well into the twentieth century.[5]

European states also met the resistance of the Church, which struggled to retain its traditional control over education. In Italy, liberal governments saw their promotion of national identity in primary schools severely challenged by the Catholic Church, which steadily and successfully opposed the educational expansion of the central state. It was not until Mussolini and the Vatican reached a compromise in the 1920s that the problem was partially solved, and even then, tensions in educational prerogatives between the Catholic hierarchy and the fascists remained throughout the 1930s.[6] In France, the secular educational policies of the Third Republic finally triumphed at the turn of the century, only to produce a strong reaction from the right, which promoted a clericalist view of a 'true' France as the only hope for national renewal.[7]

The Spanish education system faced very similar problems to those of its European neighbours. The lower classes realized that child school attendance meant a lost day of income from her/his labour and schoolbooks and materials were a serious burden on many family budgets.[8] However, Spain had a lower number of children attending school and illiteracy rates were the highest in Western Europe at the beginning of the twentieth century.[9] Chronically under-funded, the national education system could not make much progress in expanding the Castilian language in rural areas of Catalonia, Galicia and the Basque Country. In addition, the battle among those advocating a secular education and the clericalists in the second half of the nineteenth century did not end in a decisive victory for either, though the Catholic Church was granted a prominent voice within the Restoration system. As in the Italian case, the Catholic hierarchy acted as a parallel and independent power from the state. The Church had a fundamental say in the national school curricula and priests sat in the national Public Instruction Council and all municipal and provincial educational councils. Priests were responsible for censoring schoolbooks and teaching the mandatory subject of Catholic religion in both public and private schools.[10] Hence the promotion of civic values associated with the preponderance of the nation as the ultimate source of state legitimacy was seriously hindered.

Notwithstanding its shortcomings, the state seriously improved the education system in the first two decades of the twentieth century. Public schooling expanded all over the country and a series of institutions were created to improve the services of the Ministry of Public Instruction. This had an added ideological factor. The role of education as the key for national renewal had been at the centre of the political debate for decades – acquiring a special impetus after 1898. The *primorriverista* restructuring of the education system has to be understood as a strategic part of the Marquess of Estella's plans for national regeneration via indoctrination of children and teachers in counterrevolutionary ideas. Changes in the national curriculum, indoctrination of teachers, development of state schools and expansion of Castilian language became the hallmarks of a reform aimed at increasing the nationalization of the masses. As ever, nationalization and counterrevolution went hand in hand in the *primorriverista* agenda.

Espionage and repression of primary school teachers

In his role as the 'iron surgeon', Primo believed that to 'cure' the education system he first had to remove the 'cancerous cells' from the national body. The first measures taken by the Dictatorship aimed to stop the spread of 'unpatriotic doctrines' in the schools and impose Castilian as the only language in the classrooms. Issued less than a week after the coup, the so-called 'Decree against separatism' contemplated prison sentences for those propagating secessionist doctrines in schools.[11] One month later, a circular reminded primary school teachers that it was compulsory to teach in Castilian and forbade Catalanist books and schools.[12] In October 1925, a Royal Order perfectly encapsulated the ideas behind the *primorriverista* educational policy: the main goal of the state was to seek its own preservation and the government had to pursue this objective above all others. The state demanded an obligatory co-operation from all citizens, most especially from public officers who had the duty to serve it loyally in every single moment of their lives. Teachers had to be 'a paladin of civic virtues' in and outside the school.[13] Those publicizing ideas against the unity of the fatherland (whether actively or by omitting 'essential facts in the explanation of Geography and History'), or attacking Catholicism, private property and family values would be accused of committing crimes against the state and the nation.[14]

In order to secure an adequate implementation of the above legislation, the Dictatorship created mechanisms for monitoring teachers. Once again, the figure of the *delegado* became paramount in terms of both propaganda and repression. The delegates were soon commissioned with the task of inspecting public and private schools and penalizing those teachers propagating 'antipatriotic ideas'.[15] Indeed, throughout the entire Dictatorship, Primo and Martínez Anido encouraged the delegates to devote their efforts to mass indoctrination.[16] As shown in Chapter 5, the delegates were extremely active in delivering official propaganda and organizing nationalist ceremonies in rural and urban areas. They were also keen to gain the much-needed teachers' support for the organization of patriotic lectures for adults and children, something they managed to obtain on many occasions.[17]

Primo took a personal interest in controlling teachers. He set up a surveillance scheme that sought to reward and punish teachers according to their political loyalty towards the Dictatorship and their competence in propagating Spanish nationalist ideas. In 1924 and again in 1925, Primo ordered Martínez Anido to collect the names of those state teachers (*maestros nacionales*) who had shown an extraordinary zeal at work.[18] Primary school inspectors nominated candidates for the rewards and the governmental delegates supervised and authorized the names proposed. Then the delegates handed the file to the Civil Governors who reported to Martínez Anido and General Luis Navarro, the Military Directory 'minister' of education.[19] What lay behind the idea of rewarding competent *maestros* was not only to gain teachers' support for the regime, but actually to draw up a census of loyalist and opposition educators in Spain. These investigations on the 'best' teachers were complemented with enquiries about those *maestros* that were not following the *primorriverista* legislation. On many occasions, the reports sent to Madrid included sanctions imposed upon teachers.[20]

Purges of teachers from public and private schools were a constant throughout the Dictatorship. Initially fuelled by accusations from the public, the delegates inspected schools and the civil governors punished dozens of teachers from late 1923, on the grounds of recommending Miguel de Unamuno's books, teaching liberal doctrines or refusing to gather pupils for the visit of the Bishop.[21] The formation of the Civil Directory did not lead to a lessening of the inquisitorial role of the delegates. On 27 May 1926, the General Director of Primary Education Ignacio Suárez Somonte declared schools 'must be nationalized' and threatened to shut down 'every single one, whatever the type', in which children were not indoctrinated in Catholicism and love for Spain.[22] The new civilian team in charge of education really meant it. The day after Suárez's comments were published in the press, the Minister of Public Instruction Eduardo Callejo wrote to Martínez Anido enquiring whether the delegates were still legally entitled to inspect schools, and requested further involvement of the military in the persecution of *maestros* with 'irregular behaviour'.[23]

The Interior Minister reassured Callejo and replied that the governors would keep on supervising and sanctioning teachers via delegates and inspectors to 'correct those irregularities'.[24] The record suggests that Martínez Anido was right and dozens of teachers were expelled, fined and removed from their posts for political reasons during the Civil Directory, while some others were rewarded for their loyalty to the regime.[25]

In the long term the military control imposed upon *maestros* had the same negative effects as the *primorriverista* persecution of other public employees. Teachers grew increasingly frustrated by the despotism of the delegates. In 1927, diverse associations of teachers wrote to Primo advocating a different and pedagogic model of inspection as opposed to the repressive one established by the Dictatorship.[26] In some exceptional instances, the actions of the delegates led to outbursts of violence. In the town of Moya (Las Palmas), for example, the father of a sanctioned teacher tried to kill the local *delegado* by stabbing him in the neck.[27] When the Dictatorship fell in 1930, teachers denounced in the press the repression they had suffered under Primo and demanded an amnesty for some of their colleagues, arguing that the *primorriverista* system did not seek to correct the faults of those expelled, but merely to get rid of those politically problematic for the regime.[28]

Scrutinizing teachers also required controlling primary school inspectors. The regime almost immediately realized school inspectors' potential to supplement the *delegados gubernativos'* work, so they were granted the power to close down public and private schools where doctrines against the unity of the fatherland or against religion were taught. Inspectors could also close down schools if they found anyone teaching in languages other than Castilian. Should they face any opposition from the headmaster or teachers, the inspector had to inform the Civil Governor, who would enforce the sanction.[29] By the Royal Decree of 13 October 1925 inspectors and school directors were again ordered to be on the alert for cases in which anti-social ideas or doctrines against the unity of the patria could be exposed. In those cases with 'enough circumstantial evidence' (*indicios suficientes de culpabilidad*), teachers could be suspended straight away.[30] The government insisted that inspectors had to thoroughly examine textbooks and students to find out whether anti-patriotic or anti-social ideas had been taught. What is more, inspectors had to enquire about teachers' behaviour outside the school. They should investigate how *maestros* conducted themselves in town and whether they spread anti-patriotic ideas among the locals.[31] This effectively turned school inspectors into spies at the service of the regime. Once more, the *primorriverista* Dictatorship blurred the frontiers between public and private spheres in the name of protecting the fatherland, while attempting to build the surveillance machinery of a totalitarian state.

As *de facto* assistants to the delegates, inspectors also played an active part in the propaganda machine, organizing patriotic lectures and establishing cultural associations.[32] However, it was the inspectors' repressive role that had a deeper impact on the *primorriverista* education system. The wave of expectations that the Military Directory initially created led many ordinary citizens and public officers to send confidential accusations denouncing teachers to the military government. In the first three months of the Dictatorship, hundreds of teachers were accused of diverse irregularities – from repeated absenteeism to running illegal businesses selling school materials in class. Trying to cope with the situation, Luis Navarro, the General in charge of the Ministry of Public Instruction during the Military Directory, quickly reacted by sending inspectors to investigate the claims.[33] By early December 1923, the cascade of accusations was such that the government issued a Royal Order attempting to harmonize the investigations.[34] The inspectors found themselves with the huge task of running hundreds of 'criminal' investigations against teachers. The latter, quite correctly, saw the inspectors as repressive bureaucrats and governmental spies and soon showed strong disaffection for them. In every single annual meeting of the *Asociación Nacional del Magisterio* throughout the Dictatorship, teachers demanded the inspection task should be carried out by *maestros* and not by 'functionaries'.[35]

Not that the impact of the *primorriverista* system was any better among the inspectors themselves. Military control and the inquisitorial tasks imposed upon the inspectors increasingly led to the complete politicization of the corps. As public officers (*funcionarios*) the inspectors lost their autonomy and became subordinate to the *delegados* and Civil Governors. The fact that the delegates were ordered to perform the same job as the inspectors also infuriated the latter, who steadily and unsuccessfully protested against military meddling.[36] The regime reacted to these demands of professional independence by further tightening the state control over the inspectors. In October 1926, the government granted the Ministry of Public Instruction with the power to transfer inspectors to different posts around the country. This flagrantly violated the principle of immobility of inspectors established in 1913, which only infuriated the inspectors further.[37] But despite the inspectors' dissatisfaction, Primo and Martínez Anido reassured the delegates in their 'educational mission' and insisted they should keep educators under close observation.[38]

These measures, in fact, complemented rather more surreptitious governmental manoeuvres. In June 1926, Martínez Anido set up an intelligence network to spy on inspectors. In a confidential letter, he instructed all Civil Governors to secretly gather information about 'the political moral and social milieu' in which the inspectors worked and lived.[39] Martínez Anido commanded the delegates to watch the inspectors closely and report their political affinity to the Governors. The Governors in turn should report to the General Director of Primary Education for possible sanctions. The following week, the first confidential intelligence reached the Ministry of Public Instruction. The Governors' reports were political files on every single inspector in Spain. They detailed the inspectors' activities outside the schools and their degree of loyalty to the Dictatorship.[40] Many inspectors not fulfilling their 'patriotic duties' were removed from their posts, especially in Catalonia where the *primorriveristas* launched a 'crusade' against the use of Catalan in primary schools.[41]

The *primorriverista* military-run surveillance system of schools proved to have unintended consequences. As in many other areas, the work of the military delegates led to a backlash by civilian professionals who grew increasingly hostile to the Dictatorship. The regime's reaction to this discontent, tightening state control and purging the *cuerpo*, only made things worse. Once Primo had fallen, the inspectors themselves publicly complained about the political policing the Dictatorship had forced them to undertake and called for a complete rearrangement of the corps and the recovery of their pedagogic task.[42] The *primorriverista* system alienated inspectors from the regime and the *maestros* from the inspectors. Two key elements in the chain of ideological control in the education system, the inspection and the teaching, were broken by the *primorriveristas*, thus seriously hampering any possibility of an efficient mass indoctrination at the schools.

Patriotic books and ceremonies

Intensive governmental activities in banning books and repressing ideas were not initially matched with serious changes in the primary education curriculum. The regime, however, was keen in selecting the 'appropriate' Spanish history texts and elaborated lists of books to be bought by public schools and libraries.[43] The Dictatorship drew upon a range of nationalist texts for children written for the 'Book of the Patria' award. Created by the Maurist Minister of Education Cesar Silió in 1921, this prize aimed to stir patriotic feelings and promote 'civic virtues' among children. Although the jury failed to choose a winner in 1922, many of the 63 works presented were later published and included in the offficial reading lists during the Dictatorship.[44] Some of the works presented to the 'Book of the Patria' award were directly backed by the regime's ideologues, such as Adolfo Villanueva's *Patria y Hogar*, a book for which Pemán wrote the prologue.[45] Some others became bestsellers, as was the case of Manuel Siurot's *La emoción de España*, a book modelled on the French patriotic reader, *Le tour de France par deux enfants*.[46] Moreover, the *primorriverista* campaign launched in 1926 to produce patriotic books did nothing but increase the number of works published aiming at fortifying national identity among children. Simultaneously, the government made sure that the editorial boom matched public demand. It included these new titles in the officially 'recommended books' for the state and municipal schools (*escuelas nacionales*), delivered them to educational centres and public libraries and gave them out to the inspectors and teachers involved in the organization of patriotic lectures in rural areas. A sort of history book that had had a good market during the Restoration now found the market expanded by state intervention.

Although the commercial success of these works certainly pleased the Dictatorship, the *primorriveristas* sought more state control over schooltexts. As early as November 1923, the Marquess of Estella ordered the Royal Council of Public Instruction to produce a report on the establishment of a single text in primary and secondary education. However, clashes between the regime and the liberal-controlled Royal Council of Public Instruction seem to have precluded the production of the report. In 1926, the Dictatorship purged the Council, filled it with *primorriverista* loyalists and ignored the institution hereafter.[47] Yet the government was determined to have a single text for primary education and ordered the Royal Academy of History to prepare a graded series of history books for mandatory use in the country's public schools. The Royal Academy of History asked the former director of the Centre of Historical Studies, Rafael Altamira, to create the series.[48] A liberal fully committed to the promotion of Spanish patriotism via history books, Altamira wrote the first manual of the series. Interestingly, the book presented the Habsburg rule as the Spanish 'Golden Age' and, much in line with the *primorriverista* discourse, emphasized the recently 'renewed prestige of Spaniards' in the international arena and the hope that the nation would be 'as important in the world as it was from the times of the Catholic Kings to the mid-seventeenth century'.[49] However, Altamira's work was not published until 1930. Berenguer's government granted the text official status in March that year and it became mandatory in all public schools.[50] Liberal teachers welcomed the book, while the Catholic right criticized it.[51] For the *primorriveristas* it was all too late. By the time the book was in the schools, Primo had been forced to resign.

If the regime's attempt to produce a single history text can only be considered in terms of failure, the Dictatorship did much better when it came to promoting patriotic ceremonies. Whether introduced in the curriculum or considered as extra-curricular activities, the *primorriveristas* gave a great importance to the commemoration of so-called 'patriotic events'. Anniversaries of Primo's coup, the Day of the Spanish Race and the Feast of the Somatén Flag sanctification became school festivals in which children were lectured on the nation, the Dictatorship and its leader. More often than not, these commemorations also included a ceremony in which the national flag was blessed while students sang patriotic hymns.[52] In this manner, students were encouraged to internalize images of national identity in an atmosphere of patriotic communion specifically created to excite the feelings of the youngsters. For example, after the first transatlantic aerial crossing from Spain to South America in 1926 by Spanish pilots, the state ordered public schools to explain the event in geography classes.[53] The idea behind the teaching of such an event was twofold. First, the authorities attempted to combat the inferiority complex that, according to them, some progressive regenerationist views had created among the masses. The flight of the *Plus Ultra*, the official press stated,

Figure 6   Soldiers of the Spanish Army of Africa parade in the streets of Madrid in October 1925. Girls from elementary schools are in the first row among the public.

was evidence of the fact that Spain was no backward country and could achieve great modern 'deeds'. Second, the crossing was portrayed as a contemporary Columbus' voyage, therefore underlining the *Hispanista* vision of the Dictatorship. In an atmosphere of nationalist exaltation, teachers not only explained the aviators' adventure in class, but many schools also organized public homages to the 'heroes of the *Plus Ultra*'.[54]

The Dictatorship was also keen on inventing and reinventing traditions. The official establishment of the Day of the Spanish Book (*Fiesta del Libro*) was unquestionably the *primorriveristas*' greatest innovation. Created by the Royal Decree of 6 February 1926, the Fiesta was to be celebrated in all educational institutions on 7 October, the anniversary of the birth of Cervantes. The government was completely resolved to direct the festivity and carefully instructed primary and secondary schools, universities, polytechnics and professional colleges on how they had to observe the event. Every educational institution in the country was legally obliged 'to commemorate the Day of the Spanish Book with solemn public events, dedicated to praise and popularise national publications and the culture of the fatherland'.[55] Primary schools should devote 'at least, one hour to explain to students the importance of books as instruments of culture, civilization and [spiritual] richness'.[56] To make sure the celebrations took place in the manner the government had planned, three weeks before the first Day of the Spanish Book, Martínez Anido mobilized civil governors and delegates for the occasion.[57] The Interior Minister ordered all provincial governments (*diputaciones provinciales*) and municipalities to co-operate with the celebration and organize public lectures in the high schools. In addition, all public corporations had to assign a certain percentage of their budget to buy books to be donated to poor children and 'popular' (public) libraries had to be built in every Spanish province.[58]

Behind the promotion of libraries and the donation of books lay the regenerationist idea of educating the masses in patriotic values as a way to build a strong national identity.[59] But the *Fiesta del Libro* had further implications. Above all, it was a vindication of the Castilian language. Restoration liberal governments had promoted Castilian as the national language in public schools and turned *Don Quixote* into a national emblem. In 1912 and again in 1920, the educational authorities ordered the mandatory reading of *Don Quixote* in public schools on a daily basis. The *primorriverista* establishment of the *Fiesta del Libro* was the heyday of the linguistic policies of Spanishization (nationalization in Spanish values or *españolización*). It was also the National-Catholic response to similar celebrations peripheral nationalists and regionalists held, such as the

Day of the Catalan Language. It was no coincidence, then, that Primo's government made significant efforts for the promotion of the *Fiesta del Libro* in Catalonia.[60] At the same time, the regime's ideologues were always eager to stress the universal character of the Castilian language, linking it to their *Hispanista* policies and the revival of Spanish imperialism. The figure of Cervantes, himself a soldier who had participated in the battle of Lepanto, was a permanent reminder of the sixteenth-century Spanish imperial glories.[61]

According to the conservative press, the celebration of the *Fiesta del Libro* was an important achievement for the Dictatorship.[62] In Santander, for example, three new libraries were opened in the province to commemorate Cervantes on 7 October 1926. In addition, school trips were organized to the library of Menéndez Pelayo. Once there, children were lectured on the historian's life and said a prayer for the soul of the traditionalist thinker, the honour of the nation and the Spanish book in front of the statue of Menéndez Pelayo.[63] One of the reasons for this success lay in the teachers' support for the celebration. Teachers welcomed the initiative from the very first day and took an active role in the celebrations. *El Magisterio Español* praised the Fiesta as follows: '[This is] one of the government's best ideas. And, it has not been just an initiative, like many others that are later forgotten, but [the government] has done its best since the very first day and has mobilized all possible elements for the Fiesta to produce positive results.'[64] Martínez Anido's network turned out to be highly effective in mobilizing teachers.

Nevertheless, for all the *primorriverista* use of the state apparatus, the success of the *Fiesta del Libro* in terms of mass mobilization should not be exaggerated. According to Gómez Baquero, a liberal educationalist, the general public scarcely attended the events organized in schools and academies nor did bookshops increase their sales during the 1927 celebrations. In his view, the main problem was that the regime had put too much stress on public rites to commemorate the *Fiesta del Libro*, but these were newly created artificial ceremonies and the public did not respond. 'The *Fiesta del Libro* began imposing a liturgy and two years later it is already old, wasted, decrepit', he concluded.[65]

Not all patriotic ceremonies in the schools were recent *primorriverista* inventions. In some cases, the regime revitalized old rituals and transformed them into new National-Catholic ceremonies. First celebrated in the 1890s, the Day of the Tree (*Fiesta del Árbol*) was a salutation of nature and the fatherland, in which school children planted trees and teachers gave patriotic discourses. Planting trees symbolized the growth of the locality as part of the regeneration of the whole nation. For many conservative regionalists, the *Fiesta del Árbol* became the main exponent of how the 'little patria' could regenerate the 'larger patria' and the ceremonies spread throughout Spain in the first decade of the twentieth century. In 1904 the *Fiesta del Árbol* was officially established and in 1915 it was declared a mandatory celebration in all national schools. However, the 'official-ization' of the fiesta signalled its decline since many municipalities saw it as a centralist imposition from Madrid. By the early 1920s, the Day of the Tree was in clear decay.[66]

Primo decided to revive the ritual as a means of patriotic child indoc-trination. The original conservative regionalist message of promoting the 'little patria' had to be modified, for it antagonized the *primorriverista* uni-tarian concept of Spain. Unsurprisingly, the regime called upon the *del-egados* to modify the message.[67] Since the very beginning of the Dictatorship, they organized the Day of the Tree in their districts as part of their gen-eral task of promoting patriotic feelings among the population.[68] The delegates organized the fiesta in the same manner as other patriotic rit-uals: they assembled the local authorities, hoisted and blessed the national flag and gave patriotic speeches. The teachers were also invited to utter some patriotic words and children read poems and sang nationalist songs composed for the event. On many occasions, the local priest recited a public mass, sanctifying the flag and the trees as the symbolic and organic representations of the patria. In this 'patriotic communion', the *delegados* certainly fulfilled their role of 'apostles of the fatherland', while teachers became the 'priests of the nation' addressing their young 'flock'. As with the *primorriverista* ceremonies for soldiers, Catholic imagery and rhetoric were integrated into civic patriotic rituals in schools. Like all the other National-Catholic ceremonies, this integration was in terms of subordination to the supreme deity: the nation.

It is beyond question that the regime saw schools as the most important vehicle for the transmission and consolidation of nationalist images, symbols and discourses. Whether drawing upon liberal icons (*Don Quixote*) or conservative rituals (the Day of the Tree), the *primorriveristas* transformed messages and rituals of the Restoration and turned them into specific National-Catholic celebrations. Control from the Interior Ministry and the use of *delegados* also homogenized *primorriverista* patriotic and civic rituals in terms of ceremony and discourse. In these celebrations of the nation, the school became the church of the fatherland and the com-memoration of 'civic saints', such as Miguel de Cervantes, was entrusted to teachers in their role as lay priests.[69] However, the effective transmis-sion of National-Catholicism as a 'civic religion' in the school needed something more than patriotic lectures and rituals. Improving the material conditions of schools and teachers became indispensable for the success of the indoctrination policies of the regime.

The demographic trap

The Dictatorship adopted the battle against illiteracy as one of its main educational priorities. Like the regenerationists, the *primorriveristas* considered the high number of illiterates in Spain as a symptom of the country's backwardness and accused the *caciques* of deliberately keeping the masses ignorant so that the local elites could maintain their political power.[70] Since the beginning of his regime, Primo directed the delegates to create cultural associations, which would provide reading classes in towns and villages.[71] He also demanded public co-operation in this task, especially from teachers and priests, and mobilized the UP militants for the organization of 'anti-illiteracy campaigns'.[72] Although these measures may have had some sort of temporary effect and certainly scored a propaganda victory for the government, they could not solve the problem of illiteracy in Spain. As Primo's much-admired Joaquín Costa had noticed at the turn of the century, only by tackling the chronic shortage of schools and improving the salaries of teachers could illiteracy rates go down in the long term.

The regime was fully aware of the need to promote the construction of new schools and in November 1923 facilitated credits to the municipalities with this specific aim in mind.[73] In April 1924, the government created the Junta for the Promotion of Public Schools, an agency in charge of co-ordinating state funds for school constructions, and, seven months later, the state gave more credits to the municipalities for building schools.[74] What all this legislation shows is that the regime advanced towards extensive state intervention in public education, reinforcing the role of the central government in terms of financial and legal control to the detriment of the municipalities. In other words, the Dictatorship furthered the process of nationalization of public education, by bringing schools under the direct control of the central state. It soon paid off in terms of the number of new schools constructed. In the last three months of 1923, 78 new schools were built. Throughout 1924, 652 schools were inaugurated and this figure had risen to 857 by 1925.[75]

For the *primorriverista* team in charge of education during the Civil Directory school building became a major task not only for improving the appalling pedagogic conditions of the country, but also in terms of political propaganda. For a technocratic Dictatorship, building schools was seen as a material justification of the regime and a way to gain popular support. In 1926, Suárez Somonte stated that increasing the number of schools was the number one objective. The reason was simple:

> [Of all works of the Dictatorship] the one that raised the people's enthusiasm most [. . .] has been the increase in the number of teachers with 2500 schools created and the intensification of school constructions. Every school created or built in whatever locality is a town gained for the regime.[76]

Suárez might have been under the illusion that building schools in a locality was tantamount to gaining its political support, but there can be no doubt that the regime took advantage of the constructions to promote itself. The governmental delegates turned every single opening of a new school into a nationalist ceremony. In the purest *primorriverista* style, they gathered the population, delivered patriotic speeches, and sanctified the national flag. As in the case of the *Fiesta del Árbol*, school teachers were also invited to utter some patriotic words for the occasion and children sang nationalist anthems. Almost invariably the new schools were named after Primo de Rivera.[77]

By 1926 the regime was seriously behind schedule in constructing the schools it had promised. Suárez calculated 2000 new *escuelas* had to be built in 1927 simply to catch up with the government's original plans.[78] He presented a proposal for accelerating the number of school-building projects that included a series of measures all of which called for a further state funding of the education system. The Director General of Primary Education realized that the current legislation favoured urban centres in terms of government's subsidies and proposed the state should pay for 50 per cent of the cost of schools in villages and small towns. This was a radical policy. In Spain, municipal councils traditionally paid for the cost of local schools. For extremely poor localities the Director General of Primary Education intended the central government to take full responsibility for funding schools, since these municipalities 'needed a more energetic, efficient and complete state protection, imposed by force'.[79] Suárez's plans were to partially find legal expression in 1927 when the Section of School Constructions (*Sección de Construcciones Escolares*) was created in the Department of Primary Education to co-ordinate school building.[80] The following year, a Royal Decree facilitated state direct funding to the poorest municipalities and established a Committee for School Constructions (*Comisión de Construcciones Escolares*) in every Spanish province, in order to evaluate their diverse material necessities.[81]

More importantly, Suárez's project found monetary backing in the government's 'special budget' (*presupuesto extraordinario*), the 1926 ten-year plan by which the state borrowed 3539 million pesetas to fund works in the public sector. This allowed the Ministry of Public Instruction to heavily invest in school buildings. Thus the state spent 9 million pesetas in school constructions in 1927, 12 million in 1928 and 14.5 million in 1929, a rather substantial increase when considering that in 1920 the central government had spent just 1.5 million in building schools.[82]

Although this injection of money led to an important increase in the number of *escuelas* built, it far from solved the problem of the schools shortage in Spain. In 1927, out of the 2000 schools needed according to Suárez, only 950 materialized. The shortfall infuriated teachers who bitterly complained about the broken promises and the fact that the regime had decided to reduce the target of schools to be built the following year.[83] In effect, things just worsened from then onwards. In 1928, only 671 new *escuelas* were inaugurated, beginning a serious downswing in the number of schools constructed. By 1929, the numbers had plummeted to 562.[84] Although initially the *primorriverista* propaganda machine could have deceived some sectors of the public, it did not mislead teachers, who insisted on the necessity of increasing the number of schools and improving the budget for their maintenance.[85] After the fall of the Dictatorship, *El Magisterio Nacional*, alarmed after Berenguer had announced a cut in the public instruction budget, angrily grumbled:

> the Spanish state has to spend more on primary education. People were led to believe that *Maestros* were well paid and that is not true. [The *primorriveristas*] repeated so often that thousands of schools were being created, that many think that need is fulfilled already, and this is not the case.[86]

Why did teachers consider *primorriverista* investment insufficient? After all, the regime expanded the number of *escuelas nacionales* from 27 080 in late 1923 to 33 446 at the end of 1930.[87] Yet it is important to note that this 23.5 per cent increase in the number of schools could not have had a decisive impact on improving the ratio of schools to students, since, as a result of the demographic boom of the 1910s, the number of children attending primary school grew an impressive 22.9 per cent during the period 1924–1930.[88] By 1932–1933, only 51.2 per cent of school-age children were in fact on a school roll.[89] In other words, for all the *primorriveristas'* efforts, the construction of schools during the

Dictatorship merely palliated the pressures imposed upon the education system by the country's demographic growth. Paradoxically, the upgrading of the education system in the 1920s, which was itself a response to the process of socio-economic modernization of Spain in the first two decades of the twentieth century, became a victim to the demographic growth produced by that very process of socio-economic development.

Increasing the number of teachers and improving their training and material conditions was a necessary complement to the *primorriverista* quantitative structural reform of primary education. During the Military Directory, the regime promoted the creation of new primary teacher posts in an attempt to match the intended growth of new schools. As early as November 1923, the government identified the need to 'create new *Maestros* and *Maestras* posts for primary schools', to be paid for by the state.[90] Thus, the state created 1500 new posts in 1924 and 1000 more in 1925, an increase of 8.64 per cent in the total number of *maestros nacionales*.[91] Following the same pattern of nationalization of the education system applied to the construction of schools, the Dictatorship committed the central government to funding teachers.

During the Civil Directory, however, the creation of teaching jobs soon slowed down and by the end of 1926 the number of new *maestros* had plummeted to 300.[92] The decrease was mainly due to a reduction in the 1926 Public Instruction budget and the chaotic situation produced in the allocation of those teaching posts created in 1924 and 1925. Suárez was fully aware of the need to seriously increase the number of teachers if he was to, first, modernize the education system and, second, gain support from the educators. In his report on the 1927 education budget, the Director General of Primary Education stated that Spain was in a dramatic situation with only 1.5 teachers per 1000 inhabitants, whereas France had 3.05 per 1000 inhabitants; Italy 2.3; and Germany 4.32. He concluded that to catch up with Europe, 'we need 23 000 *maestros* more, so there would be one teacher for every 60 children'.[93]

Suárez's recommendations seem to have had an immediate effect and, in 1927, the state created 1500 new teaching posts. The following year, 700 men and women became *maestros nacionales*, 1000 more teaching posts were created in 1929, and plans to generate 1000 new posts in 1930 were achieved.[94] Altogether, the number of *maestros nacionales* grew from 28 924 in 1922 to 34 680 at the end of 1930, a 19.9 per cent increase.[95] Yet the fact that the government passed legislation creating teaching posts did not necessarily mean that all those new *maestros* actually ended up teaching. The public competitions by which *maestro* posts were allocated were chaotic. In the 1923 and 1925 public competitions, hundreds of candidates who had passed their exams had to wait months, if not years, until they were assigned a school, while some others were never given a post. As a result of this incompetent organization of public competitions, *El Magisterio Español* denounced in late 1927 the fact that Spain had 'thousands of vacant schools without *Maestros*, and thousands of *Maestros* without schools'.[96] When the regime regulated the public competition system in 1928, it established a two-year interim period before a *maestro* was finally assigned to a school and a very complicated system of examination, which led to further confusion and irregularities.[97] Consequently, the number of teachers without a school increased, as did the outrage of candidates, teachers' associations and parents of school children, who flooded the Ministry of Education and the Office of the Prime Minister (*Presidencia del Gobierno*) with hundreds of complaints.[98] By the end of the Dictatorship, 4722 schools were vacant.[99]

It is hardly surprising that teachers felt outraged about this chaotic situation and things were no better with regard to their economic conditions. For all the Dictatorship's repeated promises of improving teachers' salaries, most of the teachers did not receive a wage rise. True, the Dictatorship raised the salary of a small minority of the worst paid *maestros* – those earning 2000 and 2500 pesetas per year. Yet the majority of the teachers did not get any kind of increase and most of them had to survive on 3000 pesetas per year throughout the Dictatorship.[100] No other single issue united teachers more than salary improvements. From the pro-*primorriverista El Magisterio Español* to the liberal *El Magisterio Nacional*, from Catholic to socialist journals, all education publications demanded urgent improvements in teachers' salaries.[101] Professionally, teachers associations of all sorts, directors of *escuelas* and mayors signed dozens of petitions from 1926 onwards, as promised improvements failed to materialize.[102] But despite the cascade of complaints, the government did not substantially improve teachers' salaries. As Callejo privately acknowledged to Máximo Cuervo, *jefe* of the Bureau of the President, the state simply did not have the money to give in one go decent salaries to all those it intended to be the 'preachers of the Patria'.[103]

The government also developed important plans seeking to instil patriotic feelings in teaching students. Suárez took up a policy of modernization of the Teacher Training Colleges (*escuelas normales*). He wanted them to became '*maestro*-making laboratories', educating teachers 'on the lights of the truths of our holy Religion and the [. . .] equally holy love for the Fatherland'.[104] An entirely new curriculum was designed stressing the history and geography of Spain and Hispanic-America, 'with special emphasis on the discovery and conquest of America, crystallizing in this teaching the greatness of Spain and the natural love of those nations to the mother Patria'.[105] The Director of Primary Education conceived the teaching profession as a 'priesthood' of the nation. As any other priesthood, he argued, the main bulk of the recruits would come from the lower classes; hence, the state should provide the means to facilitate teaching by vocations funding teacher schools.[106] However, the *primorriveristas* failed to carry out a legal reform of the *escuelas normales* and the 1914 curriculum remained in place throughout the entire Dictatorship. More importantly, the record suggests that the quality of teaching in the *escuelas normales* seriously deteriorated. The number of students in teacher colleges grew from 16 905 in the year 1923–1924 to 35 760 in 1929–1930, an increase of 111.53 per cent.[107] Yet the number of teaching colleges went up from just 91 to 93 in the same period, a clear indication of overcrowded *escuelas normales* in which the training of 'patriotic priests' became an impossible task.

In terms of mass nationalization, the *primorriverista* reforms of primary education had patchy results. It was in the battle against illiteracy that the government made serious improvements. Illiteracy rates fell from 39 per cent in 1920 to 27 per cent in 1930, in part due to the growth in the number of schools and teachers.[108] Yet the regime failed to turn the education system into the indoctrinating machine it intended. A combination of structural and political factors explains the outcome. The process of nationalization of the education system was under-funded and the regime proved unable to build enough schools and improve teachers' economic conditions sufficiently so as to operate the transformation it sought. Despite an increase in the educational budget during the Dictatorship, the Restoration legacy of underdevelopment and the population growth of the 1910s and 1920s seem to have been too heavy a burden.[109] The promise of great changes initially gained the *maestros'* support for the regime, but as these failed to materialize teachers increasingly turned against the *primorriveristas*. Conservative teachers continued to demand more money from the state, while liberal *maestros* resented the fact that the government used public money to sponsor private education.[110] *Primorriverista* military control and repression of educators only rubbed salt into the injury and alienated teachers further. Without adequate funding, educational structures and co-operation from those professionals called to be the 'priests of the fatherland', the nationalization of primary education was doomed to fail. In early January 1930, some three weeks before the fall of the regime, a progressive teacher, José María

Villegas, perfectly expressed the failure of the *primorriverista* educational policies in terms of nationalization:

> Happily, Spanish schools do not have that nationalist trait, so characteristic of many other European schools [. . .] Spanish schools, in this sense, are the real representative of society's thoughts and feelings. Not only are they not imperialist but they do not even have a great influence on the pupil's patriotic formation [. . .] Not in texts, nor in curricula, nor in personnel, is there a desire to inculcate the pride of the patria in the Spanish child.[111]

7
The Catholic Trap: Secondary Education and the Battle for Catalonia

Teaching Spanish is the only effective means of widening and strengthening the spiritual and racial basis of the Great Spain
(Primo de Rivera to Cambó)[1]

Whilst the nationalization of primary education concentrated on monitoring teachers, extra-curricula patriotic celebrations and structural improvements, the transformation of secondary education focused on a curricular reform and the imposition of a single national textbook for each level and area of instruction. As early as November 1923, the Dictatorship demonstrated its intention to carry out a series of changes in secondary and university education and ordered the Council of Public Instruction to produce a report.[2] Published in March 1924, the report recommended modernizing the system to facilitate the 'full development of all physical, moral, and intellectual adolescent activities', turning secondary education into an autonomous form of education and not merely a preparation for university.[3] However, clashes between the dictator and the Council ended up with the advisory body being purged by the regime and the transformations postponed for almost two years.

It was not until the formation of the Civil Directory that the reform began to take shape. In December 1925, the Marquess of Estella established the General Bureau of Secondary and University Education, an agency directly controlled by the Minister of Public Instruction and created with the specific aim of restricting the power of the liberal-dominated Junta for Further Studies (*Junta para Ampliación de Estudios*).[4] During the first half of 1926, Wenceslao González Oliveros, Director of the General Bureau of Secondary and University Education, Eduardo Callejo and Primo himself all worked on the reform. By June 1926, Callejo presented to Primo his blueprint of a royal decree for the reform of secondary education. Much in the same manner as the UP ideologues, the project emphasized the need to adapt the educational reform to Spanish 'national psychology' and systematized the teaching periods seeking to improve the relations between primary and secondary education, on the one hand, and high schools with universities, on the other. What lay underneath this proposal was an attempt to unify all educational institutions under state control and avoid the 'atomization' (*cantonalismo*) produced by the liberal programmes of the past.[5]

The Royal Decree of 25 August 1926 initiated the reform of secondary education. When compared to the 1903 programme it replaced, the 1926 curriculum showed significant changes. First, it put more emphasis on scientific and technical teaching, much in the same way as Bottai, the Italian fascist Minister of Education, was to attempt in his 1930s educational reforms.[6] Likewise, this 'scientific drive' was in perfect accord with the UP ideologues' modernizing discourse, which claimed to have scientific bases and advocated technical education in order to improve national productivity. Second, and not surprisingly, the new syllabus heavily stressed the teaching of history. Whilst the 1903 programme included history courses in the 3rd and 4th years, the *primorriveristas* made history obligatory throughout the first four years of secondary education, increasing the number of hours per week from six in two years to fifteen in four. Compulsory courses included World History, Spanish American History, Spanish History and History of Spanish Civilization, a clear indication of the regime's determination to instruct teenagers in *Hispanista* imperial values.

The most controversial change in the curriculum concerned the teaching of Catholic doctrine. Since 1895, the subject of religion had been optional in Spanish high schools and no exams on Catholic doctrine were required to graduate. The *primorriveristas* made Catholic doctrine compulsory in the first two years of high school (*Bachillerato Elemental*). As the dictator explained, religion had to be mandatory since inculcating Catholic principles was as important as instruction in patriotism and honour.[7] It is fairly evident that the government sought to incorporate religion in the curriculum as a means to reinforce patriotic education in high schools, following the *primorriverista* conception of Catholicism as an instrument to imbue the population with ideas of authority, order and hierarchy. However, religion did not become a standard subject in the curriculum. The Callejo Plan, the secondary and university education reform named after the Minister of Education, stipulated that no exams had to be taken in the subject to obtain the secondary education degree and, more importantly, students whose parents had declared they did not want their children to attend religion classes would be exempted.

This middle-way which turned religion into a compulsory subject but did not grant it the same status as the rest of the subjects in the curriculum predictably pleased very few. Progressive educationalists criticized the measure, arguing that the state should not impose any religious dogma.[8] The Catholic right, which had been campaigning for the mandatory imposition of religion in secondary education, had mixed responses. While the Social Catholics of *El Debate* welcomed the changes, some others considered the reform was not good enough and restarted the campaign to force the Dictatorship to establish compulsory religious education without exceptions.[9] In November 1927, the reactionary Marchioness of la Rambla, for example, claimed in the National Assembly that religion was not really compulsory in Spanish secondary education and urged the Minister of Public Instruction to abolish all exceptions. Callejo responded that the government considered the study of Catholic religion as the key element in the spiritual improvement of the 'Spanish race', but the Dictatorship never acceded to the ultramontane demands and legislation remained unchanged.[10]

No other measure, however, triggered as much anger as the imposition of a prescribed single textbook in secondary education. Parallel to the secondary education reform, the Primo–Callejo team engineered the creation of the single state-approved textbook for each course of study – the so-called *texto único*. In early 1926, the dictator gave guidelines for the eventual legislation on the single text for both primary and secondary education: books must be inspired by 'the principles of state religion, a fervent love for Spain and a profound respect for the established political system'.[11] Primo foresaw the potential controversy that such a state imposition of nationalist, religious and pro-Dictatorship principles could provoke, but the Marquess of Estella was not willing to compromise over the role of the state in the nationalization of the masses. Weeks later, in a new report, he insisted on the patriotic principles that should guide the single texts and designed a system by which the state would have absolute control of the selection, production and sales of the textbooks. Moreover, Primo ordered his Minister of Public Instruction to draft a royal order on the *texto único* 'in virile and uncompromising language, defending the undisputable right of the state to conduct and adjust education'.[12] In August 1926, Callejo presented his project to the dictator and the Royal Decree on the *texto único* was finally approved later that month.

The *primorriveristas* soon faced problems with the implementation of the *texto único*. Initially, Primo wanted the single text to be in the schools by the academic year 1926–1927, but the Ministry of Public Instruction's delay in producing the Royal Decree on the *texto único* forced the regime to postpone its implementation until the following year. Once the system was functioning, the publication of official text-books still did not follow immediately. Textbooks for the courses in Spanish Civilization and American History were not distributed until 1929 and those for Spanish History and World History never saw the light of day. Not surprisingly, in those cases where the official books were published, they reproduced the *primorriverista* interpretation of Spanish history. For example, Francisco Yela's textbook on Spanish Civilization portrayed Menéndez Pelayo as the 'wisest scholar of nineteenth-century Spain', described the 'discovery and civilization of America' as 'one of the greatest deeds of human history', and, based on Juderías, attacked jealous foreigners for fabricating the Black Legend.[13]

Yet the existence of an official textbook did not necessarily mean that students were using it. Some had predicted before the legislation was approved that the appearance of 'official little bibles' for every subject would only bring confusion to the education system, since teachers would continue to use their own materials.[14] As the regime soon came to know, this prediction proved right and many high school teachers kept on rec-ommending their own books even after the official ones were published. The government reacted by publishing a Royal Order in September 1928 emphasizing the teachers' obligation to use only official texts, but this legislation seems to have had very little impact and denunciations of professors using their own works in the schools continued.[15]

While the efficacy of the single text as an instrument of nationalization was extremely limited, the political storm it provoked was unprecedented. Progressive educationists opposed the single text mainly on pedagogic grounds, claiming it diminished the figure of the teacher and hampered students' learning processes, for it denied the plural nature of know-ledge.[16] Liberals did not overlook the fact that the Dictatorship was using the state apparatus to instruct the masses in National-Catholic values, something they strongly disapproved: 'the state is the worst of all churches when it comes to fabricating dogma', wrote Gómez Baquero, envisaging the failure of the *primorriverista* task of doctrinal unification.[17]

Contrary to what has sometimes been suggested, the single text far from satisfied the clerical ambitions of the right.[18] Catholic teachers felt uneasy about the imposition of a single text and even some pro-*primorriverista* publications, such as *El Magisterio Español*, opposed the new measure.[19] The state monopoly on the contents and production of schoolbooks became a core problem for the Church. The Augustinian Father Delgado described the single text as 'tyrannical' and 'against Natural Law', but he especially resented the fact that no cleric had been appointed to the tribunals in charge of determining the content of the books. In his view, the Church, as the constitutional guarantor of the Catholic faith, had the right to oversee the single text.[20] The reference to the 1876 constitution should not come as a surprise, for it indicates that the ecclesiastical elites had begun to realize they were better off under the Restoration. What the words of Father Delgado revealed was the Church's willingness to maintain ecclesiastical autonomy and its ability to intervene in public educational matters at the same time, as had been the case from 1876. But what the *primorriverista* reforms sought was subordination of the Church to the state.

Speaking for the Jesuits, Father Teodoro Rodríguez went a step further in his criticism of the *texto único* and denied the state had the right to select books or teachers. In the name of 'freedom of education', he proposed leaving the education system entirely to the law of supply and demand, which would 'eliminate those [schools] with no right to exist; so the paying public could freely choose'.[21] Behind this Social Darwinist approach to education, there was an unmistakable reaction against the *primorriverista* policies which effectively reinforced the state as the supreme educational authority. The Church had expected, and indeed received, direct economic support from the state but now that the implications of this official sponsorship became clear alarm bells were ringing in ecclesiastical quarters. As soon as the legislation on the *texto único* was approved, the integrist Catholic daily *El Siglo Futuro* launched a campaign against it, accusing the government of appropriating ecclesiastical prerogatives.[22] More importantly, Social Catholics, who constituted much of the UP social base, also objected to the reform on very similar grounds.[23] By late 1928, *El Debate* called Catholics to resist the process of *primorriverista* state control. A common technique to avoid censorship was criticizing Mussolini when the intended object was Primo. *El Debate* severely condemned fascist interventionism in education and clearly expressed that co-operation with, and not subordination to, the *primorriverista* regime was the aim of the Catholic right:

> In these difficult and anarchic times, Catholics must, on the one hand, support governments and civil authorities; strengthening established powers. But on the other hand, [they] must be ready to defend the freedom and legitimate rights of the Catholic Church, against the intrusion of the civil power.[24]

When in 1928 Primo granted the right to issue degrees to the religious university colleges of Deusto and El Escorial, thus breaching the monopoly of the state over higher education, the rift between the Church and the regime was already too wide to comfort Catholics. The Church certainly welcomed the measure but was fully aware that Deusto and El Escorial had a restricted curriculum and were very small compared to the state universities. This was a minuscule gain that did not bring the education system under Church control – the aspiration of the ecclesiastical authorities in September 1923.[25] True, the concession of legal parity to the Catholic university colleges united liberal scholars, the left and students in their opposition to the regime. University reform led to unprecedented student demonstrations, severe governmental repression and the resignation of the most prominent scholars in Spanish universities (Ortega y Gasset, Fernando de los Rios, Luis Jiménez de Asúa); all of these factors catalysed the fall of the regime. Yet, for the Catholic Church, the concessions could not balance the loss of 'freedom of education' and the imposition of the single text in secondary education, the ecclesiastical stronghold which assured its ideological control over the middle classes.

In late 1929, Catholics received new ammunition from Rome in their battle against the Dictatorship. Pius XI's *Divini Illius Magistri* was a fierce attack on state intervention in educational matters. In exactly the same Social Darwinist line that Spanish Catholics had been arguing in the 1920s, the encyclical defended the 'freedom of private education' and denied the state the right to interfere in educational matters, let alone to prioritize state schools.[26] After the fall of the Dictatorship, Catholics went on the offensive. They created new associations to defend the 'educational rights' of the Church and soon demanded from Berenguer a total reform of the *primorriverista* education system, the 'most violent, unjust, and un-educational regime of LEGAL OPPRESSION in Europe (except Russia)'.[27]

The clash over education between the Dictatorship and the Church reflected an essential ideological division between the *primorriveristas* and the Catholic right. For the latter, Catholicism was the supreme value-system and religious doctrine the main tool of political socialization. Patriotism was a complementary element of Catholic doctrine, but state expansion was viewed as a threat to the Church's privileges. For the *primorriveristas* the nation was the supreme sacred value and state agencies the necessary tools for mass nationalization. As in the case of Italy, the policies of mass indoctrination required a process of nationalization of the education system that inevitably led to serious tensions with the Church. In no other place did this become more obvious than in Catalonia, where the regime concentrated its efforts to 'Spanishize' (that is, to nationalize in Spanish values or *españolizar*) the education system, only to provoke ecclesiastical outrage and thus deepening the cleavage between Church and state.

The 'Spanishization' of Catalonia

The process of mass nationalization acquired specific connotations in those territories where regional languages co-existed with Castilian. Primo saw the propagation of the Spanish language in Catalonia and the Basque Country as 'the only effective means to widen and strengthen the spiritual and racial bases of the Great Spain'.[28] The regime believed 'separatists and regionalists' had used schools during the Restoration to 'de-Spanishize Catalan children by teaching exclusively in Catalan' and, therefore, it was the Dictatorship's duty to foster an utterly Castilian education.[29] The aim of *primorriverista* linguistic policy was twofold. First, it used language to transmit Spanish national identity in Catalonia and the Basque Country. At the same time, it sought to preclude regionalists and nationalists from using Catalan and Basque languages as tools for the political socialization of children in schools.

As we saw in Chapter 6, during the first weeks of the Dictatorship the regime imposed teaching in Castilian in every single public educational institution in Spain and established prison sentences for teachers propagating secessionist doctrines in schools. But the regime also wanted to curb the influence of regional languages outside schools and after his return from a state visit to Italy in November 1923, Primo began to toy with the idea of prohibiting the clergy to preach in regional languages. The initiative was not new. Already in 1902, the liberal Minister of Education, the Count of Romanones, had issued a decree requiring the teaching of catechism in Castilian. But the wave of opposition this provoked from the clergy and the Catholic right all around Spain eventually forced the entire liberal government to resign. The new conservative government of Francisco Sivela abolished the controversial decree only a month after the liberals had approved it.[30] Like Romanones, for Primo teaching the catechism in Spanish was an important issue, since Castilian was considered the guarantor of national unity and the main hope for cultural homogenization. As had been the case in France, the Spanish Church promoted the teaching of catechism in regional languages and dialects, not only because it wanted to make sure that children would correctly understand religious postulates, but also because it granted priests a privileged position in children's education, compared to the state.[31] Thus the issue of language was directly related to the power of the Church and the state to effectively indoctrinate the masses in non-Castilian speaking areas.

In the Basque Country, the *primorriverista* policies of Spanishization were far less controversial than in Catalonia. The *ikastolas*, schools where all the teaching was in the Basque language, were closed and some teachers arrested for teaching in Euskera. In Tolosa, for instance, a school was shut down and the *maestra* put on trial because she taught in Euskera only.[32] But, in most cases, the regime was lenient and pragmatic when approaching the issue of languages. In early 1924, General Echagüe, the Military Governor of Vizcaya and a Basque speaker himself, published an official note stating that the Basque language could be used in all those areas where Castilian speakers were a minority. No punishment, the note followed, should be taken against those speaking or writing in Euskera.[33] During the entire Dictatorship, the *primorriveristas* not only allowed the publication of works in Euskera but also tolerated moderate Basque nationalists' activities for the promotion of the Basque language and culture.[34]

One of the main reasons for this *primorriverista* approach in the Basque provinces was the relative willingness of the Basque Church to co-operate with the Dictatorship. Although some priests were reprimanded and fined by military officers for preaching in Basque, the Bishops of Vitoria during the Dictatorship, Zacarías Martínez and Mateo Múgica, were staunch monarchists with very few sympathies for Basque nationalism, and no episcopal protest greeted the prohibition of catechism classes in Euskera.[35] They recommended priests to preach in Spanish or Euskera depending on which language was that spoken by the majority of the population in their parishes. As a consequence, during the Dictatorship, preaching in Basque continued to be habitual in Basque-speaking areas, something the regime tolerated together with the publication of cultural magazines in Euskera sponsored by the Church. Moreover, to the dismay of Basque nationalists, a good number of rural priests in Vizcaya joined the UP, a move that certainly pleased the *primorriverista* authorities and strengthened the bond between the Basque Church and the Dictatorship.[36] Finally, the fact that *primorriverista* repression against members of the Basque nationalist movement was selective, as opposed to the indiscriminate actions in Catalonia, indicates that the regime was far less concerned with the impact of Basque nationalism than with the spread of Catalanism.[37]

In Catalonia, the *primorriverista* strategy of nationalization coupled with the one used for the renewal of the education system, first repressing teachers and institutions considered guilty of spreading regionalist or nationalist doctrines and, then, promoting schools, education centres, fiestas and lectures to cultivate Spanish nationalist values among the population. A letter from Alfonso Sala, then leader of the *españolista* UMN, to the *Presidencia del Gobierno* perfectly illustrates the inquisitorial character of some of the regime's supporters in Catalonia. In November 1923, Sala demanded the urgent abolishment of the Barcelona Municipal Cultural Commission, which he considered Catalanist, and the punishment of the 'separatist' *Federación de Maestros de Cataluña* and the *Associació de Mestres Oficials de Barcelona*.[38] He also insisted on the need to purge the inspectors, whom the leader of the UMN accused of not defending properly 'the state's rights' and of being lenient with regionalist teachers. Moreover, Sala wanted all teachers in the province of Barcelona to pledge loyalty to 'the interests of Spain'. Those under suspicion of not fulfilling their 'sacred duty' should be sanctioned for life or sent to some other town in Spain outside Catalonia. Only with these measures, Sala concluded, 'would the phantom of Catalan separatism go away for ever; [and] Spanish schools would achieve the miracle of inculcating love for the larger Patria in the masses'.

The regime moved fast to purge teachers considered Catalanists. As early as October 1923, teachers and inspectors were instructed to denounce colleagues who were teaching in a different language than Spanish.[39] Dozens of state-school *maestros* were denounced by their colleagues, inspectors or, simply, by private individuals.[40] Actions were also taken against inspectors considered too lenient, who, as recommended by Sala, were sent to other Spanish provinces outside Catalonia and replaced by *primorriverista* loyalists.[41] The regime targeted non-state schools too. Military and Civil Governors, with the assistance of the *delegados*, played an essential role by, first, purging municipal councils of those considered regionalists and, later, dismissing municipal employees accused of being Catalanists, which tightened the control over municipal schools and libraries.[42]

The *Mancomunitat* was initially put under temporary military supervision. The cultural and teaching institutions controlled by the *Mancomunitat* were rapidly purged, the Universidad Industrial closed down and Roman Sol, the *Mancomunitat* culture councillor and member of *Acció Catalana*, jailed.[43] Putting linguistic policies in the forefront, General Losada, interim director of the institution, ordered all schools and cultural centres sponsored by the *Mancomunitat* to teach exclusively in Spanish, on 24 January 1924.[44] A week later, Losada named Sala president of the *Mancomunitat*, a post the leader of the UMN would hold until Primo decided to abolish the institution in March 1925.

Nor were state universities free from the *primorriverista* 'crusade' against the Catalan language in educational institutions. Although Spanish was the customary language in Catalan universities, the Dictatorship specifically prohibited the use of the regional language in Catalan and Valencian higher education. This measure was especially important in teacher training colleges (*escuelas normales*), where state-sponsored courses on the Catalan language had been free for all students since 1916. The *primorriveristas* saw these classes as a clear threat to their project of indoctrinating teachers in Spanish nationalist values and, during the first months of the Dictatorship, the courses were brought to an end in the *escuelas normales* of Lérida, Tarragona and Gerona.[45]

Dictatorial control of the University of Barcelona also became evident quickly. In November 1923, Primo appointed as its director Andrés Martínez Vargas, a well-known conservative and anti-Catalanist. His appointment provoked the opposition of liberal professors and the members of the *Federació Catalana d'Estudiants Catolics*, who complained about the non-democratic election of the new director. The regime reacted by creating an information network within the University of Barcelona. Staunch *primorriveristas* sent secret reports to Martínez Anido and Máximo Cuervo in Madrid, denouncing the political activities of professors, lecturers and student associations.[46] On the basis of these denunciations, the Dictatorship dismissed professors, closed down publications and even imprisoned the director of the journal *Vida Universitària*, when he refused to publish the magazine in Castilian as ordered by the Civil Governor of Barcelona General Milans de Bosch.[47] When in 1925 the Minister of Public Instruction and the Medical Faculty of the University of Barcelona clashed over the language issue, the government temporarily closed it down. In April 1929, when the revolts in the universities were at their height and the conflict had spread all around Spain, Primo closed down the University of Barcelona.

The Catalan Church, considered not merely a vehicle of linguistic and cultural transmission but a propagator of nationalist ideas, did not escape *primorriverista* repression. Throughout the entire Dictatorship, the government closed down ecclesiastical associations, arrested and exiled dozens of priests, banned religious processions and purged Catholic schools. What lay behind these constant attacks on clerics was not merely the purging from the Catalan Church of 'separatist' elements, but the control of an institution considered a challenge to the power of the state. At stake also was the whole *primorriverista* project of Spanishization in Catalonia and for these proposals the regime tried to force the Catalan clergy to preach in Castilian. Primo had this idea in mind since the early months of the Dictatorship, but he knew that achieving it in practice would not be easy. The Vatican had defended the preaching in vernacular languages since the Council of Trent in the sixteenth century and Catalan bishops had reaffirmed their commitment to the provision of religious services in Catalan just a few months before Primo's coup. Thus the dictator's suggestion to preach in Castilian found strong resistance both in Rome and Catalonia. Leading the opposition to this measure was Cardinal Vidal i Barraquer, the supreme Catholic authority in Catalonia. He declared himself open to co-operation with the regime but he was unwilling to order priests to preach in Castilian.[48]

Facing resistance, Primo took action on three different fronts. First, the Marquess of Estella personally intervened to obtain the appointment of non-Catalans to rule the region's dioceses and secure the transfer of Catalan clerics to outside of Catalonia. Even anti-Catalanist clerics, such as the Archdeacon of Tarragona Isidro Gomá y Tomás, were, as Catalans, precluded from promotion inside Catalonia and sent to non-Catalan dioceses.[49] Although the dictator publicly denied the existence of a policy of 'marginalization' of Catalan priests, the truth is that this idea constituted a main element of the *primorriverista* process of nationalization. In a private letter to his loyal friend Admiral Magaz, Primo stated that if the Catalan clergy mobilized its nationalist supporters, the solution would be to organize 'a terrific raid and send [the priests] to serve in Andalusia, before their actions could have any effect'.[50]

The second front was indeed in Catalonia itself, where actions against priests preaching in the vernacular language continued to be organized from the Captaincy General of Catalonia. The creation in 1927 of the *Junta de Acción Ciudadana* in Barcelona provided Generals Barrera and Milans with the possibility of co-ordinating the repression of dissident clerics with civilian *primorriveristas*. The *Junta de Acción Ciudadana* actively conducted detentions of priests, penalized religious educators teaching in Catalan and fined ecclesiastical institutions accused of propagating anti-Spanish ideas, increasing even further the climate of political repression in Barcelona.[51] The confrontation between civil and ecclesiastical authorities became extremely tense in Barcelona, where the Bishop of the province, Josep Miralles, refused to order his priests to preach in Castilian. Despite pressure from Barrera and Milans, Miralles maintained that the Vatican orders were to preach in the vernacular language and constantly declined sermonizing in Castilian. Moreover, he denounced the anti-clerical repression of the Civil Governor in Barcelona to Rome, urging the Vatican to defend the Catalan Church against state interference. However, the complaints of the Bishop of Barcelona to the Vatican were to no avail. In 1930, after heavy lobbying by the Spanish government in Rome, the Vatican transferred Miralles to the less important diocese of Majorca.[52]

Rome became the third front of *primorriverista* action. Since the Holy See had the right to appoint and dismiss cardinals and bishops in Spain, the Dictatorship launched a diplomatic offensive to compel the Vatican to abandon its protection of the Catalan episcopate. In 1926, during one of his visits to Italy, Eduardo Aunós, the Spanish Labour Minister, met the Papal Secretary of State, Cardinal de Gasparri, and demanded more co-operation from the Vatican with the *primorriverista* task of Span-ishization. Aunós requested from the Pope a public condemnation of Catalan regionalism, the transfer of Vidal to the first available archdio-cese outside of Catalonia and the appointment of Spanish nationalist (or *españolista*) bishops in all Catalan dioceses.[53] Primo seemed determined to make the Vatican change its policies even if it meant risking a schism. He informed Vidal that Rome had to choose between his dictatorship and Catalonia and threatened 'to expel the Nuncio and move straight away to the constitution of a National Church', should the Vatican take the 'wrong side'.[54] One can only speculate on whether Primo would have gone as far as to create a Spanish National Church, but the truth is that diplomatic pressures soon began to pay off. In 1927, the Nuncio, Federico Tedeschini, exhorted the Catalan clergy to preach in Castilian and Vidal was threatened with a transfer to Zaragoza or Granada. Furthermore, Admiral Magaz, the Spanish ambassador to the Vatican since 1926, con-vinced De Gasparri to open an investigation on Vidal and the use of Catalan language in pastorals. The Papal Secretary of State sent the Nuncio and the Head of the Jesuits to enquire into the Catalanist propa-ganda by priests.[55] As a result of the investigation and the pressures from the Spanish government, the Vatican ordered the Catalan clergy that no seminarist 'contaminated with Catalanism' should be allowed to enter the priesthood.[56] Although Rome did not establish Castilian as the pastoral language, it instructed Catalan priests to underline Spanish patriotism in their sermons and required that the Catalan catechism include new passages stressing love for the Spanish *patria*.

The new Vatican regulations were a Pyrrhic victory for the regime. Changes in liturgies, catechism and sermons had been achieved at a very high price. Even after all the repression and its diplomatic efforts, the regime could not force the Catalan clergy to preach in Castilian. In turn, the Catalan clergy and laity considered the *primorriverista* policies anti-cler-ical and severely resented dictatorial repression. Moreover, the cleavage between the regime and the Social Catholics widened due to the *primor-riverista* hostility towards the Catalan Church. In February 1928, *El Debate* claimed *primorriverista* actions were a clear violation of the Church's right to choose the language in which the divine word was to be transmitted.[57] As in the case of educational policies, the intensification of state-led pol-icies of nationalization deepened the *primorriverista*–Social Catholic divide.

The *primorriverista* strategy of nationalization was not based solely on the repression of doctrines considered anti-Spanish. It also required the promotion of National-Catholic values in schools and cultural institutions. After the dissolution of the *Mancomunitat* in March 1925, the government concentrated all its efforts into promoting cultural *españolista* policies from the provincial governments. In Barcelona, Primo put Milá i Camps, the Count of Montseny and a well-known Spanish nationalist, in charge of the *Diputación*. The provincial government became the official centre of the *primorriverista* cultural programmes. The Department of Education of the *Diputación* organized the donation of books, sponsored cultural associations, arranged patriotic lectures and granted scholarships for a variety of courses. The importance of the institution for the *primorriveristas* becomes obvious when the education budget of the *Diputación* is compared to that of the *Mancomunitat*. In the year 1922–1923, the *Mancomunitat* had a budget of 2 401 872 pesetas allocated to its Department of Public Instruction; while, in 1929, the *Diputación* resources for education amounted to 2 550 233 pesetas – a figure all the more significant if we consider it relates to just the province of Barcelona, whereas the *Mancomunitat*'s budget covered all four Catalan provinces.[58]

The Department of Education of the *Diputación* of Barcelona devoted much of its efforts and resources to buy books and distribute them amongst schools and public libraries. The nature of these works was essentially patriotic, devoted to hailing the dictator, the *Somatén* or the Spanish race, although Spanish and Hispanic-American literary classics and religious publications were also included among the donations. Special attention was also paid to the preparation of patriotic fiestas. In 1925, for example, editions of the *Revista Hispanoamericana* were distributed among libraries and schools to commemorate the *Fiesta de la Raza*.[59] As instructed by the *primorriverista* legislation, the *Diputación* annually organized patriotic lectures in all public libraries and educational centres of the province and donated hundreds of books to national and municipal schools to celebrate the *Fiesta del Libro*.[60]

For all the promotion of the Castilian language by the *Diputación*, it is important to note that books in Catalan were not expressly excluded from the donations and, in some cases, they constituted around 30 per cent of the lots bestowed.[61] Nor did the *Diputación* exclude sponsoring research on the Catalan language. After the dissolution of the *Mancomunitat*, the Chair of Catalan Grammar was transferred to the *Diputación* of Barcelona, which continued to fund the institution and different research projects on the Catalan language.[62] This funding of Catalan studies was in agreement with some other measures taken by the regime, such as the creation of a Chair at the University of Barcelona for studying the work of the Catalan philosopher Ramón Llull in 1925, or the appointment of eight academics to study the Catalan, Basque and Galician languages at the Real Academia de la Lengua in Madrid in

1926.[63] It is therefore fairly evident that the *primorriveristas* did not seek to 'exterminate' Catalan language, as is at times suggested.[64] The regime imposed Castilian as an instrument of nationalization in schools and public institutions, yet the *primorriverista* conception of regional languages as folkloric relics did not preclude the promotion of their studies in academia, while press and publications in Catalan, Basque and Galician were also tolerated.

The Civil Government of Barcelona acquired in the *Diputación* a key instrument of the *primorriverista* nationalization programme and indoctrination of teachers was not overlooked. Since 1926, the Department of Public Instruction organized patriotic pedagogic courses in the Barcelona teacher training college specifically aimed at teaching how to lecture on patriotic values.[65] Nor was women's education neglected by the *primorriveristas*. The provincial government maintained the funding of the Woman's Popular Library and created new grants for study at the Women's Professional College of Barcelona.[66] As in the cases of the *primorriverista* plans for women's political and physical indoctrination, it is possible to observe here the regime's belief that women should be integrated into the labour market as well as nationalized. Once again, this approach to the social and 'patriotic' role of women clearly differed from the fascist model in Italy, which condemned women to a passive role at home.[67]

What was the overall impact of *primorriverista* policies of Spanishization in Catalonia? In October 1929, Primo stated in an official communiqué that his policies had eradicated Catalan nationalism and awoken a deep love for Spain among the people of Catalonia.[68] Nine months later, General Berenguer abolished the notorious 'Decree against separatism', arguing that the circumstances that originally led to its imposition did not exist anymore. In fact, nothing could be further from the truth. The dictatorial repression in Catalonia was intensive and arbitrary. This was to alienate those sectors from which Primo sought much of his support: the Church and the bourgeoisie. As a result of the repression important sectors of the middle classes and the clergy began to move towards Catalan nationalist options. Moreover, the monarchists in Catalonia, who had been strongly anti-Catalanist before the Dictatorship, began to change their views and, once the dictator fell, embraced regionalism.[69] The suppression of political liberties led Catalan regionalists to take refuge in cultural activities. Publications in Catalan rocketed during the Dictatorship: in 1923, there were six newspapers published in Catalan, while in 1927, ten newspapers and 147 magazines were published in this language. By 1930, 10.2 per cent of all books published in Spain were in Catalan.[70] In other words, Primo de Rivera's policies of Spanishization put language in

Figure 7   Children's premilitary education. King Alfonso XIII and General Barrera inspect a formation of the Exploradores of Barcelona and Tarrasa.

the front line of the dialectic between Spanish and Catalan nationalism and turned education into a political battleground. When in 1932 Catalonia was granted political autonomy, the 'Catalanization' of schools became the first goal of the regional government.

At the education level, the policies of Spanishization also led to serious practical problems in teaching. The imposition of Spanish in public educational centres was certainly welcomed in those urban areas with a high number of Castilian speakers. After all, due to the steady flow of immigrants from other Spanish regions during the first two decades of the century, many Catalan towns had witnessed a rapid growth, becoming strongholds of Spanish nationalism.[71] Yet, in rural Catalonia, *maestros* found teaching in Spanish a serious burden. In a letter to *El Magisterio Nacional*, an Aragonese *maestro* working in a village in the district of Tortosa bitterly described how he had to waste much of his lessons explaining the meaning of Castilian words, such as *lentejas* (lentils), to an amazed young audience which could hardly understand him.[72] In such circumstances, he considered his teaching was 'anti-pedagogic' and demanded permission to use Catalan, or 'at least some Catalan words', when teaching. The Aragonese teacher was not alone in his petitions. Three months after the fall of the Dictatorship, the *maestros nacionales* of Barcelona, most of them non-Catalan, called for total change of the *primorriverista* linguistic policy. They unanimously demanded, first, permission 'to use regional languages in the classroom' and, second, the re-establishment of regional language courses in the teacher training colleges.[73] As in the rest of Spain, in Catalonia the Dictatorship failed to gain teachers' support for its policies of nationalization.

In many ways, the *primorriverista* failure in Catalonia epitomizes the regime's inability to turn the education system into an effective indoctrinating machine for the whole country. The regime's educational reforms had a twofold negative effect. They alienated key groups of *primorriverista* supporters (that is, the Church, Social Catholics, and much of the conservative urban middle classes) and antagonized teachers, the very state servants responsible for the transmission of the National-Catholic message. The disaffection of teachers and school inspectors with the regime due to repression and the inquisitorial education system created by the *primorriveristas* reinforces the argument of the 'republicanization' of certain professional groups under the Dictatorship. Like many doctors, clerks and state servants, teachers and school inspectors began to consider a constitutional republic as their best hope: a non-arbitrary form of power which could protect their own professional interests.

A second factor that seriously hampered the education system as a successful agency of nationalization was the *primorriveristas'* clash with the Catholic Church. This conflict was difficult to avoid. The process of nationalization of the masses from above required the expansion of the state education system, something that inevitably affected ecclesiastical interests. This put Primo in an extraordinarily difficult position, since the state's educational limitations made ecclesiastical co-operation indispensable in the *primorriverista* task of nationalization. As a result, like Mussolini, the dictator needed to make some concessions to the ecclesiastical authorities while, at the same time, expanding the public education system. Yet the confrontation is also extremely revealing of the real nature of *primorriverismo*. As we saw in Chapters 2 and 3, *primorriverista* discourse developed a sacred concept of the patria, in which the nation was placed above Catholicism and the state above the Church. When the nation was perceived to be under threat, as in the case of Catalonia, confrontation with the Church became inevitable.

For all its shortcomings, the public education system grew significantly in terms of schools and teachers during the Dictatorship. By 1931, the Second Republic could benefit from the *primorriverista* reinforcement of state education. This was, however, a poisoned legacy, for the economic situation of the 1930s made the improvement of a seriously under-funded education system a very difficult task. The Republican–Socialist coalition (1931–1933) took a similar top-down approach to the *primorriveristas* in an attempt to nationalize the masses, but this time indoctrination was in democratic and secular values. The creation of a 'new republican citizen' became a key goal in the first democratic government, which promoted lectures and readings of the 1931 constitution in small towns and villages. But financial restrictions, the revisionist policies of the period 1933–1936 and the lack of time precluded Republican–Socialist initiatives from having a significant impact.[74] Ideologically, it was the Francoist regime which ultimately gained from the *primorriverista* experience. As in the case of Primo, Franco welcomed the help of the Church with his project of 'political religion', but did not allow an ecclesiastical tutelage of his regime.[75] Once the subordination of the Church was secured and political opposition eradicated during and after the Civil War, the formation of a totalitarian National-Catholic education system finally crystallized in the 1940s.

8
Somatén Nacional: Paramilitaries and Cheerleaders

> Reason is not enough for the colossal endeavour of saving the people: we must light in it the flame of passion
>
> (Emilio Rodríguez Tarduchy)[1]

On 21 November 1923, Primo de Rivera met Mussolini for an official lunch at the Palazzo Venezia. In his speech, the Spanish dictator described fascism and *primorriverismo* as parallel movements of national salvation and presented the *Somatén* and the fascist militia as twin 'secular institutions of civilization and order'.[2] That very same day, gratefully impressed by the *Duce*, Primo proudly declared to the press that Spain would follow the fascist example. When the official delegation returned to Spain on 1 December, Primo could see his approach to fascism had generated a great deal of expectation. At Barcelona harbour, together with the whole Catalan political elite, around 300 'blue shirts' of the *Federación Cívico Somatenista* (aka *La Traza*) welcomed the King and the dictator with Roman salutes.[3] The twelve *tracista* squads followed the royal retinue through the city. The streets of Barcelona presented an atmosphere of celebration – balconies in the Ramblas displayed Spanish flags and thousands of people gathered to cheer the King and the dictator. The procession first stopped at the cathedral where Alfonso XIII and Primo were greeted by the Cardinal-Archbishop of Catalonia and all Catalan bishops before hearing a *Te Deum*. Immediately afterwards, the group headed towards the town hall. At the entrance of the San Jaime Palace the mayor welcomed the distinguished guests and the municipal band played the Spanish national anthem in the middle of a popular ovation. What followed was an hour-long military parade in which army soldiers and navy sailors marched together with the Civil Guard and police forces. At three o'clock, the King and the dictator went for lunch at the Ritz Hotel,

Figure 8 Somatén Nacional concentrates in Barcelona to honour the King and the dictator in December 1923.

where the Catalan political, military and ecclesiastical elites awaited them. In the evening, Primo and Alfonso XIII attended a banquet organized by General Barrera at the barracks of the Barcelona garrison. Both guests thanked the garrison for its leading 'patriotic' role in the 13 September coup and promised the Dictatorship would create a 'new Spain'.[4]

Yet the main event of the royal visit was scheduled for the following day. On 2 December, a quarter of a million people gathered in Barcelona to see Alfonso XIII being decorated with the *Somatén*'s 'Constancy Medal'. Perfectly organized by General Barrera, the patriotic celebration was conceived as the 'beginning of a historic period for the nation'.[5] The ceremony was meant to be the symbolic proclamation of the *Somatén* as the protector of the Spanish fatherland. Mobilization for the event was impressive. In what was reported by the press as the biggest demonstration in Spanish history, 40 000 members of the *Somatén* came from all over Catalonia to pay tribute to the monarch and Primo. Members of the Red Cross, the Boy Scouts (*exploradores*), the Barcelona police, Civil Guards, soldiers, six aeroplanes and hundreds of children from public and private schools waving Spanish flags were also mobilized for the ceremony. In an atmosphere of patriotic fervour, 250 000 people cheered the arrival of the monarch and

Primo to the royal tribune, while military bands played the national anthem and young students waved hundreds of Spanish flags. What followed in the next three hours – gun salutes, a military mass, patriotic speeches, a homage to the Virgin of Montserrat (patron saint of the militia), decoration of militiamen, and a parade of the 133 *somatenista banderas* (squads) – was to set a pattern for the *primorriverista* nationalist celebrations throughout the Dictatorship.[6] Over the next two days, Zaragoza and Madrid held similar celebrations to welcome dictator and King.

The above paragraphs illustrate the *primorriveristas'* early intentions to use the *Somatén* for pro-regime mass mobilization and to engage vast sectors of society in nationalist ceremonies. Rituals are an essential component in the creation of a community of 'patriotic believers' and in the formation of nationalism as a 'secular political religion'.[7] The sacralization of national symbols takes place in patriotic ceremonies where the nation is endowed with holy qualities and patriotic liturgies acquire a religious character previously reserved for the deity. Italian and German fascists elaborated secularized religions as the political cement of the nation, which attempted to draw the people into anti-democratic political mobilization and active participation in the national mystique as a way to foment popular consensus and social cohesion. In these new fascist religions the role of rituals, symbolism and sacralized rhetoric became paramount and were created in a syncretic manner, that is, incorporating and overlapping traditional Christian metaphors, liturgies and symbols with fascist political discourse to idealize the nation-state.[8] In these processes of nationalist mobilization the militias and the official parties were to play a key role. In the cases of Italy and Germany, the militias, together with the fascist parties, acted as the mediator between the leader and the followers to transmit both discourse and symbolized myths, while at the same time providing an instrument of social control over the masses.[9] In Spain, the *Somatén Nacional* and the UP were conceived by the *primorriverista* elites as having that very same role of connecting the dictator's discourse to the people and drawing the masses into an anti-democratic political mobilization.

The formation of the *Somatén Nacional*

The *Somatén* was certainly not a *primorriverista* invention. As a rural militia its origins can be traced back to the Middle Ages and throughout the nineteenth century it remained an important popular organization fighting French invaders, Carlists and Federal Republicans in the Catalan countryside. At the turn of the twentieth century, however, the *Somatén* steadily grew in Catalan urban centres as a bourgeois response to increasing working-class mobilization. In January 1919, Catalan regionalists of the *Lliga*, Spanish nationalists of the *Unión Monárquica* and Carlists joined forces and, with the support of the Barcelona financial elite, created the Barcelona *Somatén*, a civic guard (*guardia cívica*) under military supervision and integrated into the general framework of the Catalan *Somatén*. Its declared aims were protecting property, fighting the alleged Bolshevik menace and keeping factories and public services running during strikes. By the end of 1919, employers' organizations and different conservative groups had created civic guards in Madrid, Zaragoza, Valencia, Granada and Alicante following the Barcelona *Somatén* model. In the next two years, Palma de Mallorca, Seville and San Sebastián followed suit.

The actions of the Barcelona *Somatén* in the years before 1923 made for a real political education for the would-be *primorriverista* military elite. Generals Milans del Bosch, Captain General of Catalonia (1918–1920), Martínez Anido, Civil Governor of Barcelona (1920–1922), Miguel Arlegui, Head of the Barcelona Police, and Primo de Rivera, Captain General of Catalonia (1922–1923), provided the *Somatén* with arms and military training and co-ordinated the actions of the militia during strikes. For the military authorities, the militia proved to be extremely useful in their struggle against organized labour. First, the *Somatén* was used as a substitute for the army to repress strikers, so the military was not compromised in the eyes of the public. Second, Martínez Anido and Arlegui incorporated some *somatenistas* into the army-organized *Sindicato Libre* killing squads, which contributed to an increasing number of assassinations of trade unionist leaders in Barcelona.[10]

Primo was delighted with the work of the *Somatén* in Barcelona and as early as March 1919 publicly demanded the extension of the Catalan militia all around Spain.[11] Yet the successive liberal and conservative governments did nothing to extend the *Somatén* to all Spanish provinces under a centralized framework. Thus Primo had to wait until he personally took power to realize his dream of a *Somatén Nacional*. Not that the Marquess of Estella waited long once in office. The manifesto of 13 September promised the formation of the *Somatén Nacional* in a matter of hours. Primo stuck to his word and four days after the coup a Royal Decree extended the Catalan militia to every province of Spain and the Moroccan Protectorate. The reason for this was twofold. First, it was an initial defensive measure to endow the regime with a civilian militia capable of backing the military government in case it came under pressure. Second, the Military Directory conceived the *Somatén* as a pedagogic organization where all social classes would be indoctrinated in nationalist values.[12]

Extending the *Somatén* to all Spanish provinces was something other than the mere replication of the Catalan militia around the country. The *primorriverista* model in effect militarized the militia, by placing the *Somatén* under direct control of the army. The 17 September Royal Decree ordered each Captain General to choose a 'Commander of *Somatén*' from among his generals. Likewise, the regional Captain Generals had to select officers from among those in the reserve as military trainers of the local militias (*Auxiliares militares*).[13] The officers, in turn, were in charge of organizing the local *somatenes* and naming the militia leader (*cabo primero*). This top-down approach shows Primo's firm belief in the army as the essential institution for the creation of new agencies of mass nationalization. Similar to the establishment of the *delegados gubernativos*, Martínez Anido co-ordinated the creation of the militia from the Interior Ministry. During the first years of the Dictatorship, the regimen's second-in-command supervised the works of the Captain Generals and the *Somatén* commanders in every region and demanded Civil Governors to mobilize the delegates for the organization and regular inspection of *somatenes* in small towns and villages.[14] Therefore, the delegates became the main link between the *Somatén* commanders in the cities and the rural militias. This military tutelage was to remain throughout the entire Dictatorship, tightly interweaving the fortunes of the *somatenes* with the actions of the delegates.

With this hierarchical and militarized structure the *Somatén Nacional* expanded into the most recondite places of Spain in a matter of months. This development also had much to do with the different groups that initially supported the regime's initiative. The Social Catholic trade unions had been part of the militias in Madrid even before the Dictatorship and when the *Somatén Nacional* was established many Catholic workers joined it in other Spanish towns.[15] In rural areas the powerful *Confederación Nacional Católica Agraria* (CNCA) and the *Asociación Católica Nacional de Propagandistas* (ACNP) suggested to peasants that they join the militias, a recommendation that according to the Catholic press they followed *en masse*.[16]

The reaction of the upper classes was, however, mixed. In the cities, bankers, employers, industrialists and aristocrats fully supported the idea and funded and directed the militias.[17] In rural areas, some of the great landowners happily jumped on the *primorriverista* wagon and formed militias as their own praetorian guards, but most of the *caciques* saw the creation of *somatenes* as a direct challenge to their power.[18] Ten days after the Royal Decree establishing the *Somatén Nacional* was published, the Captain General of the Second Military Region (Andalusia) wrote to Primo explaining the difficult task he was facing.[19] The General believed he could not organize independent militias in towns of less than 3000 inhabitants until the councils were transformed because of the *caciques'* control of the municipal boards. Once the governmental delegates had taken over the municipal councils in the autumn of 1923, the formation of *somatenes* began to take place in small towns and villages. In some cases, the *caciques* sought to infiltrate the militias with stooges or simply hampered the actions of those corporals opposed to *caciquil* influence, which in turn led to denunciations by members of the public sparking military investigations.[20] On some other occasions, however, the local bosses seem to have stepped aside and 'allowed' the formation of the *Somatén* with only passive opposition. A year after the official establishment of the institution, the *Somatén* General Commander of the Second Military Region, Antonio Fernández, complained to his Captain General about the 'regretful apathy of the upper class' which did nothing to help him in creating militias.[21]

The political orientation and social strata of those groups which supported the formation of the *Somatén* from the start obviously had a severely negative impact on the readiness of some other political groups and social classes to join the militia. Thus the involvement of the upper classes and conservative elements of the lower middle classes (shopkeepers and small employers) in the urban *somatenes* alienated most of the blue-collar workers. In the same manner, the support of middle and small landowners made the integration of landless peasants (*jornaleros*) an impossible task. And yet the *primorriveristas* insisted that the government wanted to integrate all classes into the militia. To get this message across, every regional commander was commissioned with the creation of an official regional bulletin of the militia as an initial step into the political indoctrination of the paramilitaries. Subscription to the regional bulletins was made mandatory for all *somatenistas*, who had to pay a small fee for the membership and the funding of the publication.

The set of political values defended in the pages of the *somatenes'* bulletins were those of nationalism, counterrevolution and Catholicism, together with a bitter anti-communism and anti-Catalan nationalism. These beliefs were loosely defined in a discourse that, nonetheless, led to the effective sanctification of political terms, such as patria, nation and order, while including a veneer of pseudo-scientific vocabulary. The *Somatén's Decalogue*, for example, described 'Anarchists, paranoids, alcoholics, and effeminate people' as 'mentally degenerate' and 'public enemies', thus portraying the nature of the regime's political opponents as subhuman and sick.[22] Despite the obvious political implications of these postulates, *somatenista* publications always presented the militia as non-political. Mindful of the popular perception of the *somatenes* as ideologically and personally linked to the extreme right, the paramilitaries emphasized that all ideological options were welcomed, including the 'intellectual left' – the only proviso being that of supporting the Dictatorship.[23] Vague ideological definitions had the goal of attracting the largest possible number of members from different political backgrounds, especially the middle classes not connected with dynastic parties, the so-called *clases neutras*. But ideological vagueness is also telling of the nature of the *Somatén Nacional*. Created as a 'movement of citizens', the *primorriveristas* understood that in the regime's militia action should precede doctrine, and strength and decision should herald the ideological debate – a view much in line with the postulates of Carl Schmitt and the fascist theoretician Giovanni Gentile.[24] In no other field did this combination of regime's propaganda and mobilization of the masses became more important than in the public ceremonies that the *Somatén* organized throughout the entire Dictatorship.

The battle for the public arena: rituals, virgins and parades

By autumn 1924, the regime boasted the *Somatén* had more than 175 000 members all around the country.[25] Yet the actions of the militias against political opponents of the regime had been almost non-existent in the year the *Somatén Nacional* had been functioning. As Primo himself acknowledged in October 1925, many wondered about the raison d'être of the *Somatén*.[26] For the dictator the explanation was clear. First, the militia was a 'pre-emptive medicine', a deterrent for eventual social disorders. Second, the *Somatén* was a 'school of citizenship', that is, a device of social indoctrination via mass mobilization. In fact, by the autumn of 1925 the *Somatén* had been mobilized to participate in every single nationalist ceremony organized by the regime since 13 September 1923. These included not only activities related to the militia (the Fiesta of the Sanctification of the *Somatén* Flag and celebrations for the Virgin of Montserrat), but also participation in commemorations of Spanish military victories in Morocco, ceremonies for those fallen in Cuba and the Philippines, openings of school buildings, the *Fiesta del Árbol* and all sorts of pro-regime 'patriotic campaigns'. The *Somatén Nacional* had become the regime's cheerleaders.

During the Dictatorship, the *Somatén Nacional* created its own rituals, essentially developing those of the Catalan militia. The Fiesta of the Sanctification of the *Somatén* Flag was the foundational ritual of all militias and it was repeated on a yearly basis during the annual military inspection. Whether in cities or in villages it usually followed a similar pattern everywhere. It began with a military parade of the members of the army and the local *Somatén* followed by an open air mass (*misa de campaña*). Once the mass was over, the ecclesiastical authorities blessed the *Somatén* and the Spanish flags, while the military or local band played the national anthem. The sanctification of the emblems was followed by a series of speeches delivered by the *Somatén's* military commanders and the godmothers (*madrinas*) of the militia, who usually praised the paramilitaries, the war in Africa and the Dictatorship at home. After the speeches, the *somatenistas* paraded in front of the authorities while the music bands played *pasodobles*.[27]

It is worth noting the novelty that the celebration of these fiestas had for hundreds of small towns and villages where no popular patriotic ceremony had ever taken place. True, many in the countryside might have listened to patriotic discourses emanating from the pulpit or the balcony of the town hall during the Restoration. And yet, the *Somatén Nacional's* ceremonies encouraged the active participation of local men and women as never before. The militia's parades, the speeches of the *madrinas* and the corporal of the *Somatén* were all new elements of popular participation in patriotic rituals. Further, the *primorriverista* ceremonies incorporated elements of popular culture, such as *pasodobles* and Catholic masses, designed to integrate thousands of peasants into the patriotic liturgy. For the first time, many individuals in rural Spain could identify themselves with symbols designed to stress the sense of national community and could 'experience' the fatherland, with all its religious, populist and military connotations, in emotional terms.

In the cities and large towns the regime specialized in grand gatherings and parades. In these cases, the *primorriveristas* put into practice all the experience gained in Catalonia during the years previous to the Dictatorship. In the early 1920s, the Catalan elites had organized *somatenista* parades to celebrate the day of the patron saint of the institution (the Virgin of Montserrat) and the oath to the militia's flags, with support of the civil and military authorities. In 1921, the first grand gathering took place in Barcelona, where 35 000 militiamen marched in a ceremony which included an open-air mass, blessing of the flags, interpretation of the national anthem, and popular displays of Spanish and Catalan flags. The show really gained momentum when Martínez Anido and Arlegui, then Civil Governor and Chief Police Inspector of Barcelona respectively, paraded in an open-topped car throughout the Paseo de Gracia to the delight of the public.[28] In the following years new parades were organized to commemorate the Virgin of Montserrat in Barcelona and Gerona. On these occasions, the recently named Captain General of Catalonia, Miguel Primo de Rivera, attended the ceremonies.[29] Once in power, Primo was determined not only to maintain this newly invented 'tradition' but also to export it to the rest of the country.

The Royal Order of 3 November 1923 declared the Virgin of Montserrat patron saint of all *Somatenes* in Spain, as a tribute to the Catalan militia praised for its religious and 'glorious Spanish tradition' and its role in combating the French during the War of Independence.[30] In the months to come, Primo personally encouraged the celebration of the patron saint and Martínez Anido mobilized Civil Governors, delegates, captain generals and *Somatén* commanders to assure the success of the celebration. Already in the spring of 1924, the ceremonies were widespread throughout Spain.[31] In Madrid, for example, a huge altar with the figure of the Virgin of Montserrat was on display for the ceremony held in El Retiro Park, where thousands of paramilitary paraded in front of the dictator. In the following years, the Fiesta of the Virgin of Montserrat became the most important *somatenista* ceremony, frequently presided over by Primo and members of the royal family and always cautiously co-ordinated by the Ministry of the Interior.[32]

The regime's promotion of the Fiesta of the Virgin of Montserrat was not gratuitous. The decision was consistent with the *primorriverista* quest for the creation of a 'patriotic religion'. The *primorriveristas* were fully aware of the power of religion to impact on the psyche of the masses. As one of the leaders of the *Junta de Propaganda Patriótica*, Lieutenant Colonel Emilio Rodríguez Tarduchy, bluntly put it, religion was the most important factor in the transformation of the 'social psychology of the mob'.[33] The Dictatorship sought to imbue *Somatén* rituals with a strong religious flavour that in turn emphasized the sacred character of the nation. The incorporation of Christian iconography, the celebration of open-air masses, the priests' patriotic sermons and the interpretation of the national anthem during the benediction of the *Somatén* and the Spanish flags, were all elements intended to create the feeling of a mass nationalist 'communion' among the participants and the public.[34] As in the *primorriverista* nationalist ceremonies with soldiers and students, Catholic imagery and rhetoric were fully integrated into civic patriotic rituals.

The decision to declare the Virgin of Montserrat as the patron saint of the *Somatén Nacional* also had more subtle objectives: it aimed at transforming the Catalanist Virgin *par excellence* into a symbol of Spanish nationalism. By the early 1920s, the cult of Montserrat was a well-established ritual of Catalan regionalism and nationalism. By incorporating *la moreneta*, as the Virgin of Montserrat was popularly known, into Spanish nationalism's symbolic repertoire, Primo sought to deprive the Catalanist enemy of its own signs of identity. The extent to which this new tradition of celebrating the Virgin of Montserrat grew roots outside Catalonia is not difficult to determine. The Fiesta was celebrated throughout the entire Dictatorship with the support of the state apparatus, but once the regime fell, the rapid decline of the *Somatén* and the disappearance of the celebration went hand in hand.[35] More importantly, the regime was unable to strip *la moreneta* of its Catalanist connotations. During the period 1923–1930, the trend to baptise girls with the name Montserrat doubled in Catalonia.[36] The selection of the patron of Catalonia (and of a name that has no equivalent in Castilian) to baptise daughters has to be understood as an act of resistance by many Catalans who opposed the *primorriverista* policies of Spanishization. The fact that the same pattern was to be repeated in Catalonia under Francoism should not come as a surprise.

Together with the Catholic features of *Somatén*'s rituals, it was the military factor which most contributed to the creation of a sacred idea of the nation at the symbolic level. In the years before 1923, the militias had developed militarized rites in the burials of comrades, where coffins were covered with the national flag, praetorian guards were installed around the coffin and collective oaths were made.[37] This military-religious symbiosis in the *somatenistas'* last honours was to continue during the Dictatorship.[38] However, the drastic reduction of violent deaths in social clashes from 1924 onwards led to a sharp decline in the celebration of these funeral rites. Nevertheless, the regime used the *Somatén* ceremonies to honour those fallen for the patria in the colonial wars. Seeking to develop a cult of the dead, the *Somatén* celebrated ceremonies with veterans of Cuba and Puerto Rico and tributes to the fallen in the African fields were paid as part of the militia's rituals.[39] Likewise, the *Somatén* was mobilized every time the government organized a public mass to honour the Spanish army. These masses for those fallen in Africa or to commemorate Spanish victory over Moroccan rebels became a central part of the nationalist rallies.[40] In these ceremonies the nation was endorsed with the Christian symbolism of death and resurrection. Like fascist Italy, all these elements became essential ingredients for a new 'patriotic religion', which placed the nation on the main altar.

Some factors, however, acted against the successful creation of a cult of the fallen in Spain. The main problem was the unpopularity of the war in Morocco. The fact that the official celebrations of the end of the war emphasized peace over colonial greatness illustrates to what extent the regime was aware of the difficulties of imbuing the Moroccan campaign with popular jingoist fervour.[41] Second, Spain's neutrality in the First World War had precluded the formation of groups of veterans eager to experience again the comradeship of the front and honour those fallen in the battlefields – a phenomenon found in most European countries in the 1920s.[42] Unlike Italy, most of the paramilitaries in the *Somatén Nacional* had neither war experience nor had they fought the trade unionists in the streets.

Primo's *Somatén Nacional* not only deviated from the fascist militias in its lack of war ethos but also in its image. Whereas Italian and Nazi militias wore uniforms and militarized their public performances as much as possible, the *somatenistas* had no uniforms and marched without military discipline. As described by one witness, the *somatenistas* parading in Madrid in December 1923 were 'excellent bourgeois, over-40 fathers, who looked more like peaceful tourists than heroic guardians of social order'.[43] Their heterogeneous civilian clothes and peaceful image simply could not transmit 'discipline and martial ideas' to the public.[44] This lack of martial spirit and military aesthetics certainly conditioned the initial popular reception of the *Somatén*. As the dictator acknowledged, the first *somatenista* parades were met with mockery and sneers by many in Andalusia. Nonetheless, he refused the idea of creating a uniform for the militia. For Primo 'discipline and honour' were to be the distinctive features of the *Somatén* over any aesthetic consideration.[45] The decision not to give uniforms to the militias seems contradictory for a regime so eager to endow civilians with military values. But it might well have responded to the intention not to blur the external distinctions between the army and civilian supporters of the Dictatorship – something that would have infuriated military officers. The army was to remain a different, superior class within the regime apparatus.

For all the initial problems the militia experienced, Primo's confidence in the *Somatén* remained intact. During the first three years of his regime, the *Somatén* was to play a key role in the so-called 'campaigns against bad Spaniards'. These were regime-organized gatherings to show mass support for the Dictatorship when criticized by the liberal opposition in exile. As early as January 1924, the Dictatorship organized a parade outside the Royal Palace to honour the King and 'make amends' for those who had criticized the monarch and the regime. Representatives of all provinces, around 5000 mayors coming from all over Spain, hundreds of Catalan *somatenistas* and 1500 boy-scouts marched in front of Primo and Alfonso XIII. The following week Barcelona hosted yet another pro-regime celebration that was to last for three days.[46] As anti-*primorriverista* opposition grew among liberal intellectuals throughout 1924, so did the regime's resolution to mobilize supporters. The publication in France of the exiled republican Blasco Ibáñez's *Por España y contra el rey* led to a new governmental campaign against the 'bad Spaniards abroad'. In December 1924, tens of *somatenes* held parades in different towns while aristocrats and Catholic workers celebrated 'patriotic' meetings to vindicate the figures of the monarch and the dictator.[47] In Valencia, the town council opted to change the name of Blasco Ibáñez Square.[48] On 23 January 1925, Martínez Anido gathered thousands of *somatenes* from all over Spain for a grand march on the streets of Madrid in defence of the King and the nation.[49]

For a regime obsessed with its image abroad, these parades sought to demonstrate to the international community the popular support Primo had at home. In terms of objectives and even location (the Royal Palace in Madrid), they also bore a striking resemblance to those gatherings Francisco Franco was to organize when criticized by European democrats. For the *primorriveristas*, the patriotic campaigns were an important part of their endeavour to nationalize the masses via active participation in emotionally enhancing folkloric celebrations, in which King, dictator and nation were portrayed as the supreme good opposed to the evil of liberal-republican-Bolshevik-foreign-anti-Spanish critics. In other words, the campaigns sought to facilitate the symbolic popularization of the Manichean views promoted by the regime at the discursive level through the active participation of the man in the street.

The nationalization of the masses through participation in patriotic ceremonies was in absolute concurrence with the regime's attempt to 'gain' the streets. At times this was quite literal. In September 1923, General Losada ordered the Barcelona City Council to add a version in Spanish of every municipal poster, edict and street sign in the city, so hundreds of street signs with the name translated into Castilian were attached to the original in Catalan. In 1926, the City Council passed a proposal to remove the signs in Catalan but financial restrictions led to a limited application of legislation: only 15 per cent of the Barcelona streets were modified during the Dictatorship.[50] The 'conquest' of the streets as a public political space was, in turn, part of a much more far-reaching project to monopolize the symbolic universe and, hence, gain an absolute control of political discourse. Together with military censorship, propaganda and mandatory inclusion of Primo's official notes in all newspapers, the regime implemented a long-term symbolic repression to reduce the potential for organized protest. In the Dictatorship's bid for controlling the symbolic universe it is possible to distinguish three different interrelated tactics: assimilation of the enemies' symbols, creation of new symbols and rites, and banning the iconography and rituals of the opponents. The regime attempted assimilation in the case of the Virgin of Montserrat but, as noted above, *la moreneta* never fully made it into the sanctuary of Spanish nationalism. The Dictatorship also sought to monopolize some historical myths shared by both liberals and conservatives, such as the War of Independence, but they remained in dispute during the 1920s and 1930s.[51] Probably no other case encapsulates better the struggle for controlling the nationalist symbolic universe than the repatriation of Ángel Ganivet's body. Claimed by both liberals and conservatives as the intellectual doyen of their respective versions of Spanish nationalism, his burial in Madrid in 1925 ended with violent clashes between *primorriverista* supporters and opponents.[52]

In terms of inventing new symbols and rituals, the *primorriveristas* were less creative. Symbols that represented the nation – the flag and the anthem – remained unchanged. The symbolic unity of the militias was not achieved until January 1930, two weeks before the collapse of the regime.[53] Notwithstanding the fact that some new celebrations were created (for instance, the *Día del libro español* and the *Fiesta del soldado*), the regime mainly re-elaborated existing ceremonies emphasizing their military and nationalist features. The cases of the *Fiesta del Árbol* and the *somatenista* celebrations provide good examples of rites which changed their meaning under the Dictatorship – shifting from the celebration of the local community to the national one. The relevance of this 'reinvention of traditions' lay in its magnitude and geographical extension. The fact that the regime expanded regional ceremonies to the national level with the support of the state apparatus led to the multiplication of patriotic rituals all around Spain.

Nonetheless, as in many other fields, the regime proved itself more effective at destroying than at creating. The 'Decree against separatism' banned all regional flags and emblems from public display. Furthermore, in early September 1924, the Civil Governor of Barcelona forbade not only the celebration of the *Diada*, the national day of Catalonia, but also bringing bouquets of flowers to the statue of Rafael Casanova, the Catalan national hero. In 1925 the military imposed restrictions on the public performance of the *sardana*, the Catalan national dance. On the surface, repression worked, for it ended the most radical manifestations of Catalan nationalism in the streets. But, in reality, it turned out to be a spectacular own-goal for the Dictatorship. Catalan regionalists and nationalists invented new rituals and counter-rituals to oppose those organized by the *primorriveristas*. For example, on 15 April 1924, the Dictatorship opened a monument to honour the poet Verdaguer. In the inaugural ceremony Primo described the author as a staunch monarchist always loyal to Spain.

Catalanists ignored the official ceremony and, at the very same time, gathered around Verdaguer's sepulchre to read his poems and commemorate the figure of someone they considered a national hero. Similar alternative rituals to celebrate Saint Jordi, the patron saint of Catalonia, and new rituals to commemorate the figure of Martí i Julià in the Montjuic cemetery emerged during the Dictatorship, as means to reinvent Catalanist historical memory under difficult conditions. Additionally, the prohibition to use the *senyera*, the Catalan flag, had the unintended consequence of reinforcing the identification between the symbol and the Catalan fatherland. Moreover, even those critical of Catalanism, such as the Anarchist CNT, began to display *senyeras* as a way to provoke the authorities: it became the symbol of all opposition to the Dictatorship in Catalonia.[54]

Repression extended all across the political board. When the Dictatorship realized that intellectuals and Restoration political elites were turning their meetings into public acts of opposition, it reacted by forbidding the events. In the autumn of 1924, for instance, police broke up the public homage to Pedro Sáinz Rodríguez, then an anti-*primorriverista* Professor of Law at the University of Madrid.[55] Subsequent public meetings organized by liberals and conservatives to honour the former Prime Minister Eduardo Dato and Dr Gregorio Marañón were simply forbidden. The left and anti-*primorriverista* groups of the extreme right were also kept from celebrating their rituals. The commemoration of May Day was likewise forbidden 'to avoid foreign interference' in Spain, while the Interior Ministry constantly refused to authorize Carlist public ceremonies.[56] Republican ceremonies, such as the celebration of the anniversary of the First Republic on 11 February, were banned too. However, the *primorriveristas* could not avoid the emergence of alternative republican rituals. In November 1924, republicans celebrate the 100th anniversary of the federalist leader, Francisco Pi i Margall. From 1926 the cult to the 'martyrs of Sarrià' (republicans assassinated by Carlists in 1874), which had disappeared in 1917, re-emerged and slowly grew in the following years.[57] The Dictatorship's attempt to control the public space via repression led to the unintended result of promoting a rebirth of alternative rituals, consolidating the opposition's national symbols and bringing together diverse anti-*primorriverista* groups.

Problems, reforms and fall

The idea of integrating all social classes into the *Somatén Nacional* proved a difficult task from the start. For an institution that in the pre-*primorriverista* era had specialized in fighting trade unionists in the streets and supplying the services interrupted by industrial actions its appeal to the working class had to be limited. Before September 1923, dozens of trade unions had demanded to the government the dissolution of the *Somatén* in Catalonia, arguing that its existence effectively legalized the 'arming of a conflicting class in the social struggle'.[58] Some others on the left opted for more direct action. For instance, in April 1923 trade unionists exploded a car bomb during the *somatenista* celebration of the Virgin of Montserrat parade in Barcelona.[59]

The extension of the *Somatén* to the whole of Spain did little to improve the relationships between the militiamen and the working class. For all the support of the minority Catholic trade unions and the *Sindicato Libre*, the few working-class men who decided to join the militia were often scorned, ostracized and threatened by fellow workers.[60] The situation deteriorated so quickly that by September 1924 the government decided to implement special measures against those mocking or intimidating *somatenistas*.[61] Nonetheless, the legal protection of paramilitaries threatened by members of the public was to no avail. Mockery, threats and retaliations against *somatenistas* continued to be carried out not only by workers in industrial cities but also by members of the lower classes in rural areas. In the village of Catrocalbón, for instance, a great scandal broke out when two locals openly insulted the *somatenistas'* mothers during a public ceremony, yet no action seems to have been taken against them.[62]

Scorn for the *Somatén* can be explained in terms of class struggle, but most of the popular contempt for the institution has to be understood in relation to the continual abuses of power carried out by the paramilitaries. The establishment of the *Somatén Nacional* provided a golden opportunity for many 'free-riders' to pursue personal economic gains and/or advance their position in the local political arena. Soon the *Somatén* general commanders had to expel paramilitaries from the institution for a variety of reasons, including pressing false charges, business fraud and indiscriminate beatings.[63] In some rural areas, *somatenistas* organized criminal networks. As the Civil Governor of Albacete wrote to Martínez Anido, many *somatenistas* in the province were charging local peasants for crossing paths and roads in the name of 'imaginary laws', while some others simply 'shot and robbed' travellers and locals alike.[64] This situation, the Civil Governor observed, had led to the *Somatén*'s loss of prestige and was seriously hampering the possibility of integrating many citizens, 'supporters of the current regime', into the militia. Despite their illegal behaviour, the regime was always extremely lenient with paramilitary criminals. In the spring of 1927, the Dictatorship declared an amnesty for all *somatenistas* convicted of lesser crimes, providing the latter were not against property. This measure marked a sharp contrast with the arbitrary and indiscriminate political and social repression of the Dictatorship, and led to further popular hostility not only against the *Somatén* but against the regime as a whole.[65]

Erosion of the militia's public image and the 1926 rebellions against the Dictatorship convinced Primo of the need to reform the *Somatén Nacional*. In June 1926, the Sanjuanada, a coup planned by General Francisco Aguilera and supported by the Restoration liberal elites, and the radical Catalanist attempt to 'invade' Catalonia with an army of 150 volunteers from Prats de Molló in the French border in November of the same year, were easily put down by the military, the police and the Civil Guard. However, the *Somatén*'s inaction drew the ire of the dictator. After all, the institution had been created for the defence of the regime and these were the first two occasions when the Dictatorship was directly challenged. In September 1927, the formation of a *Somatén* National Council was announced and, in May 1928, a military commission was created to draft a blueprint of the new militia's statute. The main objective was to expand the militia and to increase its effectiveness, so the draft handed to Primo for approval in September 1928 included the formation of a women's *Somatén* and granted new privileges to the institution, such as the confidentiality of *Somatén* informers and the acquisition of military force legal status when on duty.[66] In December 1929, the new regulation of the *Somatén* finally became law.[67]

By the time the new regulations were implemented the *Somatén* had been undergoing a radical modification for almost a year. In January 1929, José Sánchez Guerra, the former conservative leader, led an insurrection in Valencia backed by republicans, the Artillery Corps and some Restoration politicians. The idea of the Revolutionary Committee presided over by Sánchez Guerra was to replace Primo and call for the election of a constituent assembly. However, the coup failed due to lack of co-ordination and popular support. The artillery garrison in Ciudad Real rose one day earlier, 28 January as opposed to the agreed 29th, and Sánchez Guerra found little backing from the workers and the army once he landed in Valencia in the early hours of the 29th. The insurrection made the dictator realize that he could not count on UP and *Somatén* mobilization to defend his regime.[68] In Valencia and Ciudad Real, the local *somatenes* stayed at home when the rebellion broke and it was down to the army to suppress the insurrection. Furthermore, the intensification of the students' revolt in the spring of 1929 made it clear that the opposition was retaking the streets from the *Somatén*. In terms of political socialization and nationalization, the *Somatén*'s apathy is extremely significant. Unlike

Mussolini, Primo was unable to mobilize the militia and the party when the Dictatorship was in trouble.[69] This shows not only a much lower level of political commitment to the regime of the Spanish paramilitaries than that demonstrated by the *fasci*, but also less popular support.

Nevertheless, under growing political pressure, Primo decided to turn the *Somatén* and the UP into espionage and police institutions. The Royal Decree of 4 February 1929 bestowed the party and the militia with 'additional functions of vigilance and information' and called upon the *Somatén* for a further intervention in political repression.[70] Among the new measures, the regime created the 'Citizens' Investigation and Information Centres' (centres for political denunciations made by the public) under UP control, organized an espionage network whereby the *Somatén* corporal of every 'district, village or neighbourhood' was to collect information and establish databases of political opponents at the local headquarters of the party and the militia, and authorized the paramilitaries and UP affiliates to carry out searches in the homes of those suspected of opposing the regime.[71] The *somatenistas* were also encouraged to use violence against those compromising 'public order' and authorized to close down those clubs in which 'political debates' were taking place.[72]

These measures marked a qualitative drive towards semi-totalitarian positions by the Dictatorship.[73] Party, militia, security forces and army were interlinked in the service of *primorriverista* repression in what constituted the *de facto* creation of a police state. The distinction between public and private political spheres became blurred as paramilitaries were encouraged to invade the homes and organizations of political opponents. In terms of the *Somatén*'s public image, the consequences of the regime's radicalization were catastrophic. Not surprisingly, the regime's 'blank cheque' to the militia led to more abuses of authority, an increasing number of anonymously made false accusations and *en masse* imprisonments of political adversaries.[74] The slight but steady decline in the number of affiliates throughout 1929 is telling of the counter-productive effects of the *primorriverista* totalitarian drive.[75] The fall of the regime in January 1930 did nothing but accelerate *Somatén* disintegration. Accusations of impunity and abuses of authority were made in the press and dozens of demands to disarm the militias poured onto the Interior Minister's desk.[76] Fully aware of its ideological and political connotations, the provisional Republican government abolished the *Somatén*, except in Catalonia, the day after it took power. The decree of 15 April 1931 justified the dissolution of the *Somatén Nacional* on the grounds of the militia's lack of popular support, the paramilitaries' abuses and the threat to the social order that the institution posed.[77]

In no other place was the negative effect of the *Somatén Nacional* more evident than in Catalonia. Since the beginning of the Dictatorship the number of *somatenistas* had consistently decreased in the region, falling from 65 735 members in September 1923 to 62 850 in August 1928.[78] By 1929, the decrease in popular support of the militia was also obvious in terms of street celebrations. In a letter to Primo, General Barrera acknowledged that only 22 000 *somatenistas* took part in the 1929 street march in Barcelona – a reduction of almost 50 per cent when compared to the parades of December 1923. This decline in the number of Catalan *somatenistas* can be explained as a by-product of the downturn in social clashes in Barcelona during the Dictatorship.[79] But it was also the transformation of the militia into an agency of Spanish nationalization and the *primorriverista* control of the institution that alienated many from the *Somatén*. From 1924, as part of the Catalan oligarchy distanced itself from the Dictatorship, the support for the institution began to decrease. More importantly, Primo's mistrust of the rural *somatenes*, always under suspicion of harbouring Catalanist feelings, led General Barrera to carry out a purge of suspected Catalanist members in the militia, which certainly hampered the popular backing of the *primorriverista Somatén*.[80]

Few documents epitomize better the level of popular alienation produced by the *primorriverista Somatén* than the collectively drafted letter sent by the mayors of the Falset constituency in Tarragona to the new Republican Interior Minister in September 1931. The mayors demanded the abolition of the *Somatén* in Catalonia, for the Dictatorship had perverted the institution's original 'dignified local Catalan spirit' and turned the militia into a 'vulgar tragicomedy performed by a bunch of gunmen', servile to dictator and King.[81] In the view of the mayors:

It is well known that in the last eight years [the *somatenes*] acted with a totally inverted morality. Thus, instead of a citizens' institution in defence of the Catalan people, it turned into its quasi-executioner, giving unconditional help and resolute collaboration to those who vexed, trampled on and tried by all means to humiliate the most intimate and respectable aspects of the citizen's consciousness and Catalan sentiments.

The *primorriverista* attempt to 'de-Catalanize' the *Somatén* seems to have been successful, yet at a very high price, as popular contempt for the institution grew in rural Catalonia during the Dictatorship. The picture was no better in some other Spanish regions. The avalanche of public accusations against members of the *Somatén* in 1930 illustrates the deep grievances produced by the institution. During the first months of the Second Republic, socialist associations demanded the total disarmament of the individuals who had belonged to the *Somatén*, arguing that they posed a danger to the newly established democratic system.[82] The link between the institution and *primorriverista* anti-democratic values did not escape anyone. Contemporary observers also understood the failure of the *Somatén* as a state-controlled 'pedagogic' agency. As the conservative Gabriel Maura noted in 1930, 'the state cannot produce citizens like it coins money, but it can educate and train them; and to that effect, a tidy exercise of liberties is considerably better than the *somatenista* tactic.'[83] An institution created to indoctrinate the masses in the nationalist ideal had ended up dividing the population. As in the case of the delegates, the paramilitary combined the role of propagandists and repressors in the same figure, which certainly undermined popular acceptance. Like the *delegados*, the *Somatén Nacional* was the creation of a military state whose fate was interwoven with the fortunes of the regime. Once the Dictatorship faced its final crisis in 1929, the disgrace of the militia went hand in hand with the discrediting of the authoritarian idea of Spain promoted by the *Somatén*.

9
Unión Patriótica: the Official Party

> [. . .] the issue now is Fatherland or Soviets, the nation is attacked by communism, separatism and terrorism [. . .] peoples are now in the Communist destructive bloc or the National constructive bloc. In Spain the latter is the Unión Patriótica neither Liberal nor Conservative, but Patriotic
>
> (José María Pemán)[1]

The warm welcome the squads of the *Federación Cívico Somatenista* (FCS) gave to Primo and the King in Barcelona in December 1923 when returning from their visit to Italy should not come as a surprise. The leaders of the pro-fascist group had held conversations with Primo and Martínez Anido in late October that year seeking to turn the FCS into the regime's official party and were eager to show the dictator that they had the capacity to mobilize popular support.[2] Captivated by fascist Italy, Primo initially seemed delighted with the idea of having the FCS as his main power base to build a *primorriverista* nation-wide party. The *tracistas* were well connected with the military officers of the Barcelona garrison and had shown their devotion to the regime since its very beginnings. However, the dictator soon changed his mind. In late January 1924, a new meeting of the dictator with the *tracistas* did not lead to the creation of the official party desired by Primo.[3] The FCS might have had supporters, if only a few, in Barcelona, but it was virtually unknown outside the Catalan capital. The grand ambition of creating an official party able to mobilize all sectors of society required a further amalgamation of conservative groups. When the UP was finally created in Barcelona in April 1924, the 'blue shirts' of the FCS were included, but so were the members of the *Unión Monárquica Nacional* (UMN) and many others ranging from former liberals to moderate regionalists.

Seeking to gain broad social support for his official party, Primo turned to the Social Catholics. Since early November 1923, the Social Catholic mouthpiece *El Debate* had begun to question the effectiveness of the FCS as the basis for the eventual official party.[4] At the same time, Ángel Herrera, one of the Social Catholic leaders, had formed a commission with the specific goal of founding a new party that would mobilize social support for the regime.[5] On 30 November 1923, members of the *Acción Católica Nacional de Propagandistas* (ACNP) and the *Partido Social Popular* created the *Unión Patriótica Castellana* in Valladolid, as an alternative candidate to become the Dictatorship's party.[6] In the following weeks new *Uniones Patrióticas* were created throughout northern Castile. In April 1924, Primo decided to unify the Social Catholic political movement and turned the *Unión Patriótica* (UP) into the official party. The implications of the choice were clear: by opting for the Social Catholics over the pro-fascist members of the FCS, the dictator aimed at benefiting from the already proven ACNP's capacity to mobilize the masses and, hence, to integrate large sectors of society into the *primorriverista* project.

Events would prove the validity of Primo's judgement. Throughout 1924, the members of the *Confederación Nacional Católica Agraria* (CNCA), such as José María Gil Robles, mobilized its affiliates and founded tens of *Uniones Patrióticas* in both Old and New Castile.[7] Granting the initiative to the Social Catholics did not mean, however, that the regime renounced to its customary top-down approach when it came to the creation of new institutions. As in the case of the formation of the *Somatén Nacional*, Primo instructed civil governors and *delegados* to set up the Dictatorship's party.[8] Like on many other occasions, the work of the delegates seems to have been patchy when creating new institutions. In the summer of 1924, the Interior Ministry sent new guidelines for the formation of the UP in all provinces, emphasizing the need to intensify the propagandist effort and be vigilant of those 'old politicians' trying to infiltrate the party. The official orders established a system in which governmental authorities would set up local organizational commissions including members of all social classes. These commissions were to elect a local committee, which in turn was to send representatives to the District Committee (*Comité del partido judicial*). Finally, the District Committee's members were to choose delegates for the Provincial Committee, the top institution ultimately responsible to the soon-to-be-created UP National Council in Madrid.[9]

Two points are significant in the official guidelines. First, the absence of regional committees in the UP pyramidal framework was very much in line with the regime's idea of the Spanish nation-state. By emphasizing the direct links between the province and the state, the idea of regional representation was bypassed, thus underpinning the very notion of region. Second, and more importantly, the governors were endowed with the power of imposing or removing any person from any committees, while all mayors were named directors (*vocales*) of their respective UP district committee. In this manner, the top-down approach to the establishment of the UP led to the entanglement of the party with the state structure.

The *primorriverista* choice of the Social Catholics as the main basis on which to build the UP and the process of incorporating the party into the state apparatus were to have obvious consequences in attracting membership from certain social backgrounds. Those provincial middle and lower-middle classes affiliated to the organizations controlled by the ACNP, such as the CNCA and *Acción Católica*, joined the UP *en masse* during the years 1924 and 1925.[10] State and municipal public officers constituted the second largest group in the party's rank and file, becoming an important contingent of support for the regime. Finally, for all the apparent restrictions that the delegates had to impose on those related to the 'old regime' wanting to become UP militants, many landless peasants under the political control of the *caciques* were allowed to join the party. This clearly seems to have been the case in provinces with a strong *caciquil* tradition, such as Huelva or Cáceres, which had the highest number of UP members in Spain.[11]

It is important to note that for all the Social Catholic organizational and human contribution to the formation of the party, the ideological tenets of the UP were based on the principles of military nationalism. Most significantly, Castilian regionalism, so latent in the founding manifesto of the *Unión Patriótica Castellana* of November 1923, was to fade away totally once the Dictatorship took over the party.[12] Ideologically, as in many other fields, the military was calling the shots. As in the case of the *Somatén*, the *primorriveristas* initially presented vaguely defined values of patriotism, tradition and order as the ideological guidelines of the UP, seeking to attract the largest number of militants. The regime always insisted that all ideologies and classes were welcomed in the UP. As in the case of the militia, there was a genuine attempt by the *primorriveristas* to integrate the lower class into the state-controlled party.[13] Much in the same way as Mussolini and his fascist party, Primo presented the UP as an 'anti-party', as a 'league', as a 'movement of citizens', aiming at differentiating the organization from traditional political parties.[14] After all, the UP was meant to be a radically new political organization. First, the UP was created to legitimize the perpetuation of an illegal regime.[15] The party was to be living proof of the Dictatorship's popular support, that is, Primo sought a 'populist' legitimacy as a 'substitute' for the legal legitimacy that he never won at the ballot box. Second, the 'pedagogic' aspect of all *primorriverista* agencies was also present, conceiving the UP as a 'school of citizenry'. As the ideologues of the regime acknowledged, the means to achieve these goals was to mobilize the masses following the Italian example.[16] To what extent this mobilization was to be effective heavily depended on the structure and resources the regime was to endow the party with.

Party structure and propaganda machinery

Setting up the official party posed a series of difficulties to Civil Governors and delegates alike. To begin with, some *caciques* opposed the creation of an alternative power base in their constituencies and used their political connections to hamper the creation of the UP.[17] But some other *caciques* saw the creation of the UP as a golden opportunity to jump onto the *primorriverista* wagon and many of them managed to gain control of local branches of the UP. Whether this was due to the delegates' lack of knowledge of the local political arena or out of sheer necessity in the absence of political personnel unconnected to the *caciquil* system is difficult to determine. Whatever the reason, it seems that in many rural areas the delegates had to choose between two rival factions when creating the UP, which effectively meant handing a 'blank cheque' to one of the groups to chase its opponents under the Dictatorship's official umbrella.[18]

The poor results obtained by the Civil Governors in the spring and summer of 1924 led Martínez Anido to intensify the pressure on the delegates. In August, the new guidelines for the formation of UP branches were sent to all Civil Governors and in October the first delegates were dismissed for failing to rally support for the party in their districts.[19] The link between the delegates and the party, although initially presented as temporary, was never totally broken by the regime. Documents from the Interior Ministry show that Martínez Anido continued to monitor the activities of the party throughout the Dictatorship. As late as 1929, Civil Governors, delegates and UP leaders (*jefes*) alike were reporting to the Interior Ministry and the Prime Minister's Office (*Presidencia del Gobierno*) different problems the party faced on a regular basis.[20] In the long run, the UP subordination to the delegates was to have an important negative effect in terms of public acceptance, for when the delegates fell into disgrace in the eyes of the people, this was going to have a knock-on effect on the public's appreciation of the party.

In the cities, the regime's attempt to integrate diverse political groups and social classes led to a series of problems. In Barcelona, the formation of the UP brought together members of the so-called 'military party' (the pro-fascists of the FCS, *mauristas*, former republicans and military officers of the Barcelona garrison), the UMN and many Carlists. Although these groups were all Spanish nationalists, they differed on the political framework that they wanted for Catalonia. While the 'military party' opposed any regional institutions and defended a provincial structure for Spain, the Carlists and the members of the UMN still considered the *Mancomunitat* as a valid organization once it had been purged of Catalanists. The result was a struggle for power within the UP in Barcelona and Gerona throughout 1924 that culminated in the suppression of the *Mancomunitat* and the victory of the 'military party' in the spring of 1925. The price of the infight was, nevertheless, high: it weakened the support for the official party of the upper classes linked to the UMN from its early stages.[21] In Bilbao, the Basque oligarchy represented in the *Liga de Acción Monárquica* simply refused to merge with the UP. Thus the official party that emerged in Vizcaya was basically run by middle-class members with no previous political experience, as was the case in many other provincial capitals.[22] In Madrid, since the very moment the dictator announced the creation of the official party, both liberals and conservatives opposed it on grounds of ideology. For both the liberal *El Sol* and the conservative *La Época*, the UP was an extreme-right party and its creation a serious burden for the eventual return to a constitutional regime.[23] In the capital by early 1924, liberals and conservatives began to understand the implications of the dictator's move. For all his comments on the temporary nature of his position in power, Primo was there to stay.

Internal squabbles, the delegates' inefficiency and ideological opposition mounted by those who had at first supported the regime certainly hampered the consolidation of a strong UP during the Military Directory. Yet it is important to notice that, initially, the dictator did not seem terribly eager to endow the UP with a relevant function in the regime and prioritized the power of the army over the party. It was only by the autumn of 1925, once he had decided to form the Civil Directory, that the Marquess of Estella increasingly began to promote the role of the UP, declaring it 'independent' from governmental control and ready to rule Spain.[24] It was also then that the UP ideologues arrived in the public arena; the Dictatorship was endowed with a nation-wide mouthpiece, *La Nación*; and the founding (or buying) of provincial pro-government newspapers increased.

The UP created the most sophisticated propaganda network known by any Spanish political party. In 1926, the Madrid UP divided the party into five main sections, including one for 'Culture, Propaganda and Publicity'.[25] By early 1927, this section had formed Propaganda and Political Action Commissions in every district of the capital, which in turn created diverse neighbourhood propaganda sub-committees.[26] In addition, the Madrid UP provincial headquarters were divided in four sections: propaganda, provincial affairs, local affairs and statistics. Conceived as a centre of information, the headquarters had their own census, a press archive on political and social issues and collected data on every single militant.[27] The UP structure in Barcelona also shows a modern and extremely hierarchical concept of party structure being implemented by the *primorriveristas*. The provincial *jefe*, Andrés Gassó y Vidal, former secretary of the *Cámara de la Propiedad Urbana de Barcelona*, directed the party with the assistance of the Provincial Committee. Under direct control of the Provincial Committee there were ten district committees, covering all of Barcelona's urban area. In four of the most populated districts sub-committees were formed so that the party could reach every single neighbourhood of the city. In addition, over ten UP cultural centres were opened all around the Catalan capital to improve the propaganda work and counterbalance the appeal of leftist *casas del pueblo*. On top of this, youth, women's and workers' sections of the UP were created, seeking to attract new members by appealing to specific sectors of the population.[28] The power of Gassó extended the boundaries of the city. He commanded thirteen Delegates of the Provincial Leader (*Delegados del Jefe Provincial*), who, in turn, were aided by a plethora of Assistant Delegates (*Delegados Asesores*). The Provincial Delegates' mission was to tour around the province checking the development of tens of local committees and UP cultural centres in towns and villages and reporting back to Gassó.[29]

The creation of such a vast network in the cities was indicative of the Dictatorship's will to form a modern party able to reach many different sectors of society. Notwithstanding the many problems that the regime initially found in the creation and organization of the party, the UP dramatically increased its membership throughout 1925. By July 1926, when the UP Great National Junta (*Gran Junta Nacional de la Unión Patriótica*) was established, Primo declared that 'more than 700 000 individuals, including women', were affiliated to the party.[30] A year later, an editorial in *Unión Patriótica* claimed that the number of members was 1 319 428.[31] Although these figures have to be taken with more than a few grains of salt, there is little doubt that the regime had formed the largest right-wing political party in the history of Spain.

Ceremonies and mobilization

Together with the official press, the military and the *Somatén*, Primo increasingly relied on the party to carry out propaganda tasks. In line with their 'pedagogic' mission, UP cultural centres all around Spain organized hundreds of 'patriotic lectures'. As in the case of the Sunday lectures given by the governmental delegates, the *upetistas* not only talked about the greatness of the Spanish nation and the goodness of the regime, but also covered professional, technical and cultural topics in their dissertations. A more sophisticated version of the 'patriotic lectures' were the so-called 'patriotic affirmation acts'. These usually included a lecture followed by a banquet, speeches and an afternoon party, where the public danced to traditional folkloric music such as *jotas*.[32] Food and dancing were combined here with patriotic indoctrination creating a festive atmosphere and thus attempting to make the nationalist discourse more appealing to the popular classes.

While some of these acts took place indoors, it is important to notice that the *primorriveristas* developed a taste for open-air ceremonies. Popular banquets, dances and the opening of public buildings were all considered good opportunities to celebrate 'patriotic affirmation acts'. The idea behind these ceremonies was using the party to help the regime to monopolize the public political sphere – a task, as we have seen, to which the army and the *Somatén* also contributed significantly. In fact, the *primorriveristas* were prepared to go a long way to succeed in their endeavour. At a time when Basque nationalists and Catalan regionalists were increasingly turning to hiking, as part of the few 'cultural' activities that they were allowed to carry out without risking sanction, the *upetistas* countered and began to organize patriotic fieldtrips to the countryside.[33]

The party was also behind the official campaigns to promote the consumption of Spanish products. Launched almost on a yearly basis, these campaigns 'in defence of Spanish goods' significantly targeted women and presented the purchase of products 'Made in Spain' as a 'patriotic duty'.[34] It is evident that these campaigns were in accord with the regime's economic nationalism. Yet, on closer examination, it is possible to detect a subtler goal behind the promotion of domestic products. The campaigns constantly emphasized the fact that Spanish products were 'as good or better than foreign ones' and heavily criticized those Spaniards who assumed foreign goods were of a higher quality than Spanish ones just because they were manufactured abroad. At the heart of this criticism lay not only a vindication of Spanish products, but also of Spain as a nation. By claiming the superiority of Spanish goods over foreign ones, the regime aimed at ending what it saw as a Spanish inferiority complex – a complex that led Spaniards to assume the superiority of their fellow Europeans in many different fields. It was not by chance that the magazine of the UP had a section called 'Successful Spaniards Abroad', which reported the professional achievements of Spaniards in Europe and the Americas as evidence of the international respect for Spain as a nation. The regime, of course, tried to capitalize on these 'successes' and presented them as part of Spain's revitalization under the Dictatorship.

This triumphant representation of Spain has to be understood within the new positive image of the nation fostered by the regime both at discursive and symbolic levels. As a reaction to the 'pessimistic nationalism' of the Generation of 1898, the *primorriveristas* heralded the immediate rebirth of the Spanish nation. Likewise, official propaganda began to represent the nation in more positive terms. The regime reproduced nineteenth-century paintings representing key moments in Spanish history in stamps, postcards, almanacs and even the packaging of sweets.[35] This representation of the so-called 'history painting' sought to popularize pictures of a victorious Spain against Muslim infidels, while simultaneously emphasizing the Catholic nature of the fatherland. In addition, the *primorriveristas* were resolute in endowing the image of Spain with a more festive character and hence the official press began to depict bullfighting and *romerías* as the expression of the real national character. What is interesting when looking at personifications of Spain as a female figure during the Dictatorship is the process of 'Andalusization' that the image of the patria underwent. In clear opposition to the nineteenth-century icon of the *Mater Dolorosa*, the suffering motherland, *primorriverista* propaganda represented Spain as a joyful and beautiful Andalusian young lady.[36] Against the Castilian sense of austerity, restraint and drama represented in the paintings of the artists of the Generation of 1898, the *primorriverista* icons portrayed joy, youth and beauty in bright colours, much in consonance with the official idea of a rejuvenated nation. Paradoxically, in doing so the *primorriveristas* partially perpetuated in the Spanish collective imaginary the 'orientalist' representation of Spain as Andalusia created by foreign travellers throughout the nineteenth century.

Whilst foreign 'recognition' of Spanish achievements became an essential propaganda tool to nationalize Spaniards at home, the UP also explored xenophobic routes to mobilize the man in the street. To begin with, the aforementioned 'campaigns against bad Spaniards' not only targeted those Spanish citizens publicly denouncing abroad the abuses the Dictatorship, but also the foreigners who, 'jealous of the Spanish resurrection', gave them credit and support.[37] On other occasions, the *upetistas* were mobilized to protest against 'anti-Spanish campaigns' following criticism of the regime in the foreign press. The campaigns were a way to show the world that the Spanish people stood by their dictator and no 'foreign intervention' whatsoever would alter the nation's destiny to regain its place in the sun. After all, the *primorriveristas* repeated again and again, it was the envy of Spanish greatness that led foreigners to invent the Black Legend. The moral of the story was that foreigners could not be trusted and Spanish liberals' admiration for French and British political systems posed a threat to the very essence of the nation. Probably no one put it in blunter terms than Rodríguez Tarduchy, when he wrote that praising foreigners equalled 'de-Spanishizing Spain'.[38] Paradoxical as it may seem, the *upetista* discourse and ceremonies had a strongly contradictory character. On the one hand, the *primorriveristas* copied the ideas and ceremonies of the Italian fascists and the French extreme right and show an acute need to be positively recognized by foreigners – which in a way indicates that the *primorriveristas* suffered from the same inferiority complex that they intended to cure Spaniards of. On the other hand, the regime needed to create a 'foreign threat' in order to be able to play the xenophobic card in the game of mass mobilization. For all the *primorriverista* contradictions, it is important to notice that both discourse and ceremonies perfectly suited the *upetista* Manichean view of a world divided between Good and Evil. And this clear-cut dichotomy was probably more useful to stir nationalist emotions than any other complex political analysis.

Like fascist Italy, and later Nazi Germany, the official party in Spain acted as the mediator between leader and the masses to transmit both discourse and symbolized myths.[39] Discursively, the *primorriverista* press propagated the image of the dictator as a prophetic leader and a national saviour in religious terms.[40] Additionally, the official media constantly printed pictures of the national leader (*caudillo*) in newspapers, magazines, pamphlets and brochures, while portraits of the Marquess of Estella were frequently displayed in UP centres and public ceremonies.[41] Furthermore, tens of towns and villages named streets and squares after the dictator and, from 1926 onwards, the vast majority of new elementary schools chose as their namesake Primo de Rivera. Admittedly, Primo lacked the oratory skills of Mussolini and the UP did not have the propagandistic strength of the fascist party, but this was no impediment for the regime's attempt to create a personality cult of the dictator. It was Primo's showmanship concept of politics that fuelled this cult of personality. In Madrid, the UP regularly held rallies in front of Primo's house, the Palacio de Buenavista, to show their support for the dictator, a liturgy which reminded the British ambassador to Madrid of fascist gatherings at the Palazzo Venezia.[42]

Primo's constant tours around Spain provided UP provincial branches with a good opportunity to mobilize supporters. On some occasions, the presence of the dictator led to the organization of grand gatherings. On 29 May 1924, for instance, 30 000 people gathered in Medina del Campo to hear the speech of the Marquess of Estella.[43] In January 1926, liturgies during his visit to Barcelona included a gargantuan parade of 20 000 *upetistas* marching in front of Primo and a separate rally at the Olympia Theatre which gathered together 7000 'selected supporters'.[44] In September 1928, the celebrations of the fifth anniversary of the coup set in motion the entire party network. For a week, the *upetistas* organized meetings, lunches and parades in hundreds of towns and villages throughout the country.[45] The central focus of the celebrations was, however, to be in Madrid. Thousands of UP militants all over Spain were given free train tickets and boxed lunches to travel to the capital. According to the official press, 100 000 *upetistas* marched on the streets of Madrid on 13 September 1928 to commemorate the anniversary.[46] Three days later 40 000 *primor-riveristas* paraded in Barcelona.[47]

Perhaps no other celebration epitomizes better the eclectic character of the *primorriverista* ceremonies than the *Fiesta de la Raza*. The 12 October celebration provided the Dictatorship with an excellent opportunity to disseminate its anti-Black Legend discourse, to emphasize the supremacy of the Castilian language and to present the legacy of the Spanish empire in a positive light.[48] In clear opposition to the pessimist and pro-European

Figure 9   Unión Patriótica members from all over Spain parade in the streets of Madrid, on 13 September 1928, to celebrate the 5th anniversary of Primo's coup.

views of the Generation of 1898, the *primorriveristas* celebrated the nation in a optimistic fashion looking towards America. Additionally, the *Fiesta de la Raza* emphasized the sacred character of the nation. The twelfth of October coincided with the popular celebration of the Virgin of Pilar, the patron saint of Spain. Together with military parades, open-air masses placing the patria under the protection of the Virgin of Pilar became a common event of the *Fiesta de la Raza* all over Spain. Again, religion was considered to be 'the most powerful engine to reach the heart of the masses' and Catholic iconography and rituals were used to stir the emotions of the people in favour of the national ideal and the Dictatorship alike.[49]

From 1918 to 1923 the celebrations had on many occasions taken place indoors and the *Fiesta de la Raza* had gained relatively little popular support.[50] The widespread celebration of open-air masses and military parades, together with the regime's mobilization of UP members, *somatenistas* and school children to march in the streets as part of the ceremonies, transformed the commemoration of the fiesta during the Dictatorship. In order to achieve this transformation Primo used party and state resources alike. In early 1925, the dictator declared that the UP had among its missions to stir the people's 'spiritual vibrations [of] love for the race'.[51] As a result, diverse sections of the party issued manifestos mobilizing *upetistas* and organized public UP flag sanctifications as part of the *Fiesta de la Raza* celebrations.[52] Conceived as a ceremony especially suitable for the indoctrination of young people and children, the Dictatorship fostered the incorporation of students into the celebration of the *Fiesta de la Raza*. Provincial administrations devoted part of their resources to propagate the *Hispanista* ideal in education centres and public libraries, teachers were instructed to devote some hours to explain to pupils the grandeur of *Hispanismo*, while the regime carefully organized the participation of children from public and private schools in the *Fiesta de la Raza* parades.[53]

There can be little doubt that the *primorriverista* efforts to popularize the fiesta paid off. By 1928, Madrid witnessed huge parades with 30 000 children marching in the streets, while the Barcelona press also noted that the massive celebrations showed the *Fiesta de la Raza* had taken a firm root in the Catalan capital.[54] Furthermore, hundreds of villages celebrated the *Fiesta de la Raza* for the first time during the Dictatorship, proving once again the key role of the governmental delegates in spreading patriotic rituals. Yet the use of the *Fiesta de la Raza* as a device for governmental propaganda and the continual representation of nation and Dictatorship as conterminous were soon to prove costly for the *primorriveristas*. As in the *Somatén* ceremonies, once the regime entered its final crisis in 1929 the participation in the ceremonies decreased remarkably.[55] More importantly, notwithstanding *primorriverista* efforts, the impact of the *Fiesta de la Raza* on the population was at best dubious. In an editorial of October 1930, *La Nación* bitterly acknowledged that some were not convinced of the efficiency of the celebrations while others simply considered the *Fiesta de la Raza* useless.[56] The following year, Berenguer's government removed the militarist connotations of the *Fiesta de la Raza* and opted for a more low-key celebration.[57] The Republican-Socialist government of 1931–1933 declared the fiesta a national holiday, but removed the Catholic masses from the celebration and shifted the emphasis of the official discourse towards liberal *Hispanismo*.[58] Democratic principles and the Spanish language, and not Catholicism and militarism, became the dominant themes of the celebration in the first years of the Second Republic.

Radicalization and fall

In 1928, Primo created the *Junta de Propaganda Patriótica y Ciudadana* (JPPC). A special branch of the Press and Censorship Cabinet, the JPPC was directed by Lieutenant Máximo Cuervo, *Jefe* of the Bureau of the President. Cuervo, Eduardo Hernández, the head of the censorship department, and a team of fifty military officers, soon centralized *primorriverista* propaganda efforts and began publishing books and pamphlets. In the spring of 1929, the JPPC published *Cursos de Ciudadanía* (a compilation of lectures by regime ideologues) and produced a series of pamphlets and postcards to be distributed among public officers and the general public at large.[59] At the same time, the JPPC co-ordinated massive publication of the dictator and the *primorriverista* ideologues' books. These works were later sent to all Civil Governors, who in turn distributed them among schools, cultural organizations, town councils, libraries, military barracks and UP centres.[60]

In addition, the JPPC orchestrated a series of 'patriotic demonstrations' to protest against the 'conspiracy' of the foreign press and the student revolt.[61] With the help of the Civil Governors, the JPPC mobilized UP militants to participate in patriotic acts in which signatures of support for the regime were collected and thousands of pamphlets were distributed. As the Civil Governor of Lugo crudely put it, these acts were a good opportunity 'to flood the province with [pamphlets] and make citizens swallow their concepts'.[62] Domestic propaganda was coupled with international promotion of the Dictatorship. Cuervo tried to intensify the regime's presence in the international media and prepared a series of new publications to be sold abroad. Seeking to counter the increasingly negative image the regime was gaining in Europe and Latin America, the JPPC co-ordinated its activities with *Plus Ultra* – the propaganda agency established by Primo in Paris in 1926 to promote the regime in the international arena.[63] As a result of this collaboration, the JPPC launched *La España de Hoy. Periódico editado en español, francés, alemán e inglés para propagar en todo el mundo el resurgimiento actual de España* and *España Nueva*, and funded the translation into French of propagandists' works, such as Pemartín's *Los valores históricos en la Dictadura*.[64]

The JPPC also supported private propagandist initiatives in defence of the regime. The most notorious case was *Propagandistas de España*, a civil nationalist organization devoted to 'inspire the masses to praise the Spanish Race' which, according to the official records, had 'had almost no activity whatsoever' since its foundation in 1927.[65] In July 1929, however, *Propagandistas de España* was granted official recognition by Primo and the JPPC began to assist the patriotic association.[66] The reason for this backing was the JPPC's urgency to promote the Seville and Barcelona international exhibitions of 1929. In June that year, the Bureau of the President had received a shocking report from the Commissioner of the Ibero-American Exhibition in Seville stating that the event desperately needed more visitors. The Commissioner pointed out that many foreigners would not visit the exhibition due to the political 'atmosphere in the country' and 'the alarming situation' created abroad by the *primorriverista* opposition.[67] More importantly, the report suggested not enough Spaniards were visiting the exhibitions in Seville and Barcelona and, hence, the people could not grasp the 'patriotic effort' carried out by the regime in organizing the events. The proposal by the Commission was an 'integral plan' to publicize Seville and Barcelona exhibitions both in Spain and abroad. The plan was an example of a modern approach to propaganda similar to that put into practice by Mussolini in the 1932 Exhibition of the Fascist Revolution.[68] It included the participation of embassies, public officers, publicity agencies and other private companies, such as travel agencies, hotels, restaurants and health resorts, and emphasized the use of posters, cinema and flyers as the most effective means of attracting visitors.

The report constituted a serious blow to a project that Primo himself had passionately endorsed since his first days in power. For all the money and propaganda the Dictatorship had put into the exhibitions throughout the years the results were a fiasco. It was not only that the actions of the opposition were having a knock-on effect in restraining the number of foreign visitors but, crucially, the fact that Spaniards were not visiting the exhibitions deprived the regime of a political success at home. Unlike

Italy, where the 1932 Exhibition of the Fascist Revolution constituted a key event in the construction of the so-called 'culture of consent' and encouraged mass support for Mussolini's dictatorship, the Seville and Barcelona exhibitions elicited the wrath of Spanish republicans. In their view, the Seville and Barcelona exhibitions were nothing but clear evidence of Primo's megalomania and a deceitful manifestation of the decadent monarchic system.[69] Far from attracting the population towards the national ideal, the exhibitions seem to have further exacerbated the divisions among Spaniards.

In many senses, the *primorriverista* propaganda offensive came too late. By the time the JPPC was formed the UP was losing members and the Dictatorship was in crisis. At the heart of the party's problems lay its very official nature. This had attracted many opportunists who hoped to benefit from their affiliation but were not committed to the regime – ideologically or otherwise.[70] Evidence of this lack of political commitment is to be found in the party organs. For a party which claimed to have over a million militants, the fact that *La Nación* and *Unión Patriótica* had circulations of 50 000 and 6000 issues respectively shows that the UP affiliates did not even bother to read the official press. By 1926, it was clear to senior figures in the regime that the UP was a breeding-ground of personal ambitions for many members. In December, Milans del Bosch and Barrera publicly called for a purge of the party and 'elimination of all those that had joined in bad faith'.[71] Nevertheless, the task of reorganizing the UP on 'purer' ideological bases did not begin until January 1930, when both party and Dictatorship were collapsing.[72]

The factor that most significantly contributed to the fall of the UP, and to a large extent to the collapse of the regime, was the loss of Social Catholics' support for the party. From 1928, the Social Catholics grew increasingly disaffected with the Dictatorship. As we saw in previous chapters, the exclusion of Catholic trade unions from the *comités paritarios* and the educational reforms granting more power to the state to the detriment of the Church were all indicative of the divergent route the Dictatorship was taking from the Social Catholics' goals. Social Catholic discontent can be detected in the pages of *El Debate* from the autumn of 1928, when the newspaper questioned the regime's attitude towards the Catholic Church, demanded more state money for the clergy and attacked fascism.[73] In April 1929, following the censoring of an editorial in *El Debate*, its director Ángel Herrera wrote a letter of complaint to Máximo Cuervo explaining that the article was pro-monarchical and aimed at 'destroying the republican atmosphere that four Republican intellectual politicians were trying to spread in Madrid'.[74] Crucially, Herrera added that the newspaper's campaign to promote the figure of the King, sought to facilitate 'an easy transition to a different regime'. In the spring of 1929, the rift between the Dictatorship and the Social Catholics was widening by the day.

The consequences of the split were catastrophic for the official party. Throughout 1929, both Social Catholic cadres and rank and file militants increasingly left the UP as the Dictatorship faced one crisis after another. The Social Catholics' gradual withdrawal led the radical authoritarian wing of the party to take absolute control over the UP.[75] Moreover, all this happened in a moment when Primo had turned the UP and the *Somatén* into espionage and police institutions, seeking to make political repression more efficient. However, the results of this 'totalitarian drive' were counter-productive, for it was not only ineffective in curbing opposition to the Dictatorship, but it also made the UP and the *Somatén* more unpopular.[76] Especially damaging for the UP was the new legislation to repress suspected dissidents from among public servants.[77] Functionaries constituted one of the largest sectors of the party's rank and file, and indiscriminate arrests and random legislation alienated public servants from the regime.[78] No less important was the attack on professional groups, such as lawyers, doctors and architects, which turned against the Dictatorship due to the *primorriverista* interventionism in their associations and the repressive measures taken against political dissidents.[79] As a result, the integration of middle-class professional groups into the regime, which Mussolini gradually achieved in Italy, never happened in Spain.

In the spring and the summer of 1929, Cuervo and Martínez Anido orchestrated a series of 'patriotic acts' to 'demonstrate' to the opposition at home and the foreign press abroad that popular support for the regime remained unchanged.[80] Yet the fact that Civil Governors and delegates were once again in charge of organizing the gatherings is indicative of the low level of independence the UP had gained throughout the years and, indeed, of the little trust the government had in the party's capacity to mobilize the masses. Primo's scepticism towards the UP was not unfounded. In April 1929, the Barcelona UP's provincial *Jefe* bitterly informed the Marquess of Estella about the inaction of the militants. In a frank letter to Primo, Gassó wrote that 90 per cent of the members were either 'indifferent' or 'disappointed' with the regime. Another 5 per cent, Gassó explained, went to party centres just to read the newspaper and play cards, and around 5 per cent of the militants wished 'to act in good faith, but owing to the lack of assistance by their *jefes* [their] enthusiasm could not materialize [. . .] It can be said that *Not doing* is the tenet of the UP in Barcelona'.[81] Furthermore, the establishment of a branch of the JPPC in Barcelona did not make things any better for the *primorriveristas*. On the contrary, Gassó saw the establishment of a JPPC committee in Barcelona as a challenge to his position and became remarkably uncooperative.[82] Under such circumstances of lack of interest and disappointment of militants and internal struggles between the *primorriverista* cadres, it is hardly surprising that the UP failed to mobilize its members when it was most important for the survival of the regime.

The decadence of the party was implicitly admitted by Primo in late 1929. In an official note dated 17 December, the dictator boasted that the UP had '600 000 or 700 000 affiliates'.[83] Regardless of the more than dubious correctness of the figure, the statement implied a loss of around 50 per cent of UP militants in two years, compared to the 1.3 million affiliates *Unión Patriótica* claimed the party had in 1927. Two weeks later, the Marquess of Estella stated the obvious and conceded that different sectors of society were disaffected with the regime, including Catholic political groups and functionaries – the two backbones of the UP rank and file.[84] After Primo was compelled to resign on 29 January 1930, the party simply collapsed. Once Berenguer ordered the Civil Governors to cut all support to the UP, the desperate calls for unity from the pages of *Unión Patriótica* were to no avail.[85] In April 1930, ex-ministers and ideologues of the regime gathered together to form the *Unión Monárquica Nacional* (UMN) in an attempt to replace the UP. The same month the UP Provincial Leaders' Assembly recommended the *upetistas* to join the UMN on an individual basis. During the summer of 1930 the last sections of the UP were dissolved.[86] Created from above, the official party could not survive without the *primorriverista* regime.

In 1923 Primo claimed he was to follow the example set by Mussolini. Seven years later his regime had collapsed while the fascist dictator had consolidated his power and enjoyed a certain level of popular support.[87] When comparing the development of the fascist party and the UP, the picture that emerges is one of two regimes travelling in opposite directions. In Italy, the fascist party gradually integrated different conservative groups and increasingly accommodated Catholic rhetoric into its discourse throughout the 1920s.[88] In 1929, the Lateran Agreements effectively integrated the Catholic Church into the fascist state. Conversely, the UP increasingly radicalized its discourse, political goals and political personnel throughout the 1920s, a process which led to the gradual alienation of conservative groups from the regime. In 1929, the departure of the Social Catholics from the UP paved the way for the fall of the Dictatorship.

A poisoned legacy

How successful might the UP be considered as an agency of nationalization? An overall consideration of the actions of the party indicates that the UP's attempt to indoctrinate the masses was a failure. The very official nature of the UP and the tight military control exercised over it linked the public's image of the agencies to the Dictatorship's popularity. This meant that when the dictator and the military began to lose popular support by 1928 the public's image of the party soon deteriorated. This process was abetted by the regime's 'totalitarian drive' of 1929. By transforming the party and the *Somatén* into repressive police institutions, the agencies' popularity severely decreased. The discrediting of the UP had a knock-on effect on the public's perception of the National-Catholic idea of Spain. Since the *primorriveristas* constantly presented the Spanish nation and the Dictatorship regime as the very same thing, the drop in popular support for the regime led to the fall of support of the official idea of Spain. Thus, as in the case of the army and the *Somatén*, the actions of the party led to a 'negative nationalization', in which increasing opposition to the state agents propagating the official canon of the nation was accompanied by the rejection of the very idea of nation defended by those agents. The fact that the disaffected middle classes, who had initially supported the regime, increasingly turned towards the defence of a democratic and republican idea of Spain (or towards alternative nationalist movements in Catalonia and the Basque Country) has to be understood as a reaction to the monarchist authoritarian canon promoted by the UP. Unlike Mussolini, by the late 1920s Primo had failed to create a 'culture of consent' that could integrate diverse social classes into the national ideal.[89]

The negative impact of the UP as an agency of mass nationalization was obvious as soon as the Dictatorship fell. Liberals criticized the UP's 'secret denunciations and illegal arrests' and called for a democratic citizenry based on 'the public exercise of rights and duties'.[90] Just six days after the fall of Primo, José Ortega y Gasset condemned the Dictatorship's policies for fostering the divisions among Spaniards and 'de-nationalizing' the state agencies.[91] The state apparatus, Ortega observed, was not at the service of all Spaniards but exclusively of the *primorriveristas*. For the *madrileño* philosopher, the formation of a 'great national party' integrating all social classes was the only way to 'renationalize' Spain.[92] A similar emphasis on democracy and civil rights is to be found in the socialists' discourse. Against the *primorriverista* militarized concept of citizen, the socialists presented 'the people' as the essence of the nation and asserted the need to educate the masses in civil and democratic values in order to create a new democratic regime.[93] Significantly, the socialists challenged the Social Catholics' claim to speak for the nation, arguing that the 'real Spain' was liberal and democratic and not the reactionary, backward-looking patria the right represented. 'Do they [the Social Catholics] really deceive themselves thinking they are Spain?', *El Socialista* ironically wondered.[94] Far from consolidating a uniform national identity the Dictatorship led to the fragmentation of it, with different competing Spanish identities fighting to become hegemonic among the masses.

Yet the *primorriverista* nationalist rituals and top-down mobilization were to have a long-lasting impact. Like the fascists, the *primorriveristas* built a symbolic universe taking the liturgy and the language from the Christian tradition in order to endow the nation with a sacred aura. This facilitated the 'internalization' of the nation as a sacred value by thousands of Spanish Catholics perfectly familiarized with Christian liturgy and symbolism. What is interesting when looking at the rites developed during the Dictatorship is the extraordinarily high number of them. The thousands of patriotic ceremonies celebrated all around Spain were unprecedented and reached the most remote corners of the country, hence reinforcing the dominance of the Catholic-Monarchic symbolic universe in the public political sphere. This in turn constituted a poisoned legacy for the Second Republic, for the democratic forces found it extremely difficult to transform the National-Catholic symbolic universe constructed in the 1920s. As a result, the Second Republic was to suffer a 'representation crisis' for the political authority of the democratic parties was not integrated into a wider social order that could create a sense of national community.[95] On the other hand, the experience the Social Catholics had gained during Primo's regime in terms of mass mobilization, party organization and nationalist rituals was vital during the 1930s, when most of the former cadres of the UP entered *Acción Popular*, first, and, later, CEDA.[96] The Catholic right not only incorporated much of the *primorriverista* discourse (for instance, counterrevolution, the cult of the leader, an organic and hierarchical concept of nation and the myth of the Anti-Spain) but also the sacred symbolic universe developed during the Dictatorship.[97] Furthermore, some *primorriverista* rituals (such as the *misas de campaña* consecrating the national flag), and myths (*Hispanidad*) became essential tools to mobilize support for the rebels during the Civil War.[98] And it was the same *primorriverista* top-down approach to mobilization that Franco was often eager to use to orchestrate grand gatherings against 'bad Spaniards' and critical foreigners all the way through his 40-year-long dictatorship. The Manichean discourse of both dictatorships had their equivalent Manichean rituals.

10
Conclusion: From Negative Integration to Negative Nationalization

In the aftermath of the First World War, some European elites resorted to dictatorships as a way to halt the advance of the left. In these cases nationalism and counterrevolution were two sides of the same coin. Repression of political opponents went hand in hand with vast programmes of mass indoctrination in nationalist values designed to gain the hearts of the population, diminish the appeal of the left among the lower classes and legitimize the dictatorships simultaneously. The Dictatorship of Primo de Rivera has to be understood within this counterrevolutionary European context as a nationalist regime which attempted a vast process of mass nationalization in National-Catholic values. Like many other dictators of the interwar period, the Marquess of Estella realized that the liberal oligarchic system would not hold in the post-1918 world and envisaged the need to create a new authoritarian state that could integrate the masses without paying the toll of a real democracy. In Spain, and elsewhere, this required the creation of a new political discourse that would redefine the traditionally dominant liberal canon of the nation and rally the people around the Dictatorship via 'negative integration', that is, the assimilation of the lower and middle classes through nationalist ideas that emphasized foreign and domestic foes.

Seeking to reach a wide audience, the *primorriverista* discourse during the Military Directory was intentionally vague and populist. It blended elements from regenerationists, Maurists, Social Catholics, Carlists and, above all, military nationalism in a 'negative discourse' that attempted to integrate different political groups from the opposition to common enemies (such as *caciques*, regional nationalists, trade unionists, Moroccans and so on). In the first two years of the regime, the *primorriverista* discourse sought to justify the existence of the Dictatorship on a temporary basis. During the Civil Directory, once the dictator had announced his intention to build a new state, the *primorriverista* discourse shifted to ensure the disparagement of the Restoration and the transformation of the *canovista* structures. National-Catholicism was created from above in an attempt to endow the regime with a solid doctrinal basis and increase social support for the Dictatorship. It merged French integral nationalism, Italian fascism and vitalist philosophy with diverse postulates of the Spanish anti-liberal right to formulate a new discourse which heralded the end of democracy, defended a sacred concept of the fatherland and promised a national rebirth via an authoritarian corporative state. The result was a new highly *fascisticized* nationalist ideology in line with the European radical right.

The *primorriveristas* promoted a series of political myths (such as the messianic leader of the fatherland, the Anti-Spain and so on), displayed a religious rhetoric, fostered national symbols in the public sphere and invented a series of nationalist rituals. The goal was nothing less than the moral and physical improvement of the 'Spanish race', the making of 'new Spaniards', and to this end state agencies were mobilized to an unprecedented extent. Yet the results of this process of state nationalization were patchy. Although the Dictatorship managed to mobilize sectors of Spanish society hitherto uninvolved in politics, create a catch-all inter-class party and organize scores of nationalist rituals in the most remote corners of the country, its effectiveness was poor. The regime failed to turn the National-Catholic concept of Spain into the hegemonic one, let alone to create any sort of consensus among Spaniards about the nation and the Dictatorship. On the contrary, the more the regime radicalized its discourse the more social support it lost.

Reasons for this failure lie in the functioning of the state agencies as much as the policies implemented by the *primorriveristas*. First of all, it is possible to detect a pattern in the work of state institutions under Primo: both the education system and the army lacked the necessary funds to carry out the ambitious plans of mass nationalization. Here the *primorriveristas* were caught in a sort of 'demographic trap'. The economic development of the first two decades of the twentieth century had led not only to the rise of a working class which challenged the Restoration system, but also to an important demographic growth. The *primorriverista* programmes of mass nationalization were precisely an attempt to neutralize the threat of a changing society by integrating the lower classes into the national ideal. Consequently, Primo reformed the state agencies, seeking to turn them into modern efficient indoctrinating institutions. Yet the modernization of the state agencies could not keep pace with the demographic growth which put extra pressure on these already obsolete institutions, thus hampering their functioning as effective indoctrinating machines.

A second factor which seriously undermined the efficiency of the state agencies as institutions of nationalization was the alienation of public sector officials and workers. *Primorriverista* policies of purging, surveillance and repression of teachers and public servants antagonized the very personnel the Dictatorship needed for an effective transmission of the official message. To make things worse for the regime, Primo did not merge the UP with the state bureaucracy but rather used military officers to control the state apparatus. Unlike Mussolini, the Marquess of Estella did not create a bureaucracy linked to the official party and thus precluded the emergence of a new political clientele dependent on the regime. Hence, the *primorriveristas* could not be assured of the political loyalty of the UP's social bases nor the so-called 'passive popularity' that Mussolini achieved in Italy.

Thirdly, the implementation of *primorriverista* policies of nationalization severely undermined the initial support of many on the right. Indiscriminate repression in Catalonia towards all those labelled 'separatists' led to the detachment of the regionalist sector of the Catalan bourgeoisie and the Carlists from the regime, while the linguistic policies of 'Spanishization' brought direct confrontation between the Catalan Church and teachers, on the one hand, and the *primorriveristas* on the other. As in many other cases, language teaching policies proved to be counterproductive rather than a unifying factor in the process of state nationalization. As Calvo Sotelo observed as early as 1924, the regime's policies of nationalization in Catalonia made things worse, turning many sectors of the population, hitherto opposed to of all sort of Catalanism, into Catalanist sympathizers.[1]

In the case of the Social Catholics it was not so much the *primorriverista* anti-regionalist policies as the incorporation of the UGT into the *comités paritarios* and the increasing power of the state in education issues that led to the gradual breach with the government from 1928 onwards. This proved costly for the *primorriveristas*, as the Social Catholics constituted the main social bases of the UP and the *Somatén*, but it was in many ways a logical product of the *primorriverista* ideological understanding of the leading role the state should have in the process of nationalization. While the incorporation of the socialists into the corporative state was essentially a *primorriverista* move to co-opt the moderate sector of the working class, Primo always considered the Church as subordinate to the state. He was determined to extend state control over education to secure an effective process of nationalization which necessarily collided with ecclesiastical interests. The dictator had to trade off some concessions (such as granting the right to issue decrees to religious colleges), yet he held firm in more important issues in terms of mass nationalization, such as the *texto único* and the creation of new public state-controlled secondary schools.

Governmental policies of nationalization also proved counterproductive in the rural areas. The public image of the *delegados* soon deteriorated owing to indiscriminate repression, accusations of corruption, the officers' inability to deal with municipal issues and the financial strains put on local councils. When the regime created a permanent institution specifically devoted to mass indoctrination in the rural areas in 1929, the SNEFCP faced the same old problems of under-funding and had no time to make an impact. The overall effect of the actions of the 'apostles of the fatherland' was to undermine the regime, the military as a whole and the National-Catholic idea of Spain, since *primorriverista* officers constantly presented nation, Dictatorship and army as the very same thing. A similar negative effect on the urban and rural population is to be observed in the cases of the *Somatén* and the UP. The abuses of the militia and the transformation of the party into a repressive police institution created hostility towards the regime and discredited the *primorriverista* idea of Spain. If the *primorriverista* discourse sought a 'negative integration' of the entire population against the 'enemies of the fatherland', the actions of the agencies propagating that message led to a 'negative nationalization'.

The different political proposals that emerged immediately after the fall of the Dictatorship are evidence of the discredit into which the *primorriverista* idea of Spain had fallen and, ultimately, of the regime's failure to nationalize the masses in National-Catholic values. In Catalonia, different nationalist and regionalist factions came together in their struggle against the Dictatorship, and cultural production in the Catalan language increased, while left-wing republican Catalanist tendencies gained mass backing. In the Basque Country, the two factions of the Basque nationalist movement reunited in the PNV and soon increased their popular support. In other areas of Spain regionalist movements mushroomed in the early 1930s. Some of these movements were the continuation of the late 1910s and early 1920s conservative regionalism, but some others had acquired a more democratic veneer. More importantly, as a reaction against the Dictatorship, the idea of a republican democratic Spain took root among many in the urban centres. As soon as the *primorriverista* regime collapsed, democratic Spanish nationalism re-emerged stronger than ever. From February 1930, liberals and socialists argued in favour of the formation of a new constitutional system based on universal suffrage and an active participation of the 'Spanish people', as the only way to heal the divisions originated by Primo's dictatorship. In December 1930, Spanish liberals, republicans and socialists reached a political agreement with Catalan nationalists to establish a secular, democratic and decentralized republic.

The *primorriverista* ideological legacy to the Spanish right was rich and complex. Throughout the Second Republic, the Social Catholics of *Acción Popular* adopted the *primorriverista* sacred anti-democratic concept of Spain, together with its symbolic elements and liturgy, as a central part of the conservative discourse. Nevertheless, the fact that the Social Catholics and the Catalan monarchists returned to their pre-1923 regionalist postulates as soon as Primo fell illustrates how unpopular the *primorriverista* centralist policies had become. Only marginal parties on the extreme right, *Renovación Española* and *Falange Española y de las JONS*, stridently opposed all forms of regionalism and defended the centralist policies of the Dictatorship. Yet electoral oblivion did not mean political insignificance. The generals who revolted against the Second Republic in July 1936 were highly influenced by the National-Catholic postulates elaborated during Primo's dictatorship. In fact, the military rebels declared they sought to achieve what Primo could not: 'to nationalize and to deintoxicate the masses, to create a new state and to reorganize society'.[2]

This second attempt of mass nationalization was to be much more radical and brutal. The Francoist regime differed from the *primorriverista* in two main aspects. First, as in 1923, the 1936 military coup was welcomed by most conservative groups, but this time the democratic experience of the early 1930s and the Great Depression had frightened many on the right who had become much more extreme in their determination to halt social change and political reform. Second, Francoism emerged from a civil war, unlike the bloodless coup that brought Primo to power. Franco's refusal to recognize the rights of the defeated after the war and his determination to establish a reign of terror with large-scale executions and mass imprisonments made the political conditions of the 1940s very different from the *primorriverista* era. Yet, for all these differences, it is important to note that the ideological principles behind both Primo and Franco's bid to regenerate Spain and nationalize the masses bore a close resemblance. This was not only owing to the fact that the former ideologues of the *primorriverista* regime played a leading role in the merging of different conservative groups in the *FET y de las JONS* and were soon integrated into the Francoist government during the Civil War. It was also that many ideological postulates, myths, ceremonies and 'traditions' invented and/or consolidated during the Dictatorship of Primo de Rivera became part of the Francoist regime from its conception. The organic concept of the nation as a supreme and sacred political value, the idea of Spain as conterminous with Catholicism, *Hispanismo*, the corporative state, the idealization of the military leader as the saviour of the fatherland and the myth of the Anti-Spain were all essential elements in a Francoist discourse soaked in religious and medical vocabulary, whose ultimate goals were the nationalization of the masses in authoritarian and militarist values and the creation of a 'New State'. In many respects, Francoist National-Catholicism was ideologically born during the Dictatorship of Primo de Rivera.

Notes

Introduction

1. Wehler, 1985, pp. 100–37.
2. Preston, 2002, pp. 137–65.

1.   The Roots of National-Catholicism

1. Cited in Vilar, 1984, p. 13.
2. The manifesto in Casassas, 1983, pp. 81–5
3. Núñez Seixas, 1999, pp. 22–30; Blas, 1994a, pp. 105–67.
4. Herrero, 1971, p. 14.
5. Álvarez Junco, 2001a, 405–64; Foard, 1979, pp. 83–97.
6. Núñez Seixas, 1999, p. 23.
7. Vilar, 1984, p. 13.
8. Fox, 1999, pp. 21–36.
9. Cacho, 1986, pp. 54–62.
10. The thesis of the 'weak nationalization of the masses' was first sketched by Linz in 1973, pp. 32–116. De Riquer further developed the thesis in 1990, pp. 105–26 and 1994, pp. 97–114. The thesis of weak nationalization has also been supported, among others, by Beramendi, 1998, pp. 187–215; and Álvarez Junco, 2001b, pp. 29–51; 2002, pp. 13–36.
11. Andrés de Blas was one of the first critics of the 'weak nationalization' thesis. He argued that the emergence of Catalan and Basque nationalism at the turn of the century was not due to a failure of the Spanish nationalist project but rather it was evidence of the impact Spanish nationalism had made on Catalonia and the Basque Country. See Blas, 1994b, pp. 39–52. In recent years the most vehement criticism of the 'weak nationalization' thesis has come from historians of the Universitat de València. See the collective article by Ismael Saz, Ana María Aguado, Joan del Alcazar, Isabel Burdiel, Manuel Martí, María Cruz Romero and Nuria Tabanera, 1998, pp. 139–48. The 'Valencian school' also questioned the general assumption that the permanence of strong regional identities by the turn of the nineteenth century was a sign of the weak nationalization of the masses. Rather, it presented regional identities as compatible with the idea of a unified nation. See, for example, Martí and Archilés, 1999, pp. 173–90; Archilés and Martí, 2002a, pp. 779–97; Archilés, 2002, pp. 302–22; On the lack of a Spanish exceptionalism in Western European terms see Núñez Seixas, 2001a, pp. 93–115 and Archilés and Martí, 2002b, pp. 245–78.
12. Fusi and Palafox, 1997, pp. 87–152.
13. De Riquer, 2000, pp. 91–112.
14. Burdiel, 2003, pp. 101–33.
15. Manzano and Pérez, 2002, p. 261; Pérez Garzón, 2002, pp. 53–86.
16. Boyd, 2001, pp. 859–78.

17. Álvarez Junco, 1996, pp. 99–100.
18. Fusi, 1990a, p. 34.
19. Archilés and Martí, 2002b, p. 251; Molina, 2005, pp. 129–46.
20. Balfour, 1997, p. 134.
21. Radcliff, 1997, pp. 306–25.
22. Serrano, 1999, pp. 114–15; Juaristi, 1997, pp. 19–31.
23. Mann, 1993, vol. 2, p. 5; Núñez Seixas, 2001a, pp. 93–115.
24. Manzano and Pérez, 2002, p. 262.
25. Alonso, 2000, pp. 261–9.
26. Storm, 2000, pp. 392–400.
27. See, for example, Maeztu, 1998 (1st ed. 1899), pp. 187–202; Ortega, 1993 (1st ed. 1922), pp. 39, 46, 69.
28. Balfour, 1995, pp. 412–13.
29. Balfour, 1997, p. 171; Jensen, 2000, pp. 257–74.
30. González Calbet, 1987, p. 49.
31. Balfour and La Porte, 2000, p. 314.
32. Boyd, 2000, pp. 300–1.
33. Fernández Bastarreche, 1988, p. 233.
34. *El Ejército Español*, 12.9.1923.
35. For the positive response of the military press to the coup see *El Ejército Español*, 14.9.1923; *Ejército y Armada*, 14.9.1923; *Revista Hispano Africana*, September–October, 1923; *La Correspondencia Militar*, 14.9.1923.
36. Cited in Balfour, 1997, p. 188.
37. González Hernández, 1990, pp. 149–61.
38. Romero, 1996, p. 130.
39. *La Traza* Manifesto in González and Rey, 1995, pp. 326–7.
40. Fusi, 1990a, pp. 38–9.
41. Serrano, 1991, p. 187.
42. González Cuevas, 1998, pp. 47–8.
43. Castillo, 1977, p. 278.
44. Castillo, 1979, pp. 340–4.
45. Montero, 1983, pp. 120–1; Winston, 1996, pp. 85–101.
46. Blinkhorn, 1975, pp. 33–5.
47. *El Siglo Futuro*, 4.11.1898 and 5.11.1898.
48. Andrés, 2000, p. 58.
49. Vázquez de Mella, 1915, pp. 73–5, 85–95.
50. This concept of race was a cultural one. Race is understood here as being shaped more by common culture, historical experiences, tradition and language, than by blood. See Pike, 1971, pp. 1–2.
51. Juderías, 1997 (1st ed. 1914), p. 24.
52. Salaverría, 1917, pp. 14–19, 21, 30–41, 48, 123–32, 136–7. See also his articles in *ABC*, 20.8.1914; 18.10.1917; 15.8.1922.
53. Sepúlveda, 1994, pp. 317–36.
54. Fusi, 2000, pp. 21–52.
55. Capitán, 1994, vol. 2, pp. 385–92.
56. *Ibid.*, pp. 394–5.
57. Silió, 1914, pp. 224–5.
58. *Ibid.*, pp. 181–2.
59. Pozo and Braster, 1999, pp. 82, 89.

60. Núñez Seixas, 1999, pp. 24–5.
61. Serrano, 1999, pp. 318–21.
62. Álvarez Junco, 2001b, p. 50.
63. Serrano, 1999, p. 199.
64. For the idea of Spain lacking a modern nationalism at the beginning of the twentieth century see Payne, 1999, pp. 3–23 and González Cuevas, 2000, p. 264.
65. For the thesis of Catholicism as an exclusive mutual identity that hampered the development of a modern nationalism in Spain see Payne, 1999, p. 14.

2. The Military Directory (1923–1925)

1. Cited in Rubio, 1974, p. 126.
2. Martínez Segarra, 1997, p. 169.
3. Primo himself acknowledged that the Spanish government paid money to the foreign press 'to look after [Spain's] interests and good name'. Pérez, 1930, p. 317. For the regime's propaganda machine abroad see Cal, 1995, pp. 177–95.
4. Reports from the Civil Governors to the Minister of the Interior on the subscription campaign in Archivo Histórico Nacional (hereafter AHN), Gobernación Serie A, Bundle 18, Folder 4.
5. Gómez-Navarro, 1985, p. 156.
6. Martínez Anido to Civil Governors, 10.10.1923 and 23.10.1923, AHN, Gobernación Serie A, Bundle 18 A.
7. Primo, 1929, pp. 166–71.
8. Primo, 1926, pp. 7–9.
9. Iglesia, 1930, pp. 75–6. On censorship under Primo see also Villanueva, 1930, pp. 146–62; Santonja, 1986; and Seoane, 1986, pp. 233–43.
10. Primo, 1926, p. 12.
11. *Ibid.*, p. 14. See also *La Nación* 18.10.1925 and 22.10.1925.
12. Primo, 1929, p. 109.
13. See, for example, Primo's official note of August 1925 in Rubio, 1974, p. 154; Primo, 1926, p. 23 and *La Nación*, 19.10.1925.
14. González Calbet, 1987, pp. 50–1, 265.
15. *El Sol*, 2.10.1923; *El Debate*, 14.9.1923; 13.10.1923; 28.9.1923; *ABC*, 14.9.1923.
16. Tens of denunciations from the public in AHN, Gobernación, Bundle 18 A, Folders 1 and 2.
17. Mask, 1925, p. 268.
18. Primo, 1926, pp. 19–23.
19. For example, Berenguer, 1894, pp. iii–iv.
20. Iradier, 1924, pp. 4–5, 8, 15, 17–19.
21. Gentile, 1996, p. 96.
22. Primo 1916, pp. xi–xv.
23. Royal Decree (hereafter RD) in *La Gaceta*, 21.10.1923.
24. RD 20.10.10, Royal Order (hereafter RO) 9.12.1923, RD 20.3.1924. See also Primo's letters to the *delegados*, 5.4.1924; 24.4.1924 and instructions from the Interior Ministry, 7.12.1923, in Archivo General de la Administración del Estado (hereafter AGA), Subsecretaría Sección de Orden Público, Interior, Box 149.
25. RD 17.9.1923 in *La Gaceta*, 18.9.1923.
26. *La Nación*, 19.10.1925.

27. Quiroga, 2005, pp. 73–4.
28. *La Nación*, 3.11.1925.
29. Balfour, 1997, pp. 230–1.
30. Primo, 1926, pp. 12–14.
31. Primo, 1917, p. 34.
32. Official note, 11.7.1925, in Primo, 1929, p. 144.
33. *Revista de Tropas Coloniales*, 31.8.1925. For the alleged Communist links with the Rifean rebels see also *La Nación*, 19.10.1925; and Primo to Sanjurjo, 4.5.1925, in Armiñán and Armiñán, 1930, p. 125.
34. Maradiaga, 1988, pp. 577–99.
35. Balfour, 2002, p. 194.
36. Cited in Casassas, 1983, pp. 156–7.
37. RD 6.10.1925.
38. For the comparisons to Mussolini and Mustafa Kemal see, *El Somatén*, August 1924. The exaltation of Primo's military talent and the comparison to Napoleon and Lenin in Mask, 1925, p. 189.
39. Rubio, 1974, pp. 161–2.
40. Reports on the celebration of 'patriotic acts' in AHN, Presidencia del Gobierno, Bundle 331, Box 2.
41. See, for example, Primo's speech at the *Fiesta del Somatén*, in *El Somatén*, May 1924.
42. See, for instance, Primo's discourse in Barcelona in October 1923 in Rubio, 1974, pp. 77–8.
43. Primo, 1926, pp. 13–14, 36.
44. Primo, 1929, p. 214.
45. *ABC*, 22.11.1923.
46. *ABC*, 22.11.1923. Sánchez Mazas had had the chance to interview Mussolini on 16 November 1923. Interestingly, the Italian dictator defended the merging of religious and national identities stating the need to achieve a 'union between the good Italian and the good Catholic' – a kind of argument used later by the *primorriverista* ideologues. The interview of Sánchez Mazas with Mussolini is reviewed in the British Ambassador to Madrid's report on the King and Primo's visit to Italy, see 'Italo-Spanish Relations', Dossiers from 1920–1923, Public Record Office, Foreign Office, 185/1743.
47. Rubio, 1974, pp. 83, 141, 145.
48. *ABC*, 25.1.1925; *La Nación*, 3.11.1925.
49. Primo to Magaz, 2.6.1925, in Armiñán and Armiñán, 1930, pp. 141–2.
50. Ben-Ami, 1983, p. 102.
51. Rubio, 1974, pp. 128–9, 143–4, 157, 161.
52. For the account of the celebration of nationalist ceremonies in towns and villages during 1924 see the dozens of letters and telegraphs from the Civil Governors and the *delegados* to Martínez Anido in AHN, Presidencia del Gobierno, Bundle 331, Box 1.
53. For the Italian case Ridolfi, 2003, pp. 72–92.
54. Primo, 1926, pp. 13–14.
55. Primo in Pérez, 1930, p. 24.
56. *Ibid.*, p. 24.
57. *La Vanguardia*, 12.10.1923.
58. Roig, 1992, pp. 91–2.

59. RD in *La Gaceta*, 1.10.1923. For the denunciations see AHN, Gobernación Serie A, Bundle 18A, folders 1 and 2.
60. Martínez Anido to the Civil Governors, 1.1.1924, AGA, Interior, Box 149. For a further discussion of the network of anonymous accusations see Chapter 5.
61. See preamble to the statute in *La Gaceta*, 9.3.1924.
62. Genieys, 1997, pp. 108–9.
63. 'Manifiesto referente a la significación de la Unión Patriótica, en relación con los problemas nacionales', 10.4.1925, in Casa, 1925, p. 841.
64. Calbet, 1987, pp. 244–5.
65. Official note, 21.3.1925, in Primo, 1929, pp. 102–5.
66. The letter is partially reproduced in *ibid.*, p. 30.
67. See official notes 21.3.1925 and 2.6.1925 in Primo, 1929, pp. 100–3; and *La Nación*, 22.10.1925.
68. 'Manifiesto a la nación', 5.9.1926, in Primo, 1929, pp. 34–6.
69. Núñez Seixas, 2001b, pp. 495–504.
70. Blinkhorn, 1975, p. 40.
71. 'Manifiesto al Pueblo Español', Paris, 1.3.1925. A copy of the document in AHN, Gobernación, Bundle 40A, n. 12.
72. For the arrest of Carlists see AHN, Gobernación, Bundle 40 A, n. 12.
73. *El Debate*, 2.12.1923; 7.12.1923.
74. Gómez-Navarro, 1985, p. 101.
75. *La Veu de Catalunya*, 14.9.1923. See also Rey, 1988, pp. 289–307 and Smith, 2007, pp. 7–34.
76. Roig, 1992, pp. 55–66.
77. RD 18.9.1923, in *La Gaceta*, 19.9.1923.
78. For the Italian case see Gentile, 1996, pp. 34–5.
79. Villanueva, 1930, pp. 114–15.
80. Rubio, 1974, p. 126.
81. *La Vanguardia*, 19.9.1923.
82. *La Veu*, 20.9.1923.
83. *El Sol*, 19.9.1923.
84. *El Debate*, 2.12.1923.
85. Barrera's comments on Catalanist priests in *ABC*, 8.9.1924; *La Publicitat*, 27.12.1924; *La Nación*, 14.12.1925.
86. Ucelay, 1993, p. 172; González Calleja, 1999, p. 357.
87. Roig, 1992, pp. 373–432; Bonet, 1984, pp. 335–52.
88. *El Ejército Español*, 19.9.1923. See also *La Acción*, 19.9.1923.
89. The letter in Casassas, 1983, pp. 111–13.
90. *El Debate*, 7.12.1923.
91. Official note, 11.4.1924, in Casa, 1925, pp. 532–3.
92. Primo, 1926, pp. 12–14.
93. RO 20.10.1923, *Boletín Oficial del Ministerio de Instrucción Pública y Bellas Artes* (hereafter *BOMIP*), 16.11.1923.
94. RO 13.10.1925, *BOMIP*, 20.10.1925, 522; RO 11.6.1926, *BOMIP*, 25.6.1926, 833–4.
95. Pozo and Braster, 1999, p. 88.
96. Traditionally National-Catholicism has referred to the political ideology of Franco's regime. The term was coined during the Civil War by one of Primo's former ideologues, José Pemartín, but it was not broadly used until the early

1960s to define the Francoist dictatorship's official doctrine. However, since the 1980s, scholars have traced the origins of National-Catholicism to the turn of the twentieth century and used the term to describe the *primorriverista* ideologues' postulates in the 1920s. See, for intance Alfonso Botti, 1992, pp. 59–71, 141–3, 151–8. Following Carolyn Boyd, I use the term National-Catholicism to refer to the ideological formulation of those intellectuals at the *primorriverista* Dictatorship's service who 'blended the reactionary cultural values of traditional Spanish Catholicism with strident authoritarian nationalism and a smattering of corporative ideas of mixed lineage, [and] legitimated the authoritarian state as the form of political organization best equipped to defend the economic interest and religious and cultural values associated with national unity and power', 1997, p. 168.

97. For the alleged liberal postulates in Primo's discourse see Beadman, 1998, p. 74. The identification of the *primorriverista* Dictatorship with conservative liberalism in Tusell and García, 1979, p. 56 and Tusell, 1987, p. 270.

98. In April 1925, the Civil Governors conducted a survey among workers' associations in all Spanish provinces enquiring about workers' demands to the government. Well co-ordinated, all associations presented a similar list of petitions demanding three things in this order: first, the return to the constitutional order; second, the end of the war in Morocco; and third, judicial and political accountability for those responsible for the military failures in Africa. Over 100 of these petitions in AHN, Presidencia del Gobierno, Bundle 353.

99. Calvo Sotelo, 1974, pp. 68–9.

100. Ben-Ami, 1983, pp. 162–4.

3.   The Civil Directory (1926–1930)

1. *La Nación*, 24.2.1927.
2. Manuel Bueno in *La Nación*, 17.11.1925.
3. On Pemán see Álvarez Chillida, 1996. On Pemartín see Quiroga, 2006.
4. Hennessy, 2000, pp. 105–17; González Cuevas, 2003.
5. For example, Pemartín in *La Nación*, 26.8.1926; 28.1.1927.
6. For the concept of 'baroque' discourse used by Falange during the Second Republic and the Franco regime see Carbayo-Abengózar, 2001, pp. 77–8.
7. Blas, 1994a, p. 57.
8. *La Nación*, 14.6.1927.
9. *La Nación*, 14.6.1927.
10. *El Sol*, 29.4.1924.
11. *La Nación*, 28.1.1927; 31.1.1927.
12. *La Nación*, 28.4.1927.
13. *La Nación*, 28.4.1927; 5.5.1927; 28.7.1927; 3.11.1927; 8.12.1927.
14. *La Nación*, 12.7.1927.
15. *La Nación*, 11.3.1927.
16. *La Nación*, 5.7.1927.
17. Pemán, 1929, pp. 71–2.
18. *Ibid.*, p. 72.
19. *La Nación*, 19.9.1928.

20. Pemartín, 1928, p. 42.
21. *Ibid.*, pp. 42–3.
22. *Ibid.*, pp. 43–4.
23. Pemán, 1929, pp. 331–2, 350–1; *La Nación*, 31.8.1928; Pemartín in *La Nación*, 16.5.1928, and 1928, pp. 70–1.
24. Spengler, 1976 (1st ed. 1918), p. 25.
25. Pemartín, 1928, pp. 27–8. Spengler's interpretation of history was also heavily influential in Pemán's explanation of European civilization. See Pemán, 1929, pp. 331–2, 350–1.
26. Ganivet, 1996 (1st ed. 1895), p. 56.
27. *Ibid.*, pp. 139, 142–3.
28. Pemán, 1929, p. 245; Pemartín in *La Nación*, 10.12.1926; 30.11.1927.
29. Pemartín, 1928, p. 97; Rodríguez Tarduchy, 1929, p. 44.
30. Pemán, 1929, pp. 107–8.
31. *Ibid.*, pp. 112–14.
32. *Ibid.*, p. 105.
33. *La Nación*, 10.2.1927.
34. Péman,1929, pp. 121, 308–9.
35. Among many examples see Pemán, 1929, pp. 28–9; Pemartín, 1928, pp. 105–6; Rodríguez Tarduchy, 1929, p. 179.
36. Pemartín, 1928, pp. 644–5.
37. *La Nación*, 24.2.1927; 24.3.1927.
38. *La Nación*, 28.2.1927.
39. *La Nación*, 24.2.1927.
40. Primo, 1929, pp. 94, 109.
41. Péman, 1929, p. 251.
42. *Ibid.*, p. 251.
43. Vilar, 1978, p. 6.
44. Fusi, 1990a, p. 41.
45. Pemán, 1929, p. 106.
46. See, for instance, Maeztu in *La Nación*, 16.5.1927; Pemán in *La Nación*, 20.9.1928; and 1929, p. 109.
47. For the French case see Davies, 1997, pp. 181–201.
48. See Pemán, 1929, p. 16; Pemartín in *La Nación*, 30.9.1927; 10.12.1926; and 1928, p. 532; Maeztu in *El Sol*, 2.10.1923; and *La Nación*, 12.7.1927.
49. Pemartín in *La Nación*, 10.12.1926.
50. Pemán, 1929, p. 255.
51. *Ibid.*, 1929, pp. 270–1.
52. Pemán, *ibid.*, p. 255 and *La Nación*, 13.10.1928 and 23.10.1928. The Dictatorship truly tried to go beyond mere oratory and developed an intense policy towards Spanish America, which included the reinforcement of cultural and economic exchanges and the propagation of Pan-Hispanic ideas in Spain. At the end of 1927, the appointment of Maeztu as ambassador to Argentina was partially an attempt to fulfil the aspirations of the conservative *Hispanismo* in South America. Pike, 1971, pp. 226–9.
53. Maeztu in *La Nación*, 4.4.1927.
54. *La Nación*, 17.3.1927.
55. *La Nación*, 12.7.1927.
56. Calvo, 1974, p. 336.

57. *La Nación* 17.11.1925; 18.11.1925.
58. González Calleja, 2005, pp. 139–40.
59. *La Nación*, 31.1.1927; 15.2.1927; 17.2.1927; 18.9.1927; 18.11.1927; 29.10.1927.
60. *La Nación*, 23.8.1927.
61. Gómez-Navarro, 1991, pp. 266–8.
62. Morodo, 1973, p. 86.
63. *El Sol,* 11.10.1927.
64. Primo, 1930a, pp. 48–59
65. Gómez-Navarro, 1991, p. 295.
66. González Cuevas, 1998, pp. 106–7.
67. Pemán, 1929, pp. 79, 332–3. See also his articles in *La Nación*, 29.11.1928; 7.12.1928; 29.12.1928; 11.1.1929.
68. González Calleja, 2005, p. 153.
69. González Cuevas, 1998, p. 108.
70. Gil, 1994, p. 51.
71. Aunós, 1928, p. 143.
72. Aunós, 1928, pp. 182–3.
73. Perfecto, 1997, pp. 177–96.
74. Ben-Ami, 1990a, pp. 71–6.
75. *El Debate,* 22.1.1929
76. Pan-Montojo, 2002, pp. 25–9.
77. González Calleja, 2005, p. 162.
78. Ben-Ami, 1983, pp. 325–32.
79. Calvo's proposal aimed at increasing upper classes' taxation and hunting down tax evasion. Calvo, 1926, pp. 10–17, 30. On the 'peseta crisis', Eguidazu, 1979, pp. 299–352.
80. Ben-Ami, 1989, p. 126.
81. See, for instance, the editorials of *La Nación*, 27.9.1926; 7.6.1928; 18.9.1929. See also C. de Iragorri in *Unión Patriótica*, 15.11.1927.
82. For instance, Maeztu in *El Sol*, 14.5.1924; and *La Nación*, 14.3.1927; 6.6.1927; 28.7.1927; Pemartín in *La Nación*, 6.12.1928; 28.11.1928; 28.1.1929; Pemán, 1929, pp. 191–2.
83. González Cuevas, 2000, p. 281. García Queipo de Llano, 1990, pp. 227–30.
84. Pemán, 1929, pp. 174–5; Pemartín in *La Nación*, 6.12.1928.
85. For the Social Catholics' criticism see the editorials of *El Debate*, 2.11.1928; 13.11.1928; 20.11.1928; 27.11.1928.
86. *La Nación*, 6.12.1928; 28.12.1928; 28.1.1929.
87. Blinkhorn, 1990, p. 2, 8; Kallis, 2003, pp. 219–49.
88. Blinkhorn, 1990, p. 1.
89. Blinkhorn, 2000, p. 6.
90. Weber, 1985, pp. 25–38.
91. Preston, 1986a, p. 20.
92. This is the view put forward by García Queipo de Llano, 1990, p. 230. In the same vein see García Canales, 1980, p. 116.
93. González Cuevas, 1998, pp. 97–101.
94. Ben-Ami, 1979, pp. 60–3.
95. Ben-Ami, 1990b, p. 79.
96. Gil, 1994, p. 102.

97. See, for instance, Maeztu, 1998 (1st ed. 1934); Pemartín, 1937 (1st ed. 1935) and his works in *Acción Española*, 1.10.1934, and 1.11.1934.
98. José Antonio Primo, 1954, pp. 49–51, 53–4, 64–9, 127, 286–7, 754, 757; Redondo, 1975, pp. 156–72. The main exception to this understanding of Catholicism as co-substantial with Spain was to be found in the writings of Ramiro Ledesma Ramos, whose secular postulates were uncommon among the Spanish fascists. See, for example, *La Conquista del Estado*, no. 10, 16.5.1931.
99. Preston, 1986a, p. 23.
100. Preston, 1986b, pp. 171–3.
101. Ben-Ami, 1979, p. 72.
102. Pemartín, 1938, pp. 32, 52, 248–9; *Acción Española*, special edition 1937, pp. 399, 402–4. Pemán in *ABC* (Seville), 23.5.1937; 1.9.1937; 20.11.1938; *Orientación Española*, 1.8.1938 and 15.8.1938.
103. Álvarez Chillida, 1996, p. 116; Quiroga, 2000, p. 198.
104. Reig, 1988, pp. 211–37.
105. Pemán, 1938.
106. For Franco's ideas see Richards, 1998, pp. 47–66.
107. Carbayo-Abengózar, 2001, pp. 75–8.

4. School of Patriots

1. Rueda, 1925, pp. 50–1.
2. Weber, 1976, pp. 292–302.
3. Gentile, 1996, p. 9.
4. Serrano, 2000, pp. 22–49.
5. Figures calculated from the *Anuario Estadístico de España 1923–1924*.
6. For instance, Escartín, 1905; García Pérez, 1906; Fanjul, 1907; Sánchez Farragut, 1913; Pérez Hernández, 1921.
7. For the different 'political cultures' in the Spanish military before 1923 see Jensen, 2002.
8. Primo, 1916, p. xiii.
9. For instance, Ruiz Fornells, 1894, pp. 110–28; Fanjul, 1907, pp. 76–91; García and Matta, 1916, pp. 37–41; Navarro, 1920, pp. 17, 22–41.
10. Espadas, 1983, p. 504
11. Fanjul, 1907, pp. 137–41.
12. For example, the RO 29.1.1926 launched the campaign of 'citizenry culture'. In *Diario Oficial de Ministerio de la Guerra* (hereafter *DOMG*), 31.1.1926, p. 249.
13. Rueda, 1925, pp. 7–8. More lectures in *Memorial de Infantería*, June 1925, pp. 384–90 and December 1925, pp. 305–12, 384–99.
14. Primo, 1927, pp. 23–4.
15. Primo to Antonio Horcada, 2.3.29, AHN, Presidencia del Gobierno, Bundle 190, Box 1.
16. The allocation of volumes in AHN, Presidencia del Gobierno, Bundle 190, Box 1.
17. RD 20.2.1927, *CLE*, 1927, no. 94, 119–24.
18. The programmes of the AGM in ROC 17.12.27, *CLE*, 1927, no. 534, 634–40. The 1882 programme in Sánchez Abal, 1992, pp. 106–10.
19. Blanco, 1989, pp. 92–106.
20. Preston, 1998, p. 79.

21. Franco also received support from Alfonso XIII in his rapid ascent into the top ranks. See Balfour, 2002, p. 157.
22. The Decalogue of the AGM in Blanco, 1989, pp. 168–9.
23. Quoted in Cardona, 1986, pp. 70–1.
24. Busquets, 1984, p. 84.
25. Preston, 1998, pp. 83–4.
26. Blanco, 1989, p. 194.
27. Rueda, 1925, pp. 50–1.
28. Italics added. *Ibid.*, p. 57.
29. *DOMG*, 30.3.1924, 985–93.
30. Data in *Anuario Estadístico de España, 1931*.
31. Martínez Anido to all Civil Governors, 'Prevenciones que para el mejor desempeño de sus cargos deben tener presentes los Delegados Gubernativo', 7.12.1923, AGA, Interior, Box 149, Folder 15. The RO 12.11.1923 and RD 29.3.1924 hardened the penalties for deserters and rewarded denunciations of runaways. Seeking rewards, it seems that many people denounced almost everyone suspected to be deserters. In April 1924, the government had to remind the public that no rewards would be given if the person denounced had been previously declared physically or mentally unfit or exempted by the army. Royal Circular Order (*Real Orden Circular*, hereafter ROC) 15.4.1924, *CLE*, 1924, no. 176, p. 258.
32. Primo, 1930b, p. 26.
33. RD 29.3.1924, *DOMG*, 30.3.1924, 985–93.
34. *DOMG*, 30.3.1924, 985.
35. Pumarola, 1928, p. 99.
36. Maura, 1930, vol. 2, p. 53.
37. Mola, 1940, p. 1029.
38. RD 29.3.1924, *DOMG*, 30.3.1924, 985–93.
39. ROC 1.12.1929, *Diario Oficial del Ministerio del Ejército* (hereafter *DOME*), 1929, no. 267, 599–607.
40. RD 31.12.1926, *DOMG*, 1.1.1927, N1, 4–5; ROC 12.1.1927, *DOMG*, 13.1.1927, no. 9, 123–4.
41. ROC 18.2.1927, *CLE*, 1927, no. 89, 114–17; RO 29.1.1926, *DOMG*, 31.1.1926, no. 24, 249; RO 24.1.1927, *DOME*, 13.1.1927, 123–4.
42. RD 29.10.1926, *DOMG*, 31.1.1926, 249.
43. See, for example, Adán and Tarrasa, 1926a, pp. 97–104; Mas, 1926, pp. 3–8; Pumarola, 1927, p. 52; Villalba Rubio, 1928, p. 14.
44. Mas, 1926, pp. 13–16.
45. Villaba Riquelme, 1928, pp. v–vi.
46. ROC 12.8.1927, *CLE*, 1927, no. 338, p. 422. See also Mas, 1926, p. 9; and Adán and Tarrasa, 1926b, p. 46.
47. *Ibid.*, p. 47.
48. Reyes, 1921, pp. i–viii.
49. González Deleito, 1911.
50. Condo, 1923, pp. 3–10.
51. ROC 18.2.1927, *CLE*, 1927, no. 89, 114–17.
52. ROC 28.4.1924, *CLE*, 1924, no. 201 and ROC 25.2.1925, *CLE*, 1925, no. 46, 69.
53. ROC 4.7.1927, *CLE*, 1927, no. 281.
54. Villalba's report in AHN, Presidencia, Bundle 217, Box 3, Folder 178.

55. The conclusions of the investigation came in a report dated 14 June 1926. The report was partially published two years later. See Aguilera, 1928.
56. Villalba Riquelme, 1927, p. 45
57. Escuela Central de Gimnasia, 1924, p. 72; *DOME*, 14.7.1929.
58. Villalba Riquelme, 1927, p. 45.
59. *Memorial de Infantería*, January 1930, 39–45.
60. ROC 31.3.1925, *CLE*, no. 83, 126–8.
61. RD 19.7.1927, *CLE*, 1927, no. 296, 372–3.
62. RD 31.3.1924, *CLE*, 1924, no. 128, p. 188.
63. RD 31.3.1924, *CLE*, 1924, no. 128, p. 188.
64. Rubio, 1986, p. 141.
65. ROC 2.6.1925, *CLE*, 1925, no. 145, 201–2.
66. *Memorial de Infantería*, September 1930, 201–8.
67. Navajas, 1991, pp. 161–2.
68. Mola, 1940, p. 1029.
69. Data in Navajas, 1991, p. 189 and RD 3.1.1929, *CLE*, 1929, 22; RD 3.1.1930, *CLE*, 1930, 22; RD 3.1.1931, *CLE*, 1931, 14.
70. The number of recruits rose from 134 410 in 1923 to 148 522 in 1930, a 10.49 per cent increase. Data in *Anuario Estadístico de España 1931*.

5.   Apostles of the Fatherland

1. Villalba to Primo, 2.2.1929, 'Minutas sobre el cumplimiento del Real Decreto de 14 de Enero de 1929 sobre conferencias patrióticas e instrucción premilitar', AHN, Presidencia del Gobierno, Bundle 190, Box 1.
2. For instance, Primo, 1916, p. xi.
3. RD 20.10.1923, *La Gaceta*, 21.10.1923.
4. Intructions to the *delegados* in RD 20.10.1923, RO 9.12.1923, RD 20.3.1924. See also Primo's letters to the *delegados*, 5.4.1924; 24.4.1924; Martínez Anido's letter to the *delegados*, 1.1.1924; Martínez Anido's telegram to the *delegados*, 4.1.1924 in AHN, Presidencia del Gobierno, Bundle 331, Box 1.
5. Art. 4, RD 20.10.1923.
6. E.T.L., 1928, pp. 52–3.
7. Dozens of these denunciations are found in AHN, Gobernación, Serie A, Bundle 18 A, Files 1 and 2.
8. Martínez Anido to Civil Governors, 1.1.1924, AGA, Interior, Box 149.
9. ROC 27.1.1924, *La Gaceta*, 29.1.1924.
10. See Martínez Anido to Civil Governors, 2.2.1924; 5.2.1924; 20.8.1924; 29.1.1926, AHN, Gobernación, Serie A, Bundle 17 A, Box 2. Further petitions of moderation in Martínez Anido to all delegates, 8.3.1925, AGA, Interior, Box 149.
11. For example, Calvo Sotelo to Civil Governors, 28.3.1924, AGA, Interior, Box 149.
12. Martínez Anido to Civil Governors, 11.7.1924, AHN, Gobernación, Serie A, Bundle 17 A, Box 2.
13. Calvo Sotelo, 1974, p. 26.
14. Martínez Anido to Civil Governors, 5.1.1924, AHN, Gobernación, Serie A, Bundle 17 A, Box 2.

15. Martínez Anido to Civil Governors, 27.10.1923, AHN, Gobernación, Serie A, Bundle 18 A.
16. Some examples of repression of leftists, liberals and conservatives in AHN, Gobernación, Serie A, Bundle 18 A, Folders 1, 2 and 5. For the repression of Carlists see Gobernación, Bundle 40 A.
17. Some reports sent by delegates informing on both collaborators and political enemies in AHN, Presidencia, Bundle 331, Box 1.
18. The institution of the *delegados* was transformed throughout the Dictatorship both in terms of numbers and duties. After one year of work purging municipalities, Primo decided it was the right moment for reducing the number of delegates. In early 1925, the number of delegates was reduced to 224. Hence, they were ordered to concentrate on their 'educational mission' and gathering popular support for the UP. The following year the number of delegates was reduced to 132. The final reduction of 1927 set the number of delegates at 79. This number was to remain static until the end of the Dictatorship.
19. Martínez Anido to delegates, 8.3.1925, AGA, Interior, Box 149.
20. Tens of reports from the delegates in AHN, Presidencia, Bundle 331, Box 1 and 2.
21. Tens of reports on diverse patriotic celebrations in AHN, Presidencia, Bundle 331, Box 1.
22. Martínez Anido to Civil Governors, 7.12.1923; 4.1.1924, AGA, Interior, Box 149. See also RO 29.3.1924, *La Gaceta*, 30.3.1924.
23. See for example delegate of Toro to Presidencia del Gobierno, 31.5.1924. AHN, Presidencia, Bundle 331, Box 1.
24. RO 29.1.1926, *DOMG*, 31.1.1926, p. 249.
25. RO 29.1.1926.
26. Almagro to Martínez Anido, 23.2.1926, AHN, Gobernación, Serie A, Bundle 61 A, Box 3.
27. Martínez Anido to Civil Governors, 24.2.1926, AHN, Gobernación, Serie A, Bundle 61 A, Box 3.
28. Martínez Anido to Civil Governors, 6.3.1926, AHN, Gobernación, Serie A, Bundle 61 A, Box 3.
29. Civil Governor of Álava to Martínez Anido, 26.2.1926, AHN, Gobernación, Serie A, Bundle 61 A, Box 3.
30. ADPB, Departament de Instrucció Pública, Bundle 4177, File 15.
31. See, for example, the celebration of Sunday lectures in Botrils, *La Vanguardia*, 27.8.1926.
32. Civil Governor of Santander to Martínez Anido, 8.3.1926, AHN, Gobernación, Serie A, Bundle 61 A, Box 3.
33. *La Gaceta*, 28.12.1927.
34. Gentile, 1996, pp. 97, 186–7.
35. After the Dictatorship, the Liberal and Conservative dynastic parties were incapable of reproducing their old political structures at the local level. Ben-Ami, 1990b, pp. 71–90.
36. 1927 and 1929 reports in AHN, Presidencia del Gobierno, Bundle 332.
37. These cases and some others in AHN, Presidencia del Gobierno, Bundle 332. There were, however, some exceptions to this policy. Two delegates in the province of Seville got commissions out of selling industrial machinery but they remained in their posts even when the Civil Governor advised Martínez Anido otherwise. Ponce, 2000, pp. 753–4.

38. Reports in Servicio Histórico Militar (hereafter SHM), Colección Adicional de Documentos, Asuntos Generales, Bundle 11, Reel 7.
39. RO 9.12.1923, *La Gaceta*, 10.9.1923; Martínez Anido to Civil Governors, 9.12.1923, AHN, Gobernación, Serie A, Bundle 17 A, Box 2; ROC 10.12.1923, *La Gaceta*, 11.12.1923.
40. Minister of Interior to Civil Governors, 17.6.1924, AHN, Gobernación, Serie A, Bundle 17 A, Box 2, File 20.
41. The letter of the Minister of War to the Interior Minister, 12.6.1926, in SHM, Colección Adicional de Documentos, Bundle 11, Reel 7.
42. The report in SHM, Colección Adicional de Documentos, Bundle 11, Reel 7.
43. Porta, n.d., pp. 213–15.
44. Cited in Montero, 1995, p. 129.
45. Hernández Mir, 1930, pp. 156–9.
46. Mola, 1940, p. 1028. Very similar views to Mola's were shared by officers Pardo González, Blanco, and Major Beta (pseudonym) in their critique of the delegates. See Navajas, 1991, pp. 99–100.
47. RD 21.2.1930, *La Gaceta*, 22.1.1930.
48. See reports by the National Assembly of the TNE in El Tiro Nacional de España, 1915, p. 74, and Tiro Nacional de España, 1918, pp. 23–7, 47–69.
49. Art. 5 and 8, RD 8.5.1925, *CLE*, 1925, pp. 151–5.
50. Art. 13, RD 8.5.1925.
51. ROC 27.6.1925, *CLE*, 1925, Appendix 6, 3–16.
52. RD 8.5.1925.
53. RD 8.5.1925.
54. The conclusions of the investigation in Aguilera, 1928.
55. *Ibid.*, p. 61; Villalba Riquelme, 1927, pp. 42–67.
56. Aguilera, 1928, p. 63.
57. 'Bases que para el desarrollo en España de la Educación Ciudadana, Física y Premilitar presenta la Comisión nombrada al efecto al Excmo. Señor Presidente del Consejo de Ministros', in AHN, Presidencia del Gobierno, Bundle 202, Box 1, File 14971.
58. 'Proyecto nacional de Educación Física Femenina. Madrid 6.6.1927, por la Inspectora de 1ª Enseñanza Cándida Cárdenas y Campo', AHN, Presidencia del Gobierno, Bundle 202, Box 1, File 14972.
59. For the Italian case see Caldwell, 1986, pp. 110–41 and Grazia, 1992. Despite the generally passive role awarded to women, the fascists attempted to mobilize female peasants in rural areas. See Willson, 2002.
60. RD 3.11.1928, *DOME*, 6.11.1928, 341–2.
61. 'Origen del excedente de la oficialidad en las escalas del Ejército', AHN, Presidencia del Gobierno, Bundle 190, Box 1.
62. RD 14.1.1929, Preamble and articles 1, 4, 7, *DOME*, 16.1.1929, 137.
63. Villalba to Primo, 2.2.1929, 'Minutas sobre el cumplimiento del Real Decreto de 14 de Enero de 1929 sobre conferencias patrióticas e instrucción premilitar', AHN, Presidencia del Gobierno, Bundle 190, Box 1.
64. *Ibid.*
65. 'Programa sobre una formación de ciudadanía española', AHN, Presidencia del Gobierno, Bundle 190, Box 1.
66. Primo to Horcada, 2.3.29, AHN, Presidencia del Gobierno, Bundle 190, Box 1.

67. 'Dossier con conferencias y demostraciones prácticas' and Primo to Carlos Guerra, director of the CSG, April 1929. Both in AHN, Presidencia del Gobierno, Bundle 190, Box 1.
68. Quoted in Navajas, 1991, p. 110.
69. RO 8.7.1929, *DOME*, 10.7.1929, no. 148, 101.
70. ROC 2.3.1929, *CLE*, 1929, no. 84, 137–8.
71. RO 12.7.1929, *DOME*, 14.7.1929, 139.
72. *Anuario Militar de España 1930* and ROC 2.12.1930, *CLE*, 1929, 537.
73. ROC 20.10.1930, *CLE*, 1930, 496–8.
74. ROC 13.11.1930, *CLE*, 1930, 537.
75. ROC 2.12.1930, *CLE*, 1930, 537.
76. Navajas, 1991, p. 113.
77. *ABC*, 29.1.1930; *El Debate*, 30.1.1930; *El Liberal*, 29.1.1930; *El Sol*, 2.2.1930; *El Socialista*, 31.1.1930.
78. *ABC*, 31.1.1930.
79. Ballbé, 1983, p. 309.
80. Gómez-Navarro, 1991, pp. 318–20.
81. Lleixà, 1986, p. 135.
82. Pemartín, 1938, pp. 15–29.
83. Blanco, 1989, p. 194.

6.   The Nationalization of Schools

1. Quoted in López Martín, 1994, vol. 1, p. 35.
2. Gellner, 1983, pp. 18–39.
3. Durara, 1996, pp. 151–77; Manzano, 2000, pp. 33–62.
4. Weber, 1976, pp. 321–6.
5. *Ibid.*, pp. 306–14.
6. Talamo, 2002, pp. 419–26.
7. Lebovics, 1992, pp. iii, 7.
8. Rial, 1986, p. 215.
9. The number of primary education students in France, Germany and Italy in 1905 was as follows: France 1422 students per 10 000 inhabitants; Germany 1577; and Italy 928. The figure for Spain in 1909–1910 is 746 students per 10 000 inhabitants. Data in Núñez, 1992, pp. 292–3.
10. Puelles, 1991, p. 197.
11. RD 18.9.1923, *La Gaceta*, 19.9.1923.
12. Circular 20.10.1923, *BOMIP*, 16.11.1923, 633–4.
13. RO 13.10.1925, *Colección Legislativa de Instrucción Pública* (hereafter *CLIP*), 1925, 569–71.
14. RO 13.10.1925.
15. RO 29.8.1924, *CLIP*, 1924, 533–4.
16. Martínez Anido to Civil Governors, 7.12.1923; Primo to delegates, 10.12.1923; Martínez Anido to delegates, 8.3.1925, AGA, Interior, Box 149.
17. See dozens of letters and telegrams from teachers to Primo in AHN, Presidencia del Gobierno, Bundle 356, Box 1.
18. See Martínez Anido to Civil Governors, 27.5.1924; Martínez Anido to Primo, 'Informe sobre profesores', 13.11.1924; General Navarro to Martínez Anido, 11.22.1925, AHN, Gobernación, Serie A, Bundle 61, Box 3.

19. See Martínez Anido to Civil Governors, 14.2.1925; Martínez Anido to Civil Governors of Alicante, Badajoz, Baleares, Burgos, Gerona, Granada, Logroño, Orense, Palencia, Santander, Teruel and Vizcaya, 27.2.1925; Martínez Anido to Primo de Rivera, 2.7.1925. AHN, Gobernación, Serie A, Bundle 61, Box 3.
20. For example, General Navarro to Martínez Anido, 22.11.1925; Martínez Anido to the Civil Governor of Almería, 14.2.1925; Martínez Anido to the Civil Governor of Castellón, 14.2.1925; Civil Governor of Pontevedra to Martínez Anido, 16.2.1925. AHN, Gobernación, Serie A, Bundle 61, Box 3.
21. Ben-Ami, 1983, p. 105.
22. López Martín, 1994, vol. 1, p. 35.
23. Callejo to Martínez Anido, 29.5.1926, AGA, Interior, Box 149.
24. Martínez Anido to Callejo, 4.6.1926, AGA, Interior, Box 149.
25. See, for example, reports from the Civil Governors to Martínez Anido in AHN, Gobernación, Serie A, Bundle 61, Box 3; 'Unión Ciudadana Anticaciquil de Villalba' to the General Director for Primary Educaction, 20.11.1927, AHN, Presidencia del Gobierno, Bundle 358; Primo to Callejo, 9.1.1930, AHN, Presidencia del Gobierno, Bundle 114, Box 2.
26. See various letters from teachers to Primo, December 1927, in AHN, Presidencia del Gobierno, Bundle 358.
27. Civil Governor of Las Palmas to Martínez Anido, 19.2.1929, AHN, Gobernación, Serie A, Bundle 17 A, Box 2.
28. *El Magisterio Español*, 14.5.1930.
29. RO 12.2.1924, *CLIP*, 1924, 84–5.
30. RO 13.10.1925, *CLIP*, 1925, 569–71.
31. RO 13.10.1925.
32. See, for instance, Civil Governor of Ciudad Real to Presidencia del Gobierno, 12.7.1928, AHN, Presidencia del Gobierno, Bundle 358; Civil Governor of Álava to Martínez Anido, 26.2.1926; Civil Governor of Santander to Martínez Anido, 8.3.1926, AHN, Gobernación Serie A, Bundle 61, Box 3.
33. For accusations between September and December 1923, see AHN, Presidencia del Gobierno, Bundle 101. More accusations for the period 1924–1930 in AHN, Presidencia del Gobierno, Bundle, 217, Box 1; and AHN, Presidencia del Gobierno, Bundle 358.
34. RO 13.12.1923, *CLIP*, 1923, 511.
35. López Martín, 1987, pp. 316–17.
36. *Ibid.*, pp. 319–20.
37. For the inspectors' dissatisfaction with the RD 22.10.1926 see *El Magisterio Español*, 20.11.1926.
38. See Martínez Anido to Civil Governors, 27.1.1926 in AGA, Interior, Box 149; and RO 28.12.1927, in *La Gaceta*, 29.12.1927.
39. Martínez Anido to Civil Governors, 'Circular Confidencial y Reservada', 24.6.1926, AHN, Gobernación Serie A, Bundle 61, Box 3.
40. See, for instance, Civil Governor of Coruña to Director General of Primary Educaction, 3.7.1926; Civil Governor of Murcia to Martínez Anido, no date; Civil Governor of Zaragoza to Martínez Anido, 1.7.1926, AHN, Gobernación Serie A, Bundle 61, Box 3.
41. López Martín, 1987, p. 321.
42. *El Magisterio Español*, 19.4.1930; 18.6.1930.
43. Pozo and Braster, 1999, p. 89.

44. Pozo Pardo, 1985, pp. 195–202.

45. Villanueva, 1927.

46. Siurot, 1924. By 1927 the book had reached its third edition.

47. The reform of the Council in RD 25.6.1926. After the reform the Council was not consulted in major educational reforms.

48. Boyd, 1997, pp. 160, 190.

49. Real Academia de la Historia [Rafael Altamira], 1930, p. 61.

50. RO 16.4.1930, *La Gaceta*, 23.4.1930.

51. For the liberals see *El Magisterio Nacional*, 6.5.1930. For the Catholic right, *Atenas*, 15.3.1931, 273–4.

52. Some examples of these ceremonies in reports from delegates and Civil Governors in AHN, Presidencia, Bundle 133, Box 1; Bundle 331, Box 1; Bundle 358. See also *El Magisterio Español*, 10.10.1928; *La Vanguardia*, 13.10.1923; *El Noticiero Universal*, 12.10.1928.

53. RO 3.2.1926, *BOMIP*, 9.2.1926.

54. See tens of teachers' reports in AHN, Presidencia del Gobierno, Bundle 358.

55. RD 6.2.1926, *La Gaceta*, 9.2.1926.

56. RO 17.9.1926, in *El Magisterio Español*, 21.9.1926, 754.

57. Martínez Anido to all Civil Governors, 20.9.1926, AHN, Gobernación Serie A, Bundle 61, Box 3.

58. RO 17.9.1926, in *El Magisterio Español*, 28.9.1926, 833–4. Further legislation insisting on the donations was issued two years later, RO 24.9.1928, in *El Magisterio Español*, 1.10.1928.

59. For a contemporary interpretation of the *Fiesta del Libro* as a means to improve the 'integral health of the race' see José Martos Peinado in *El Magisterio Español*, 1.10.1928, 1–4.

60. See Chapter 7.

61. *Revista de Segunda Enseñanza*, December 1926, 383–5.

62. *ABC*, 9.10.1928; *El Magisterio Español*, 12.10.1929.

63. *Unión Patriótica*, 1.11.1926, 24.

64. *El Magisterio Español*, 7.10.1926, 67–8.

65. *El Sol*, 12.10.1927.

66. Pozo, 2000, pp. 219–24.

67. Martínez Anido to delegates, 8.3.1925, AGA, Interior, Box 149.

68. Dozens of reports from the delegates in AHN, Presidencia, Bundles 358 and 331, Box 1.

69. For a description of the *maestros* as the 'priests of the fatherland' and the school as the 'church of the patria', in which kids worship 'Saint Cervantes', see *El Magisterio Español*, 3.10.1928, 35–6.

70. Díaz Retg, 1928, p. 54; Pemartín, 1928, p. 422.

71. RD 20.10.1923, *La Gaceta*, 21.10.1923.

72. The mobilization of the UP against illiteracy in *La Nación*, 3.11.1925. For the co-operation of *maestros* and priests see RO 28.12.1927, *La Gaceta*, 29.12.1929.

73. RO 2.11.1923, *CLIP*, 1923, 447–50.

74. RO 12.4.1924; RO 24.11.1924, *CLIP*, 1924, 245–6.

75. López Martín, 1994, vol. 1, p. 105.

76. Suárez, 'Notas para el presupuesto de 1ª enseñanza en 1927', AHN, Presidencia del Gobierno, Bundle 358.

77. Dozens of reports on the opening school ceremonies in AHN, Presidencia del Gobierno, Bundle 358.
78. 'Notas para el presupuesto de 1ª enseñanza en 1927', AHN, Presidencia del Gobierno, Bundle 358.
79. Suárez, 'Proyecto de Real Decreto para la creación de Escuelas' and Suárez to Primo, 4.12.1926, AHN, Presidencia del Gobierno, Bundle 358.
80. RD 12.12.1927.
81. RD 10.7.1928.
82. López Martín, 1997, p. 72, fn. 19.
83. *El Magisterio Español*, 31.12.1927.
84. López Martín, 1994, vol. 1, p. 105.
85 *El Socialista*, 27.11.1929.
86. *El Magisterio Español*, 30.4.1930.
87. Instituto Nacional de Estadística, 1952, p. 163.
88. Data in *Anuario Estadístico de España 1930*, 1932, xxiv.
89. Cobb, 1995, p. 135.
90. RD 2.11.1923, *CLIP*, 1923, 447–50.
91. *Anuario Estadístico de España 1930*, 1932, p. 619. For the creation of teaching posts in 1924 and 1925 see RO 28.1.1924, *CLIP*, 1923, 50–2; RO 8.8.1924, *CLIP*, 1924, 509–12; RO 7.7.1925, *CLIP*, 1925, 371–2.
92. RO 21.7.1926.
93. 'Notas para el presupuesto de 1ª enseñanza en 1927', AHN, Presidencia del Gobierno, Bundle 358.
94. López Martín, 1994, vol. 1, pp. 199–200.
95. See *Anuario Estadístico 1930*, 1932, p. 619.
96. *El Magisterio Español*, 31.12.1927.
97. Ruiz Rodrigo, 1997, p. 176.
98. Dozens of these complaints in AHN, Presidencia del Gobierno, Bundle 356, Box 1. In 1925, *maestros* without posts assigned sent dozens of complaints to Presidencia del Gobierno, AHN, Presidencia del Gobierno, Bundles 356, 357 and 358.
99. *El Sol*, 6.2.1930.
100. Ascarza, 1929, pp. 432–3.
101. Some examples in *El Magisterio Español*, 8.7.1926; 7.10.1926; 31.12.1927; 6.10.1928; 15.10.1928; and *El Magisterio Nacional*, 8.5.1930.
102. Dozens of petitions in AHN, Presidencia del Gobierno, Bundles 357 and 358.
103. Callejo to Cuervo, 15.2.1929, AHN, Presidencia del Gobierno, Bundle, 114, Box 1.
104. 'Reorganización de las Escuelas Normales para convertirlas en talleres y laboratorios de formar maestros a la luz de las verdades de nuestra Santa Religión y al calor del amor igualmente santo de la Patria', Suárez to Primo, 1926, AHN, Presidencia del Gobierno, Bundle 358.
105. 'Proyecto de decreto de reforma de la enseñanza de las escuelas normales de maestros', AHN, Presidencia del Gobierno, Bundle 358.
106. *Ibid.*
107. *Anuario Estadístico 1930*, 1932, xxiv, 620–1.
108. Núñez, 1992. p. 94.
109. The Public Instruction budget grew from 158 965 000 pesetas in 1923 to 188 114 000 in 1930. *Anuario Estadístico 1930*, 1932, xxx–xxxi.

110. For the conservative teachers' view see *El Magisterio Español*, 30.4.1930. For the liberal teachers' view see *El Magisterio Nacional*, 8.5.1930.
111. *El Magisterio Español*, 4.1.1930.

7.   The Catholic Trap

1. Primo and Cambó, 1961, pp. 3–4.
2. Presidencia del Gobierno to Council of Public Instruction, 30.11.1923, AHN, Presidencia del Gobierno, Bundle 356, Box 1.
3. 'Dictamen del Consejo de Instrucción Pública', *Boletín Institución Libre de Enseñanza*, April 1924.
4. Capitán, 1994, vol. 2, p. 518.
5. 'Proyecto de Decreto para la reforma de los estudios de segunda enseñanza', AHN, Presidencia del Gobierno, Bundle 358.
6. RD 25.8.1926, *CLIP*, 1926, 508–18. For the Italian case see Talamo, 2002, pp. 425–6.
7. Primo, 1930a, p. 336.
8. *Revista de Pedagogía*, no. 57, 1926, 431–44.
9. Díaz de la Guardia, 1982, p. 24.
10. The debate in the National Assembly in *El Noticiero*, 30.11.1927.
11. 'Estudio sobre el texto único', AHN, Presidencia del Gobierno, Bundle 358.
12. 'Bases para dictar una Real orden para el Ministerio de Instrucción Pública, referente al texto único en las enseñanzas primaria y segunda, o sea el Bachillerato', AHN, Presidencia del Gobierno, Bundle 358.
13. Yela, 1928, pp. 506, 509–12, 517.
14. Eduardo Gómez Baquero, *Revista de Segunda Enseñanza*, June 1926, 245–47.
15. RO 29.9.1928, *CLIP*, 1928, 484–5. See letters denouncing teachers in AHN, Presidencia del Gobierno, Bundle 358.
16. *Boletín de la Institución Libre de Enseñanza*, 29.2.1924, 54–6.
17. *Revista de Segunda Enseñanza*, June 1926, 245–7.
18. For the view of the single text as a victory for the right's clerical ambitions see López Martín, 1994, vol. 2, p. 32.
19. *El Magisterio Español*, 31.8.1926.
20. *Revista de Segunda Enseñanza*, no. 28, January 1927, 6–18.
21. Rodríguez, 1928, p. 16.
22. *El Siglo Futuro*, 28.8.1926; 29.8.1926; 30.8.1926.
23. Herrera Oria, 1934.
24. *El Debate*, 27.11.1928.
25. Callahan, 2000, p. 157.
26. Fernández Soria, 2002, pp. 101–2.
27. Petition of the *Federación de Amigos de la Enseñanza* to the government of General Dámaso Berenguer, 13.6.1930, cited in Boyd, 1997, p. 178.
28. Primo and Cambó, 1961, pp. 3–4.
29. Díaz Retg, 1928, pp. 229–30.
30. Pozo and Braster, 1999, 87.
31. Pozo, 2000, pp. 192–3.
32. Rubio, 1986, p. 130.
33. *Ibid.*, p. 136.

34. Ramos, 1995, pp. 145–52.
35. Callahan, 2000, pp. 161–3; Lannon, 1982, p. 582.
36. Pablo, Mees and Rodríguez, 1999, pp. 192–4.
37. The number of Basque nationalists jailed by the Dictatorship is difficult to estimate. By 1928 the Basque nationalist press claimed that 100 Basques had suffered 'persecution, exile or jail', which indicates that repression was selective and concentrated on Basque nationalist leaders as opposed to the more indiscriminate one undertaken in Catalonia. *Ibid.*, p. 173.
38. Alfonso Sala to Presidencia del Gobierno, November 1923, AHN, Presidencia del Gobierno, Bundle 356, Box 1.
39. Circular 27.10.1923, in *La Vanguardia*, 28.10.1923.
40. See AHN, Presidencia del Gobierno, Bundles 101, 217 (Box 1) and 358 and Gobernación, Serie A, Bundle 61, Box 3.
41. For example, the RO 19.4.1928, transferred seven inspectors of the province of Barcelona to some other Spanish provinces in Andalusia, Castile and the Balearic Islands. *BOMIP*, 1.5.1928, no. 35, 588.
42. See, for example, secret report of the Civil Governor of Barcelona to Martínez Anido, 7.10.1924, on the discharge of eight municipal employees in the Vich district AHN, Gobernación, Serie A, Bundle 17, Box 2, File 22. For the dismissal of the mayors of Tarrasa and Sabadell accused of separatism see *El Sol*, 19.9.1923 and *El Debate*, 20.9.1923.
43. Rubio, 1986, p. 123; Casassas, 1983, pp. 151–2.
44. *La Vanguardia*, 25.1.1924.
45. RO 21.12.1923, *La Gaceta*, 29.12.1923.
46. See, for instance, a secret report from Professors Martínez and Pérez Agudo to Presdencia del Gobierno, July 1927, denouncing collegues, AHN, Presidencia del Gobierno, Bundle 358. See also, the reports sent by Rafael Marín, from the University of Barcelona, to Máximo Cuervo on the students association during the 1929 university revolt; and the letters of Máximo Cuervo to the Minister of Public Instruction on the repressive measures taken against members of the *Federación Escolar Universitaria* in Catalonia, AHN, Presidencia del Gobierno, Bundle 114.
47. Roig, 1992, pp. 289, 298.
48. Muntanyola, 1971, pp. 144–5, 451–60.
49. Callahan, 2000, p. 159.
50. Primo to Magaz, 5.6.1925, in Armiñán and Armiñán, 1930, p. 141.
51. The activities of the Junta de Barcelona in AHN, Presidencia del Gobierno, Bundle 383.
52. Llera, 2000, pp. 103–41.
53. Quiroga and Alonso, 2004, p. 15.
54. Muntanyola, 1971, p. 146.
55. General Secretary of the Ministerio de Estado to Magaz, 25.2.1928; Magaz to Ministro de Gracia y Justicia, 25.2.1928; Magaz to Ministro de Estado, 29.9.1928; Magaz to Primo, 15.12.1928, Achivo del Ministerio de Asuntos Exteriores, Fondo Histórico, H 2824.
56. Bonet, 1984, pp. 335–52.
57. *El Debate*, 8.2.1928; 12.2.1928; and 13.2.1928.
58. Data in Ucelay, 1987, vol. 2, p. 252.
59. ADPB, Department Instrucció Pública, Bundle, 4176, File 49.

60. ADPB, Department Instrucció Pública, Bundle 4178, File 92 and Bundle 4181, Files 97, 98 and 100.
61. For example, in 1928 the *Diputación de Barcelona* donated to the library of the UP of Sabadell over 100 books, 30 per cent of them in Catalan. The list of the books donated in Diputanción to Placido Marcet, *jefe* of the UP of Sabadell, 28.2.1928, ADPB, Department Instrucció Pública, Bundle, 4184, File 50.
62. The transfer of the Cátedra de Gramática Catalana to the *Diputación de Barcelona* in ADPB, Department Instrucció Pública, Bundle, 4176, File 12. For the sponsoring of research projects on the Catalan language see, for example, the grants given in 1926 and 1927 for the 'Diccionario Balari', a Catalan lexical-graphic inventory, ADPB, Department Instrucció Pública, Bundle, 4181, File 54.
63. Roig, 1992, p. 295; Rial, 1986, pp. 218–19.
64. For example in the works of Ferrer, 1986, p. 139 and 2000, p. 241.
65. *La Vanguardia*, 27.8.1926 and 29.8.1926.
66. ADPB, FR, 246, P763–P804. For the grants see ADPB, FR 29, Department Instrucció Pública, Bundle 4176, File 59.
67. For example, Turatti, secretary of the Italian fascist party, believed that 'women were born to be at home and not to work in public offices'. His comments in *ABC*, 16.10.1928.
68. The official note in Pérez, 1930, p. 288.
69. Granja, Beramendi and Anguera, 2001, pp. 79–80.
70. Núñez Seixas, 1999, p. 95.
71. Ucelay, 1992, pp. 127–34.
72. *El Magisterio Nacional*, 8.5.1930.
73. *El Magisterio Español*, 22.4.1930.
74. Holguín, 2002, p. 196; Cobb, 1995, pp. 136–7.
75. Elorza, 2004, pp. 73–6.

8.   Somatén Nacional

1. Rodríguez Tarduchy, 1929, pp. 311–12.
2. *ABC*, 22.11.1923.
3. *El Debate*, 1.12.1923.
4. *El Debate*, 2.12.1923.
5. Barrera in Fontán 1924, pp. 52–5.
6. The ceremony in *El Debate*, 2.12.1923 and 4.12.1923 and Fontán, 1924, pp. 56–70.
7. Hayes, 1960, pp. 136–50.
8. Gentile, 1996; Mosse, 1976, Cristis, 2001; Elorza, 2004.
9. Mosse, 1976, pp. 5–6.
10. Rey, 1992, pp. 645–9.
11. Rey, 1987, p. 105.
12. RD 17.9.1923 in *La Gaceta*, 18.9.1923. See also *La Nación*, 19.9.1925.
13. RD 17.9.1923.
14. A large number of reports in AHN, Presidencia del Gobierno, Bundle 442; and Gobernación Serie A, Bundle 59.

15. Castillo, 1977, pp. 266–73.
16. Castillo, 1979, p. 344.
17. Martínez Segarra, 1979, pp. 209–24.
18. González and Rey, 1995, p. 201. A different view arguing that the *somatenes* were in the hands of the *caciques* in Tusell, 1977, p. 149.
19. Captain General of the Second Military Region to Primo, 27.9.1923, AHN, Presidencia del Gobierno, Bundle 442.
20. See reports from the *Somatén* General Commander of the Seventh Military Region to Primo, 12.2.1924, AHN, Gobernación, Serie A, Bundle 59, Box 2.
21. *Somatén* General Commander of the Second Military Region to Captain General of the Second Region, 2.9.1924, AHN, Gobernación, Serie A, Bundle 59, Box 1.
22. *El Somatén*, August 1924.
23. *El Somatén*, May 1924.
24. González and Rey, 1995, p. 181.
25. *Paz y Buena Voluntad*, September 1924.
26. *La Nación*, 18.10.1925.
27. Dozens of letters and telegrams from the Civil Governors and the *delegados* to Martínez Anido in AHN, Presidencia del Gobierno, Bundle 331, Box 1, and Bundle 442.
28. Martínez Anido to Minister of the Interior, 24.4.1921, AHN, Gobernación, Serie A, Bundle 59, Box 1.
29. Civil Governor of Gerona to Minister of the Interior, 1.5.1922, AHN, Gobernación, Serie A, Bundle 59, Box 1.
30. ROC 3.11.1923, *CLE*, no. 496, 572–3.
31. See tens of telegrams from local *somatenes* to Martínez Anido in AHN, Presidencia del Gobierno, Bundle 442.
32. See the correspondence of Martínez Anido with the provincial commanders, captains general and Civil Governors in AHN, Gobernación, Serie A, Bundle 59, Boxes 1 and 2; and Presidencia del Gobierno, Bundle 440.
33. Rodríguez Tarduchy, 1929, p. 249.
34. See, for example, *El Somatén*, May 1925.
35. The records of the Interior Ministry only show one report by a Civil Governor informing on the celebration of the Fiesta of the Virgin of Montserrat during the Berenguer government. This marks a sharp contrast with the hundreds of reports sent every year to Martínez Anido during the Dictatorship. The report dated 27.4.1930 in AHN, Gobernación, Serie A, Bundle 59, Box 2.
36. Serrano, 1999, pp. 69–73.
37. Rey, 1987, p. 130.
38. See, for example, *El Somatén*, October 1927.
39. See, for instance, the tribute paid by the Linares *Somatén* to the ex-combatants of Cuba and Puerto Rico, *El Somatén*, August 1924.
40. See, for example, the discourses of Primo and the Infante Don Fernando in front of the Monument of the Soldiers Fallen for the Fatherland on 26 January 1925, Casa, 1926, pp. 717–18.
41. The celebration of victory was named the *Fiesta de la Paz*. See its observance in *Unión Patriótica*, 15.10.1927 and 1.11.1927.
42. Mosse, 1990, pp. 71–106.
43. Aguirre, 1944, p. 314.

44. *Ibid.*, p. 314.
45. *La Nación*, 18.10.1925.
46. Rubio, 1974, pp. 127–31.
47. See telegrams of captains general and *Somatén* general commanders to Primo dated December 1924 and January 1925, AHN, Presidencia del Gobierno, Bundle 442.
48. Rubio, 1986, p. 160.
49. *Paz y Buena Voluntad*, January 1925.
50. Michonneau, 2004, p. 119.
51. Núñez Seixas, 2005, pp. 45–67.
52. García Queipo de Llano, 1988, pp. 184–96.
53. ROC 17.1.1930, *CLE*, 1930, no.13, 42.
54. Michonneau, 2004, pp. 120–2.
55. Villanueva, 1930, pp. 134–44.
56. Some examples of the prohibition of Carlist ceremonies in San Sebastián, Barcelona and Zaragoza in 1924 in AHN, Gobernación, Serie A, Bundle, 40. On May Day see Rubio, 1974, p. 141.
57. Michonneau, 2004, p. 128.
58. Telegram of Gerona railwaymen to the Ministry of the Interior, 25.6.1923. This and tens more trade union petitions in AHN, Gobernación, Serie A, Bundle 59, Box 1.
59. Chief Police Constable to Director of General Security, 24.4.1923, AHN, Gobernación, Serie A, Bundle 59, Box 1.
60. See the reports sent by the *Somatén* General Commanders, AHN, Gobernación, Serie A, Bundle 59, Box 1.
61. RD 8.9.1924, *CLE*, 1924, no. 398, 608.
62. For the incident in Catrocalbón see AHN, Presidencia del Gobierno, FFCC, Bundle 199, Box 2. More cases of threats to *Somatén* members in 1925 and 1927 in AHN, Presidencia del Gobierno, Bundle 442 and Gobernación, Serie A, Bundle 59, Box 2.
63. The cases mentioned in *El Somatén*, December 1924. More cases in AHN, Gobernación, Serie A, Bundle 59, Box 1 and 2 and Presidencia, Directorio Militar, Bundle 441, Box 2.
64. Civil Governor of Albacete to Martínez Anido, 31.5.1927, AHN, Gobernación, Serie A, Bundle 59, Box 2.
65. González and Rey, 1995, pp. 201–2.
66. A copy of the blueprint in AHN, Presidencia, Directorio Militar, Bundle 441, Box 2.
67. RD 31.12.1929, *CLE*, 1929, Appendix 19, 1–36.
68. Calvo Sotelo, 1974, p. 226.
69. For the Italian case see Tarchi, 2003, pp. 146–8.
70. RD 4.2.1929, *El Somatén*, February 1929.
71. RD 4.2.1929 and ROC 8.2.1929, *El Somatén*, February 1929; ROC, 16.4.1929, *CLE*, no. 147, 86–7.
72. ROC 8.2.1929, Additional Disposition; ROC, 16.4.1929.
73. González Calleja, 1991, p. 104.
74. For example, Emilio Casado Escobedo to Martínez Anido, 1.5.1929. Casado complained of the fact that he and 90 other people had been jailed without

charges for more than two weeks. A similar case in Manuel Ríos to Martínez Anido, 19.10.1929. Ríos demanded the release of some prisoners, 'neither political nor dangerous', who had been jailed in Barcelona for three months without charges. For examples of false accusations see Civil Governor of Valencia to Martínez Anido, 2.12.1929. All correspondence in AHN, Gobernación, Serie A, Bundle 59, Box 2.
75. González and Rey, 1995, pp. 334, 336.
76. Some accusations after the fall of the regime in AHN, Gobernación, Serie A, Bundle 59, Box 2. More cases in Martínez Sergarra, 1984, pp. 353–6.
77. Decree, 15.4.1931, *La Gaceta*, 16.4.1931.
78. González and Rey, 1995, p. 335.
79. Rey 1987, p. 113.
80. Primo to Magaz, 5.6.1925, in Armiñán, and Armiñán, 1930, pp. 141–2.
81. Collective letter of the mayors of the district of Falset (Tarragona) to the Minister of Interior, 3.9.1931, AHN, Gobernación, Serie A, Bundle 59, Box 2.
82. Various petitions in AHN, Gobernación, Serie A, Bundle 59, Box 2.
83. Maura 1930, vol. 1, p. 60.

9. Unión Patriótica

1. *Unión Patriótica*, 15.11.1929.
2. *El Debate*, 31.10.1923; 3.11.1923.
3. González Calbet, 1987, p. 131.
4. *El Debate*, 3.11.1923.
5. González Calbet, 1987, p. 131.
6. *El Debate*, 2.12.1923; 7.12.1923.
7. Castillo, 1979, p. 344; Ben-Ami, 1983, p. 127.
8. Primo to Civil Governors and delegates, 25.4.1924, in Casa, 1926, pp. 546–9.
9. 'Instrucciones para la organización de la Unión Patriótica', in *ibid.*, pp. 654–6.
10. Martín, 1959, p. 793.
11. Gómez-Navarro, 1991, pp. 232–6.
12. 'Manifiesto regionalista en Valladolid', *El Debate*, 2.12.1923.
13. For the inter-class and multi-ideological character of the party see the Madrid UP manifesto of early 1924, in Mask, 1925, pp. 139–56 and Primo's letter to the UP provincial leaders, November 1925, in Rubio, 1974, pp. 168–9.
14. *Unión Patriótica*, 15.2.1927.
15. Ucelay, 1993, pp. 162–3.
16. Pemán, 1929, pp. 25–6.
17. Some cases in Tusell, 1977, pp. 78, 136–7.
18. Blanco, 1931, pp. 119–20.
19. Some examples in AHN, Presidencia, FFCC, Bundle 202, Box 2, File 14986 and Gobernación, Serie A, Bundle 17 A, Box 2.
20. Many of these reports in AHN, Presidencia del Gobierno, Bundles 332 and 446.
21. Ucelay, 1993, pp. 169–71 and Costa, 1995, p. 7.
22. Ben-Ami, 1983, pp. 143–4.
23. Gómez-Navarro, 1985, p. 108.

24. *La Nación*, 18.10.1925.
25. *Unión Patriótica*, 15.12.1926.
26. *Unión Patriótica*, 15.1.1927.
27. *Unión Patriótica*, 1.6.1927.
28. See, for instance, *Unión Patriótica*, 1.6.1927; 15.7.1927; 'Sección Femenina de la Unión Patriótica de Terrasa', ADPB, Departamento de Instrucción Pública, Bundle 4176, File 23; Quiroga, 2005, pp. 69–96.
29. *Unión Patriótica*, 15.4.1927.
30. *Unión Patriótica*, 1.10.1926.
31. *Unión Patriótica*, 15.7.1927.
32. Tens of these lectures and 'patriotic affirmation acts' were regularly reported in the pages of *Unión Patriótica*.
33. See, for example, the fieldtrip to the Church of Santa Cruz de Olorde organized by the Barcelona UP, *La Razón*, 4.2.1928.
34. *Unión Patriótica*, 1.4.1927; González Castillejo, 1993, p. 9.
35. Álvarez Junco, 2001a, p. 258.
36. See, for instance, the front pages of *La Nación*, 28.10.1925 and 12.10.1929. See also the publicity posters of the 1929 Ibero-American exhibition in Seville in Cal, 1987, p. 88.
37. *Unión Patriótica*, 17.5.1927.
38. Rodríguez Tarduchy, 1929, pp. 309–10.
39. *La Nación*, 11.12.1925.
40. See Chapters 2 and 3.
41. For example, *El Somatén*, August 1924; *Unión Patriótica*, 1.4.1927; *La Nación*, 13.9.1927.
42. Ben-Ami, 1983, p. 157.
43. A photographic reportage of the event was published two years later in *Unión Patriótica*, 1.11.1926.
44. *Unión Patriótica*, 15.4.1927.
45. *La Nación*, 10.9.1928; 11.9.1928; 12.9.1928.
46. *La Nación*, 13.9.1928.
47. *La Nación*, 17.9.1928.
48. Vicente Gay in *El Debate*, 13.10.1923.
49. Rodríguez Tarduchy, 1929, p. 249.
50. *La Vanguardia*, 13.10.1923; *El Debate*, 13.10.1923.
51. Primo's speech, 10.4.1925, in Casa, 1926, pp. 842–3.
52. *El Noticiero Universal*, 11.10.1928 and 12.10.1928.
53. *La Nación*, 12.10.1926 and 10.10.1928.
54. *La Nación*, 12.10.1928; *El Noticiero Universal*, 12.10.1928.
55. According to the *primorriverista* press the number of children marching in the streets of Madrid dropped from 35 000 in 1926 to 20 000 in 1929. *La Nación*, 12.10.1926 and 12.10.1929.
56. *La Nación*, 11.10.1930.
57. *La Nación*, 11.10.1930.
58. *El Sol*, 12.10.1932; 13.10.1932; *El Debate*, 12.10.1932; 13.10.1932.
59. AHN, Presidencia del Gobierno, Bundle 199, Box 1 and Bundle 192, Box 2.
60. AHN, Presidencia del Gobierno, Bundle 190, Box 1, Bundle 192, Box 1, Bundle 199, Box 1, and Bundle 204, Box 2.
61. *Unión Patriótica*, 15.4.1929.

62. Civil Governor of Lugo to Cuervo, 30.7.1929, AHN, Presidencia del Gobierno, Bundle 192, Box 1.
63. Cal, 1998, pp. 72–7.
64. AHN, Presidencia del Gobierno, Bundle 204, Box 2.
65. JPPC brief to Primo 16.7.1929, AHN, Presidencia del Gobierno, Bundle 199, Box 1.
66. *Ibid.*
67. 'Propuesta de propaganda y publicidad presentada a la Comisión Permanente de la Exposición Ibero Americana en la sesión de 14 de junio de 1929', AHN, Presidencia del Gobierno, Bundle 199, Box 1.
68. For the fascist propagandist effort see Schnapp, 1992, pp. 1–37; Stone, 1998, pp. 129–76.
69. Ruiz, 1997, pp. 221–7.
70. Calvo Sotelo, 1974, pp. 331–2.
71. *Unión Patriótica*, 1.12.1926.
72. *Unión Patriótica*, 15.1.1930.
73. *El Debate* editorials 2.11.1928; 13.11.1928; 20.11.1928; 27.11.1928.
74. Herrera to Cuervo, 5.4.1929, AHN, Presidencia del Gobierno, Bundle 192, Box 2, File 13003.
75. Gil, 1994, p. 54.
76. González and Rey, 1995, p. 215.
77. RD 4.2.1929, ROC, 8.2.1929, *El Somatén*, February 1929; ROC 16.4.1929, *CLE*, no. 147, 86–7.
78. *El Sol*, 5.2.1930.
79. Villacorta, 2000, pp. 51–78; Calvo Caballero, 2004, pp. 213–28.
80. On diverse 'patriotic acts' in the provinces of Granada, Lugo, Cádiz, Jaén and Madrid see correspondence between Civil Governors and Máximo Cuervo in AHN, Presidencia, Bundle 192, Box 1.
81. 'Información de la Unión Patriótica de Barcelona', 20.4.1929, AHN, Presidencia, Bundle 446, Box 1.
82. Pérez Agudo to Cuervo, 8.4.1929, AHN, Presidencia del Gobierno, Bundle 192, Box 2.
83. Pérez, 1930, pp. 296–300.
84. *El Sol*, 1.1.1930.
85. *Unión Patriótica*, 8.2.1930.
86. Gil, 1994, p. 56.
87. Felice, 1996, pp. 1–55.
88. Pollard, 1990, pp. 32–50.
89. On the creation of a 'culture of consent' in Italy see Zunino, 1995, pp. 176–80; Grazia, 1981; and Felice, 1968, pp. 369–81.
90. *El Sol*, 2.2.1930.
91. *El Sol*, 5.2.1930.
92. This proposal was supported by Ossorio y Gallardo and Luis de Zulueta in the following days. *El Sol*, 6.2.1930 and 7.2.1930.
93. *El Socialista*, 3.1.1930; 31.1.1930.
94. *El Socialista*, 1.2.1930.
95. Radcliff, 1997, pp. 311–12.
96. Castillo, 1979, pp. 349–59. For the rituals and organization of the CEDA, with its youth and female sections, see, for example, *CEDA*, no. 38, 6; 15.2.1935, no. 40.

97. See, for instance, *CEDA*, 15.1.1935, 15.2.1935, 1.9.1935; *Revista de Estudios Hispánicos*, July 1935; September 1935.
98. Febo, 2002, pp. 46–7; González and Limón, 1988.

Conclusion

1. Calvo, 1974, pp. 68–9.
2. Jorge Vigón in Losada, 1990, p. 132.

Bibliography

Primary source material

I. Archives

Archivo General de la Administración (AGA), Alcalá de Henares
Archivo General del Ministerio de Asuntos Exteriores (AMAE), Madrid
Archivo Histórico Nacional (AHN), Madrid
Arxiu General de la Diputació Provincial de Barcelona (ADPB)
Arxiu Històric de la Ciutat, Barcelona
Biblioteca de Catalunya, Barcelona
Biblioteca Nacional, Madrid
Cañada Blanch Centre, London
Hemeroteca Municipal, Madrid
Public Record Office (PRO), Kew
Servicio Histórico Militar (SHM), Madrid

II. Newspapers, periodicals and official publications

ABC
La Acción
Acción Española
Anuario Estadístico de España
Anuario Militar de España
Atenas
Boletín de la Institución Libre de Enseñanza
Boletín Oficial del Ministerio de Instrucción Pública y Bellas Artes
CEDA
Colección Legislativa del Ejército
Coleción Legislativa de Instrucción Pública
La Conquista del Estado
La Correspondencia Militar
El Debate
Diario Oficial del Ministerio del Ejército
Diario Oficial del Ministerio de la Guerra
El Ejército Español
Ejército y Armada
La España de Hoy
La España Nueva
La Gaceta de Madrid
El Liberal
El Magisterio Castellano
El Magisterio Español
El Magisterio Nacional
Memorial de Infantería

La Nación
El Noticiero
El Noticiero Universal
Orientación Española
Paz y Buena Voluntad
La Publicitat
La Razón
Revista de Estudios Hispánicos
Revista de Pedagogía
Revista de Segunda Enseñanza
Revista de Tropas Coloniales
Revista Hispano Africana
El Siglo Futuro
El Socialista
El Sol
El Somatén
Unión Patriótica
La Vanguardia
La Veu de Catalunya

III.   Contemporary accounts, memoirs and works by protagonists

Adán, F. and Tarrasa, A. *Ciudadanía* (Valencia: Talleres de Tipografía La Gutenberg, 1926a).

Adán, F. and Tarrasa, A. *Libro de Cuota* (Valencia: Talleres Tipográficos la Gutemberg, 1926b).

Aguilera y Osorio, J. *Memoria sobre la organización de la educación física en Francia, Alemania, Suecia e Italia* (Madrid: Hernando, 1928).

Aguirre de Cárcer, M. *Glosa del año 23* (Madrid: Pace, 1944).

Armiñán, J. M. de and Armiñán, L. de (eds), *Epistolario del Dictador* (Madrid: Javier Morata, 1930).

Ascarza, V. F[ernández]. *Anuario del Maestro para 1929* (Madrid: Magisterio Español, 1929).

Aunós Pérez, E. *Las Corporaciones del Trabajo en el Estado Moderno* (Madrid: Juan Ortiz, 1928).

Berenguer, P. A. 'Prólogo', in Ruiz Fornells, *Educación moral del soldado* (Toledo: Viuda e Hijos de Juan Peláez, 1894), pp. i–iv.

Blanco, C. *La Dictadura y los procesos militares* (Madrid: Javier Morata, 1930).

Calvo Sotelo, J. *La contribución y la riqueza territorial en España* (Madrid: Imprenta del Servicio de Catastro de Rústica, 1926).

Calvo Sotelo, J. *Mis servicios al Estado* (Madrid: Instituto de Estudios de Administración Local, 1974, 1st ed. 1931).

Casa Ramos, Marqués de. *Dos años de Directorio Militar* (Madrid: Renacimiento, 1926(?)).

Condo González, A. *Manual del Instructor de Gimnasia* (Toledo, 1923).

Díaz Retg, E. *España bajo el nuevo régimen* (Madrid: Mercurio, 1928).

Escartín y Lartiga, E. *El Ejército en la acción política* (Madrid: R. Velasco, 1905).

Escuela Central de Gimnasia, *Memoria de los Cursos 1920–1921, 1923* (Toledo: 1924).

E.T.L. (pseudonym of Enrique Tomás y Lucas) *Por pueblos y aldeas: de las memorias de un delegado gubernativo* (Toledo: Católica Toledana, 1928).

Fanjul y Goñi, J. *Misión Social del Ejército* (Madrid: Imprenta de Eduardo Arias, 1907).

Fontán Palomo, J. *El Somatenista español* (Barcelona: Imprenta Moderna, 1924).

Ganivet, A. *Idearium español* (Madrid: Biblioteca Nueva, 1996, 1st ed. 1895).

García, T. and Matta, J. de la. *Elementos de educación moral del soldado* (Sevilla: F. Díaz, 1916).

García Pérez, A. *Militarismo y socialismo* (Madrid: R. Velasco, 1906).

González Deleito, F. *La educación física en Suecia* (Toledo: Viuda e Hijos de J. Peláez, 1911).

Hernández Mir, F. *Un crimen de lesa patria: la Dictadura ante la historia* (Madrid: Compañía Ibero-Americana de Publicaciones, 1930).

Herrera Oria, E. *Educación de una España nueva* (Madrid: Faz, 1934).

Iglesia, C. de la (pseudonym of Eduardo Hernández Vidal) *La censura por dentro* (Madrid: Compañía Ibero-Americana de Publicaciones, 1930).

Instituto Nacional de Estadística, *Principales actividades de la vida española en la primera mitad del siglo XX* (Madrid: n.p., 1952).

Iradier y Herrero, T. de. *Catecismo del Ciudadano* (Madrid, 1924).

Juderías Loyot, J. *La leyenda negra* (Salamanca: Junta de Castilla y León, 1997, 1st ed. 1914).

Maeztu y Whitney, R. de. *Hacia otra España* (Madrid: Biblioteca Nueva, 1998, 1st ed. 1899).

Maeztu y Whitney, R. de. *Con el Directorio Militar* (Madrid: Editora Nacional, 1957).

Maeztu y Whitney, R. de. *Defensa de la Hispanidad* (Madrid: Rialp, 1998, 1st ed. 1934).

Mas y Casterad, J. *Instrucción militar teórica* (Guadalajara: Imprenta Gutemberg, 1925).

Mas y Casterad, J. *Moral, Educación e Instrucción* (Zaragoza: El Noticiero, 1926).

Mask (pseudonym of Enrique Díaz Retg) *Hacia la España nueva* (Madrid: Sucesores de Rivadeneyra, 1925).

Martín Sánchez-Juliá, F. *Ideas claras* (Madrid: Nebrija, 1959).

Maura Gamazo, G. *Bosquejo histórico de la Dictadura*, 2 vols (Madrid: Javier Morata, 1930).

Mola Vidal, E. *Obras Completas* (Valladolid: Librería Santarén, 1940).

Navarro García, M. *Máximas de moral militar* (Madrid: Sucesores de Rivadeneyra, 1920, 1st ed. 1912).

Ortega y Gasset, J. *España invertebrada* (Madrid: Alianza, 1993, 1st ed. 1921).

Pemán y Pemartín, J. M. *El valor del hispanoamericanismo y el proceso total humano hacia la unificación y la paz* (Madrid: Imprenta del Patronato de Huerfanos de Intendencia e Intervención Militares, 1927).

Pemán y Pemartín, J. M. *El hecho y la idea de la Unión Patriótica* (Madrid: Ediciones de la Junta de Propaganda Patriótica y Ciudadana, 1929).

Pemán y Pemartín, J. M. *El poema de la Bestia y el Ángel* (Zaragoza: Jerarquía, 1938).

Pemartín y Sanjuán, J. *Los valores históricos en la dictadura española* (Madrid: Arte y Ciencia, 1928).

Pemartín y Sanjuán, J. 'Política Hispano-Americana', in E. Pérez et al., *Cursos de ciudadanía* (Madrid: Junta de Propaganda Patriótica y Ciudadana, 1929), pp. 38–91.

Pemartín Sanjuán, J. *Introducción a una filosofía de lo temporal: doce lecciones sobre Espacio-Tiempo-Causalidad* (Seville: Álvarez Zambrano, 1937, 1st ed. 1935–1936).

Pemartín Sanjuán, J. *Qué es 'Lo Nuevo'* . . . *Consideraciones sobre el momento español presente* (Santander: Cultura Española, 1938, 1st ed. 1937).

Pérez, D. *La Dictadura a través de sus notas oficiosas* (Madrid: Compañía Ibero-Americana de Publicaciones, 1930).

Pérez Agudo E. et al. *Curso de ciudadanía. Conferencias pronunciadas en el Alcázar de Toledo. Marzo 1929* (Madrid: Junta de Propaganda Patriótica y Ciudadana, 1929).

Porta Vidal, E. *La Dictadura en las aldeas: notas e impresiones* (Valencia: Imprenta Pont, n.d.).

Primo de Rivera, J. A. *Obras completas* (Madrid: Delegación Nacional de la Sección Femenina de FET y de las JONS, 1954).

Primo de Rivera, M. 'Prólogo', in T. García, and J. de la Matta, *Elementos de educación moral del soldado* (Sevilla: F. Díaz, 1916), pp. xi–xv.

Primo de Rivera, M. *La cuestión del día: Gibraltar y África* (Cádiz: Imprenta de M. Álvarez, 1917).

Primo de Rivera, M. *Discursos del Excmo. Sr. D. Francisco Bergamín, Presidente de la Academia [de Jurisprudencia] sobre Tribunales de Comercio, y del Excmo. Sr. D. Miguel Primo de Rivera* (Madrid: Talleres de la Editorial Reus, 1924a).

Primo de Rivera, M. *Discurso leído por el Excmo. Señor D. Miguel Primo de Rivera y Obraneja, Jefe de Gobierno y Presidente del Director Militar en la solemne apertura de los tribunales, celebrada el 15 de septiembre de 1924* (Madrid: Talleres de la Editorial Reus, 1924b).

Primo de Rivera, M. *Disertación ciudadana* (Madrid: Sanz Calleja, 1926).

Primo de Rivera, M. *Actuación ciudadana que corresponde al Ejército* (Madrid: Juan Pérez Torres, 1927).

Primo de Rivera, M. *Del General Primo de Rivera: documentos originales y artículos inspirados por él* (Madrid: Junta de Propaganda Patriótica y Ciudadana, 1928).

Primo de Rivera, M. *El pensamiento de Primo de Rivera* (Madrid: Sáez Hermanos/Junta de Propaganda Patriótica y Ciudadana, 1929).

Primo de Rivera, M. *Intervenciones en la Asamblea Nacional del general Primo de Rivera* (Madrid: Junta de Propaganda Patriótica y Ciudadana/Imprenta Sáez Hermanos, 1930a).

Primo de Rivera, M. *La obra de la Dictadura* (Madrid: Junta de Propaganda Patriótica y Ciudadana/Imprenta Sáez Hermanos, 1930b).

Primo de Rivera, M. *El golpe de Estado y la obra de la Dictadura, juzgados por el propio general Primo de Rivera* (Alicante: Alicantina, 1930c).

Primo de Rivera, M. and Cambó, F. *Miguel Primo de Rivera-Cambó* (Santander: Hermanos Bedia, 1961).

Pumarola Alaiz, L. *Democracia y Ejército* (Toledo: Católica Toledana, 1928).

Real Academia de la Historia [Rafael Altamira], *Historia de España, para uso de las escuelas primarias* (Madrid: Compañía General de Artes Gráficas, 1930).

Redondo, O. *Textos* (Madrid: Doncel, 1975).

Reyes Sanz, E. de los. *El Ejército y su influencia en la Educación Física Nacional* (Manresa: Antonio Esparbé, 1921).

Rodríguez, T. *El Estatismo y la Educación Nacional en los Paises Civilizados* (El Escorial: Imprenta del Monasterio, 1928).

Rodríguez Tarduchy, E. *Psicología del dictador y caracteres más salientes, morales, sociales y políticos, de la dictadura española* (Madrid: Sáez Hermanos, 1929).

Rueda y Maestro, E. de. *La moral militar* (Madrid: Sucesores de Rivadeneyra, 1925).

Ruiz Fornells, E. *La educación moral del soldado* (Toledo: Viuda é Hijos de Juan Peláez, 1894).

Salaverría, J. M. *La afirmación española* (Barcelona: Gustavo Gili, 1917).

Saldaña García-Rubio, Q. *Al servicio de la justicia. La orgía áurea de la Dictadura* (Madrid: Javier Morata, 1930).

Siurot Rodríguez, M. *La emoción de España* (Madrid: Talleres Voluntad, 1927).

Spengler, O. *La decadencia de Occidente* (Madrid: Espasa Calpe, 1976, 1st ed. 1918–1922).

Tiro Nacional de España. *El Tiro Nacional de España* (Madrid: n.p. 1915).

Tiro Nacional de España. *Libro de 1918* (Madrid: n.p. 1918).

Vázquez de Mella, J. *El ideal de España* (Madrid: Imprenta Alemana, 1915).

Villalba Riquelme, J. *Organización de la Educación física e Instrucción premilitar en Francia, Suecia, Alemania e Italia (Viaje de estudio)* (Madrid: Talleres del Depósito de la Guerra, 1927).

Villalba Rubio, R. *Método de Instrucción Integral para el recluta y Soldado de Infantería* (Toledo: Imprenta, Librería y Encuadernación de Rafael G. Menor, 1928).

Villanueva, F. *La dictadura militar* (Madrid: Javier Morata, 1930).

Yela Utrilla, J. F. *Historia de la civilización española en sus relaciones con la universal* (Madrid: Ministerio de Instrucción Pública y Bellas Artes, 1928).

Secondary source material

Adagio, C. *Chiesa e Nazione in Spagna. La dittatura di Primo de Rivera (1923–1930)* (Milan: Unicopli, 2004).

Alonso, G. 'La mirada de la izquierda. Las guerras coloniales de 1898 desde la prensa socialista y federal', in R. Sánchez (ed.), *En torno al 98* (Huelva: Universidad de Huelva, 2000), vol. 2, pp. 261–9.

Álvarez Chillada, G. *José María Pemán. Pensamiento y trayectoria de un monárquico (1897–1941)* (Cádiz: Universidad de Cádiz, 1996).

Álvarez Junco, J. 'Nation-Building in 19th-Century Spain', in C. Mar-Molinero and A. Smith (eds), *Nationalism and the Nation in the Iberian Peninsula* (Washington/ Oxford: Berg, 1996), pp. 89–107.

Álvarez Junco, J. 'El nacionalismo español como mito movilizador. Cuatro guerras', in R. Cruz and M. Pérez (eds), *Cultura y movilización en la España contemporánea* (Madrid: Alianza, 1997), pp. 35–67.

Álvarez Junco, J. *Mater dolorosa. La idea de España en el siglo XIX* (Madrid: Taurus, 2001a).

Álvarez Junco, J. 'El nacionalismo español: las insuficiencias en la acción estatal', *Historia Social*, no. 40 (2001b), 29–51.

Anderson, B. *Imagined Communities. Reflections on the Origins and the Spread of Nationalism* (London: Verso, 1991, 1st ed. 1983).

Andrés Gallego, J. *El socialismo durante la Dictadura, 1923–1930* (Madrid: Tebas, 1977).

Andrés Martín, J. R. *El cisma mellista* (Madrid: Actas, 2000).

Archilés, F. '¿Quién necesita la nación débil? La débil nacionalización española y los historiadores', in C. Forcadell, C. Frías, I. Peiró and P. Rújula (eds), *Usos públicos de la historia* (Zaragoza, 2002), vol. 1, pp. 302–22.

Archilés, F. and Martí, M. 'Ethnicity, Region and Nation: Valencian Identity and the Spanish Nation-State', *Ethnic and Racial Studies*, no. 24–25 (2002a), 779–97.

Archilés, F. and Martí, M. 'Un país extraño como cualquier otro: la construcción de la identidad española cotemporánea', in M. Cruz Romero and Ismael Saz (eds), *El siglo XX. Historiografía e historia* (Valencia: Universitat de València, 2002b), pp. 245–78.

Balfour, S. 'Riot, Regeneration and Reaction: Spain in the Aftermath of the 1898 Disaster', *The Historical Journal*, 38, 2 (1995), 405–23.

Balfour, S. 'The Lion and the Pig: Nationalism and National Identity in Fin-de-Siècle Spain', in C. Mar-Molinero and A. Smith (eds), *Nationalism and the Nation in the Iberian Peninsula* (Washington/Oxford: Berg, 1996), pp. 107–17.

Balfour, S. *The End of the Spanish Empire, 1898–1923* (Oxford: Clarendon Press, 1997).

Balfour, S. *Deadly Embrace. Morocco and the Road to the Spanish Civil War* (Oxford: Oxford University Press, 2002).

Balfour, S. and La Porte, P. 'Spanish Military Cultures and the Moroccan Wars', *European History Quarterly*, 30, 3 (2000), 307–32.

Ballbé, M. *Orden público y militarismo en la España constitucional* (Madrid: Alianza, 1983).

Beadman, C. 'Official Nationalism of the Primo de Rivera Regime: Some Findings from the Pages of *Unión Patriótica* and *Somatén*', *International Journal of Iberian Studies*, 11, 2 (1998), 69–75.

Ben-Ami, S. 'Los estudiantes contra el rey. El papel de la FUE en la caída de la Dictadura y la proclamación de la República', *Historia 16*, 6 (1976), 37–47.

Ben-Ami, S. 'The Forerunners of Spanish Fascism: Unión Patriótica and Unión Monárquica', *European Studies Review*, 9, 1 (1979), 49–79.

Ben-Ami, S. *Fascism from Above: the Dictatorship of Primo de Rivera in Spain 1923–1930* (Oxford: Clarendon Press, 1983).

Ben-Ami, S. 'La dictadura de Primo de Rivera. Una perspectiva comparativa', in *El poder militar en la España contemporánea* (Madrid: Universidad Complutense de Madrid, 1989), pp. 107–33.

Ben-Ami, S. *Los orígenes de la II República* (Madrid: Alianza, 1990a).

Ben-Ami, S. 'The Crisis of the Dynastic Élite in the Transition from Monarchy to Republic, 1929–1931', in F. Lannon and P. Preston (eds), *Élites and Power in Twentieth-Century Spain* (Oxford: Clarendon Press, 1990b), pp. 71–90.

Ben-Ami, S. 'Las dictaduras de los años veinte', in M. Cabrera, S. Juliá and P. Martín (eds), *Europa en crisis, 1919–1939* (Madrid: Pablo Iglesias, 1991), pp. 47–64.

Beramendi, J. 'Identidad nacional e identidad regional en España entre la guerra del francés y la guerra civil', in *Los Ibéricos y el mar*, vol. 3 (Madrid-Salamanca: Sociedad Estatal Lisboa 98, 1998), pp. 187–215.

Blanco Escolá, C. *La Academia General Militar de Zaragoza (1928–1931)* (Barcelona: Labor, 1989).

Blas Guerrero, A. de. *Nacionalismos y naciones en Europa* (Madrid: Alianza, 1994a).

Blas Guerrero, A. de. 'Los nacionalismos españoles ante el Estado autonómico', in J. Beramendi, R. Máiz and X. Núñez (eds), *Nationalism in Europe* (Santiago de Compostela: Universidad de Santiago de Compostela, 1994b), pp. 39–52.

Blinkhorn, M. *Carlism and Crisis in Spain, 1931–1939* (Cambridge: Cambridge University Press, 1975).

Blinkhorn, M. 'Introductuion. Allies, Rivals, or Antagonist? Fascists and Conservatives in Modern Europe', in M. Blinkhorn (ed.), *Fascist and Conservatives* (London: Unwin Hyman, 1990), pp. 1–14.

Blinkhorn, M. *Fascism and the Right in Europe* (New York: Longman, 2000).

Bonet i Baltà, J. 'L'Església catalana perseguida per la Dictadura de Primo de Rivera', in J. Bonet (ed.), *L'Església catalana, de la Il.lustració a la Renaixença* (Barcelona: Publicacions de l'Abadia de Montserrat, 1984), pp. 335–52.

Botti, A. *Cielo y dinero. El Nacionalcatolicismo en España (1881–1975)* (Madrid: Alianza, 1992).

Botti, Alfonso, 'Il nazionalismo spagnolo nella ricerca e nel dibattito storiografico', *Italia contemporanea*, no. 191 (1993), 317–23.

Boyd, C. P. *Historia patria. Politics, History and National Identity in Spain, 1875–1975* (New Jersey: Princeton University Press, 1997).

Boyd, C. P. '"Madre España": libros de texto patrióticos y socialización política, 1900–1950', *Historia y Política*, no. 1, (1999), 49–70.

Boyd, Carolyn P. 'Violencia pretoriana: del *Cu-cut!* al 23-F', in Santos Juliá (ed.), *Violencia política en la España del siglo XX* (Madrid: Taurus, 2000).

Boyd, C. P. 'El pasado escindido: la enseñanza de la Historia en las escuelas españolas, 1875–1900', *Hispania*, no. 209 (2001), 859–78.

Breuilly, J. *Nationalism and the State* (Manchester: Manchester University Press, 1993).

Burdiel, I. 'La consolidación del liberalismo y el punto de fuga de la monarquía (1843–1870)', in M. Suárez (ed.), *Las máscaras de la libertad. El liberalismo español, 1808–1950* (Madrid, 2003), pp. 101–33.

Burleigh, M. *Sacred Causes: Religion and Politics from the European Dictators to Al Qaeda* (London: HarperCollins, 2006).

Busquets, J. *El militar de carrera en España* (Barcelona: Ariel, 1984).

Cacho Viu, V. 'La imagen de las dos Españas', *Revista de Occidente*, no. 60 (1986), 54–62.

Cal Martínez, R. 'El mundo de las exposiciones (III). Del IV Centenario a Sevilla-Barcelona (1929)', *Historia 16*, 194 (1987), 86–92.

Cal Martínez, R. 'La agencia Plus Ultra: un instrumento de propaganda de Primo de Rivera', *Mélanges de la Casa de Velázquez*, 31, 3 (1995), 177–95.

Cal Martínez, R. 'Los gastos reservados y la prensa con Primo de Rivera', *Historia 16*, 271 (1998), 72–7.

Caldwell, L. 'Reproducers of the Nation: Women and the Family in Fascist Italy', in D. Forgacs (ed.), *Rethinking Italian Fascism* (London, 1986), pp. 110–41.

Callahan, W. J. *The Catholic Church in Spain, 1875–1998* (Washington DC: The Catholic University of America Press, 2000).

Calvo Caballero, P. *Las organizaciones patronales en Castilla y León durante la Dictadura de Primo de Rivera* (Valladolid: Universidad de Valladolid, 2004).

Capitán Díaz, A. *Historia de la Educación en España*, 2 vols (Madrid: Dykinson, 1994).

Carbayo-Abengózar, M. 'Shaping Women: National Identity Through the Use of Language in Franco's Spain', *Nations and Nationalism*, 7, 1 (2001), 75–92.

Cardona, G. 'La reforma de la enseñanza militar en la II República (1931–1932)', in J. Busquets and V. Fernández (eds), *La enseñanza militar en España* (Madrid: CSIC, 1986), pp. 66–80.

Casassas Ymbert, J. *La Dictadura de Primo de Rivera (1923–1930). Textos* (Barcelona: Anthropos, 1983).

Castillo, J. J. *El sindicalismo amarillo. Aportación al estudio del catolicismo social español (1912–1923)* (Madrid: Cuadernos para el diálogo, 1977).

Castillo, J. J. *Propietarios muy pobres: sobre la subordinación political del pequeño campesinado (la Confederación Nacional Católico-Agraria), 1917–1942* (Madrid: Servico de Publicaciones Agrarias, 1979).

Cobb, C. 'The Republican State and Mass Educational-Cultural Initiatives, 1931–1936', in H. Graham and J. Labanyi (eds), *Spanish Cultural Studies* (Oxford: Oxford University Press, 1995), pp. 133–8.

Colley, L. *Britons: Forging the Nation, 1707–1837* (New Haven: Yale University Press, 1992).

Collotti, E. *Fascismo, fascismi* (Milán: Sansoni, 1994).

Costa i Fernández, L. *La dictadura de Primo de Rivera, 1923–1930: Comunicació i propaganda a les comarques gironines* (Barcelona: Rafael Dalmau, 1995).

Cristi, M. *From Civil to Political Religion* (Waterloo: Wilfrid Laurier University Press, 2001).

Davies, P. 'Providence, Saviour Figures and Would-be Gods: Prophecy and the French Extreme Right', in B. Taithe and T. Thorton (eds), *Prophecy. The Power of Inspired Language in History 1300–2000* (Gloucester: Sutton Publishing, 1997), pp. 181–201.

Deutsch, K.W. *Nationalism and Social Communication* (Cambridge, Mass: MIT Press, 1966).

Díaz Barrado, M. P. *Palabra de dictador. General Primo de Rivera: análisis de discursos (1923–1930)* (Cáceres: Universidad de Extremadura, 1985).

Díaz de la Guardia, E. 'La enseñanza con Primo de Rivera', *Historia 16*, 71 (1982), 19–25.

Durara, P. 'Historizing National Identity, or Who Imagines What and When', in G. Eley and R. G. Suny (eds), *Becoming National* (Oxford: Oxford University Press, 1996), pp. 151–77.

Eguidazu Palacios, F. 'La crisis de la peseta y la caída de la Dictadura', *Cuadernos Económicos de I.C.E.*, no. 10 (1979), 299–352.

Elorza Domínguez, A. 'El anarcosindicalismo español bajo la dictadura (1923–1930)', *Revista de Trabajo*, no. 39–40 (1972), 123–477.

Elorza Domínguez, A. 'Las variantes del fascismo (1931–1936)', in J. Antón and M. Caminal (eds), *Pensamiento político en la España contemporánea (1800–1950)* (Barcelona: Teide, 1992), pp. 989–1006.

Elorza Domínguez, A. *La religión política* (San Sebastián: Haramburu, 1995).

Elorza Domínguez, A. 'El franquismo, un proyecto de religión política', in J. Tusell, E. Gentile and Febo, G. di (eds), *Fascismo y franquismo cara a cara* (Madrid, 2004).

Escribano Hernández, J. 'Formación y defensa del directorio militar de Primo de Rivera', *Cuadernos de Investigación Histórica*, 22 (2005), 373–400.

Espadas Burgos, M. 'La institución Libre de Enseñanza y la formación military durante la restauración', in *Estudios de Historia Militar* , vol. 1 (Madrid: Servicio de Publicaciones del EME, 1983), pp. 493–514.

Febo, G. di. *Ritos de guerra y de victoria en la España franquista* (Bilbao: Desclée, 2002).

Felice, R. de. *Mussolini il Fascista II. La organizzazione dello Stato fascista* (Turin: Einaudi, 1968).

Felice, R. de. *Mussolini il Duce. Gli anni del consenso, 1929–1936* (Turin: Einaudi, 1996).

Fernández Bastarreche, F. 'The Spanish Military from the Age of Disasters to the Civil War', in R. Banon and T. M. Barker (eds), *Armed Forces and Society in Spain* (New York: Columbia University Press, 1988), pp. 213–48.

Fernández Clemente, E. *Gente de orden. Aragón durante la Dictadura de Primo de Rivera, 1923–1930* (Zaragoza: Ibercaja, 1995–1998), 4 vols.

Fernández Soria, J. M. *Estado y educación en la España contemporánea* (Madrid: Síntesis, 2002).

Ferrer i Girones, F. *La persecució política de la llengua catalana* (Barcelona: Edicions 62, 1986).

Ferrer i Girones, F. *Catalanofobia* (Barcelona: Edicions 62, 2000).

Foard, D. W., 'The Spanish Fichte: Menéndez Pelayo', *Journal of Contemporary History,* 14, 1 (1979), 83–97.

Fox, Inman E., *La invención de España. Nacionalismo liberal e identidad nacional* (Madrid: Cátedra, 1997).

Fox, I. E., 'Spain as Castile: Nationalism and National Identity', in D. T. Giles (ed.), *The Cambridge Companion to Modern Spanish Culture* (Cambridge: Cambridge University Press, 1999), pp. 21–36.

Fradera, J. M. *Cultura nacional en una societat dividida. Patriotisme i cultura a Catalunya (1838–1868)* (Barcelona: Curial, 1992).

Fusi, J. P. 'Centre and Periphery 1900–1936: National Integration and Regional Nationalism Reconsidered', in F. Lannon and P. Preston (eds), *Élites and Power in Twentieth-Century Spain* (Oxford: Clarendon Press, 1990a), pp. 33–44.

Fusi, J. P. 'Revisionismo crítico e historia nacionalista (A propósito de un artículo de Borja de Riquer)', *Historia Social,* no. 7 (1990b), 127–34.

Fusi, J. P. 'Los nacionalismos y el Estado español: el siglo XX', *Cuadernos de Historia Contemporánea,* no. 22 (2000), 21–52.

Fusi, J. P. and Palafox, J. *España 1808–1996* (Madrid: Espasa, 1997).

Gallego, A. *Pensamiento y acción social de la Iglesia en España* (Madrid: Espasa, 1983).

García Canales, M. *El problema constitucional en la Dictadura de Primo de Rivera* (Madrid: Centro de Estudios Constitucionales, 1980).

García Queipo de Llano, G. *Los intelectuales y la dictadura de Primo de Rivera* (Madrid: Alianza, 1988).

García Queipo de Llano, G. 'Los ideólogos de la Unión Patriótica', in *Estudios históricos. Homenaje a los profesores José Mª Jover Zamora y Vicente Palacio Atard* (Madrid: Universidad Complutense, 1990), vol. 1, pp. 221–30.

García Queipo de Llano, G. *La dictadura de Primo de Rivera* (Madrid: Cuadernos Historia 16, 67 1996).

Garrido Martín, A. *La dictadura de Primo de Rivera, ¿ruptura o paréntesis?: Cantabria (1923–1931)* (Santander: Ayuntamiento de Santander, 1997).

Gellner, E. *Nations and Nationalism* (Oxford: Blackwell, 1983).

Genieys, W. *Les Élites Espagnoles Face à L'État* (Paris: L'Harmattan, 1997).

Gentile, E. *The Sacralization of Politics in Fascist Italy* (Cambridge, Mass.: Harvard University Press, 1996).

Gentile, E. *Il mito dello Stato Nuovo: dal radicalismo nazionale al fascismo* (Roma-Bari: Laterza, 1999).

Gil Pecharromán, J. *Conservadores subversivos. La derecha autoritaria alfonsina (1913–1936)* (Madrid, 1994).

Gómez-Navarro Navarrete, J. L., 'Unión Patriótica: análisis de un partido del poder', *Estudios de Historia Social,* no. 32–33 (1985), 93–163.

Gómez-Navarro Navarrete, J. L. *El régimen de Primo de Rivera* (Madrid: Cátedra, 1991).

González Calbet, M. T. *La Dictadura de Primo de Rivera. El Directorio Militar* (Madrid: El Arquero, 1987).

González Calleja, E. 'La defensa armada del "orden social" durante la Dictadura de Primo de Rivera (1923–1930)', in J. L. García Delgado (ed.), *España entre dos siglos (1875–1931)* (Madrid: Siglo XXI, 1991), pp. 64–108.

González Calleja, E. *El Máuser y el sufragio. Orden público, subversión y violencia política en la crisis de la Resturación (1917–1931)* (Madrid: CSIC, 1999).

González Calleja, E. 'Sobre el dominio de las masas. Visiones y revisiones en la sociografía de los regímenes autoritarios y fascistas del periodo de entreguerras', in E. Acton and I. Saz (eds), *La transición a la política de masas* (Valencia: Universitat del València, 2001), pp. 129–56.

González Calleja, E. *La España de Primo de Rivera (1923–1930). La modernización autoritaria* (Madrid: Alianza, 2005).

González Calleja, E. and Limón Nevado, F. *La Hispanidad como instrumento de combate* (Madrid: CSIC, 1988).

González Calleja, E. and Rey Reguillo, F. del. *La defensa armada contra la revolución* (Madrid: CSIC, 1995).

González Castillejo, M. J. 'Los conceptos de mujer, ciudadanía y patria en la Dictadura de Primo de Rivera. Imágenes, símbolos y estereotipos', *Mujeres y ciudadanía* (Málaga, 1993), pp. 1–17.

González Cuevas, P. C. *Acción Española. Teología política y nacionalismo autoritario en España (1913–1936)* (Madrid: Tecnos, 1998).

González Cuevas, P. C. *Historia de las derechas españolas* (Madrid: Biblioteca Nueva, 2000).

González Cuevas, P. C. *Maeztu. Biografía de un nacionalista español* (Madrid: Marcial Pons, 2003).

González Hernández, M. J. *Ciudadanía y acción. El conservadurismo maurista* (Madrid: Siglo XXI, 1990).

Graham, H. 'Community, Nation, and State in Republican Spain, 1931–1938', in C. Mar-Molinero and A. Smith (eds), *Nationalism and the Nation in the Iberian Peninsula* (Washington/Oxford: Berg, 1996), pp. 133–47.

Graham, H. *The Spanish Republic at War, 1936–1939* (Cambridge: Cambridge University Press, 2002).

Granja, J. L. de la, Beramendi J. and Anguera, P., *La España de los nacionalismos y las autonomías* (Madrid: Síntesis, 2001).

Grazia, V. de. *Culture of Consent: Mass Organization of Labour* (Cambridge: Cambridge University Press, 1981).

Grazia, V. de. *How Fascism Ruled Women. Italy, 1922–1945* (Berkeley/Oxford: University of California Press, 1992).

Hayes, C. *Nationalism: a Religion* (New York: Macmillan, 1960).

Hennessy, A. 'Ramiro de Maeztu: *Hispanidad* and the Search for a Surrogate Imperialism', in J. Harrison and A. Hoyle (eds), *Spain's 1898 Crisis* (Manchester: Manchester University Press, 2000), pp. 105–17.

Hernández Andreu, J. *España y la crisis de 1929* (Madrid: Espasa-Calpe, 1986).

Herrero, J. *Los orígenes del pensamiento reaccionario* (Madrid: Cuadernos para el diálogo, 1971).

Hobsbawm, E. *Nations and Nationalism since 1780* (Cambridge: Cambridge University Press, 1990).

Hobsbawm, E. and Ranger, T. (eds), *The Invention of Tradition* (Cambridge: Cambridge University Press, 1983).

Holguín, Sandie. *Creating Spaniards. Culture and National Identity in Republican Spain* (Madison: University of Wisconsin Press, 2002).

Jensen, G. 'Military Nationalism and the State. The Case of Fin-de-Siècle Spain', *Nations and Nationalism*, 6, 2 (2000), 257–74.

Jensen, G. *Irrational Triumph: Cultural Despair, Military Nationalism, and the Ideological Origins of Franco's Spain* (Reno: Nevada University Press, 2002).

Juaristi, J. 'El ruedo ibérico. Mitos y símbolos en el nacionalismo español', *Cuadernos de Alzate*, no. 16 (1997), 19–31.

Kallis, A. A., ' "Fascism", "Parafascism", and "Fascistization": On the Similarities of Three Conceptual Categories', *European History Quarterly*, 33, 2 (2003), 219–49.

Lannon, F. 'Modern Spain: the Project of a National Catholicism', in Stuart Mews (ed.), *Religion and National Identity*, Studies in Church History, vol. 18 (Oxford: Basil Blackwell, 1982), pp. 567–90.

Lannon, F. *Privilege, Persecution, and Prophecy. The Catholic Church in Spain* (Oxford: Clarendon Press, 1987).

Lebovics, H. *True France. The Wars over Cultural Identity, 1900–1945* (Ithaca/London: Cornell University Press, 1992).

Levinger, M. and Franklin Lytle, P. 'Myth and Mobilization. The Triadic Structure of Nationalist Rhetoric', *Nations and Nationalism*, 7, 2 (2001), 175–94.

Linz, J. J. 'Early State-Building and Late Peripheral Nationalisms Against the State: the Case of Spain', in S. N. Eisenstast and S. Rokkan (eds), *Building States and Nations* (Beverly Hills/London: Sage, 1973), pp. 32–116.

Lleixà, J. *Cien años de militarismo en España* (Barcelona: Anagrama, 1986).

López Martín, R. 'Las Conferencias dominicales. Una actividad de educación popular en la Dictadura de Primo de Rivera', in R. Bassa (ed.), *Moviment obrer i educació popular* (Palma de Mallorca: Universidad de Palma de Mallorca, 1986), pp. 111–18.

López Martín, R. 'La Inspección de Enseñanza Primaria en la Dictadura de Primo de Rivera', *Historia de la Educación*, no. 6 (1987), 311–23.

López Martín, R. *Ideología y educación en la dictadura de Primo de Rivera 1, Escuelas y maestros* (Valencia: Universitat de València, 1994a).

López Martín, R. *Ideología y educación en la dictadura de Primo de Rivera 2, Institutos y universidades* (Valencia: Universitat de València, 1994b).

López Martín, R. 'La construcción y creación de escuelas en la España del primer tercio del siglo XX', *Historia de la Educación*, no. 16 (1997), 65–90.

Losada Malvárez, J. C. *Ideología del ejército franquista (1939–1959)* (Madrid: Istmo, 1990).

Maier, C. S. *La refundación de la Europa burguesa* (Madrid: Ministerio de Trabajo y Seguridad Social, 1988).

Mann, M. *Sources of Power. The Rise of Classes and Nation States, 1760–1914*, vol. 2 (Cambridge: Cambridge University Press, 1993).

Manzano Moreno, E. 'La construcción histórica del pasado nacional', in Juan Sinisio Pérez Garzón (ed.), *La gestión de la memoria* (Madrid: Crítica, 2000), pp. 33–62.

Manzano Moreno, E. and Pérez Garzón, J. S. 'A Difficult Nation? History and Nationalism in Contemporary Spain', in R. Rein (ed.), *Spanish Memories: Images of a Contested Past, History and Memory*, vol. 14, no. 1–2 (2002), pp. 259–84.

Martí, M. and Archilés, F. 'La construcción de la Nación española durante el siglo XIX: logros y límites del caso valenciano', *Ayer*, 35 (1999), 173–90.

Martínez Segarra, R. M. 'Grupos económicos en el Somatén', *Cuadernos Económicos de I.C.E.*, no. 10 (1979), 209–24.

Martínez Segarra, R. M. *El Somatén Nacional en la Dictadura del general Primo de Rivera* (Madrid: Universidad Complutense, 1984).

Martínez Segarra, R. M. 'La Unión Patriótica', in J. Tusell, F. Montero and J. M. Marín (eds), *Las derechas de la España contemporánea* (Madrid: UNED, 1997), pp. 67–176.

Michonneau, S. 'La política del olvido de la dictadura de Primo de Rivera: el caso barcelonés', *Historia y Política*, no. 12 (2004), 115–40.

Montero García, F. *El primer catolicismo social y la Rerum Novarum en España (1899–1902)* (Madrid: CSIC, 1983).

Montero, E. 'Reform Idealized. The Intellectual and Ideological Origins of the Second Republic', in H. Graham and J. Labanyi (eds), *Spanish Cultural Studies* (Oxford: Oxford University Press, 1995), pp. 124–38.

Molina Aparicio, F. *La tierra del martirio español* (Madrid: Centro de Esudio Constitucionales, 2005).

Morodo Leoncio, R. 'La proyección constitucional de la Dictadura: la Asamblea Nacional Consultiva (I)', *Boletín Informativo de Ciencia Política*, no. 13–14 (1973).

Morodo Leoncio, R. *Acción Española. Orígenes ideológicos del franquismo* (Madrid: Alianza, 1985).

Mosse, G. L. *The Nacionalization of the Masses. Political Symbolism and Mass Movements in Germany from the Napoleonic Wars Through the Third Reich* (New York: Howard Fertig, 1975).

Mosse, G. L. *Fallen Soldiers. Reshaping the Memory of the World Wars* (New York: Oxford University Press, 1990).

Muntanyola, R. *Vidal i Barraquer. El cardenal de la paz* (Barcelona: Estela, 1971).

Navajas Zubeldía, C. *Ejército, Estado y sociedad en España (1923–1930)* (Logroño: Instituto de Estudios Riojanos, 1991).

Navajas Zubeldía, C. 'Los militares en el poder: el ejército durante la dictadura de Primo de Rivera', in *Aproximación a al Historia militar de España*, vol. 2 (Madrid: Ministerio de Defensa, 2006), pp. 583–98.

Núñez, C. E. *La fuente de la riqueza. Educación y desarrollo económico en la España contemporánea* (Madrid: Alianza, 1992).

Núñez Seixas, X. M. 'Los oasis en el desierto. Perspectivas historiográficas sobre el nacionalismo español', *Bulletin d'Histoire Contemporanie de l'Espagn*, no. 26 (1997), 483–533.

Núñez Seixas, X. M. *Los nacionalismos en la España contemporánea (siglos XIX y XX)* (Barcelona: Hipótesi, 1999).

Núñez Seixas, X. M. 'Proyectos alternativos de nacionalización de masas in Europa occidental (1870–1939), y la relativa influencia de lo contingente', in E. Acton and I. Saz (eds), *La transición a la política de masas* (Valencia: Universitat de València, 2001a), pp. 93–115.

Núñez Seixas, X. M. 'The Region as *Essence* of the Fatherland: Regionalist Variants of Spanish Nationalism (1840–1936)', *European History Quarterly*, 31, 4 (2001b), 483–518.

Núñez Seixas, X. M. 'Nations in Arms against the Invader: On Nationalist Discourses During the Spanish Civil War', in C. Ealham and M. Richards (eds), *The Splintering of Spain. New Perspectives on the Spanish Civil War* (Cambridge: Cambridge University Press, 2005), 45–67.

Oña Fernández, J. J., 'La articulación de la lucha subversiva republicana contra la dictadura de Primo de Rivera', *Cuadernos republicanos*, 56 (2004), 9–21.

Pablo, S. de, Mees, L. and Rodríguez, J. *El péndulo patriótico. Historia del Partido Nacionalista Vasco, I: 1895–1936* (Barcelona: Crítica, 1999).

Pan-Montojo, J. 'Asociacionismo agrario, administración y corporativismo en la dictadura de Primo de Rivera, 1923–1930', *Historia Social*, no. 43 (2002), 15–30.

Payne, S. G. *Fascism in Spain, 1923–1977* (Madison: University of Wisconsin Press, 1999).

Pérez, J. S., Manzano, E., López, R. and Rivière, A. (eds) *La gestión de la memoria. La historia de España al sevicio del poder* (Madrid: Crítica, 2000).

Pérez Garzón, J. S. 'El nacionalismo español en sus orígenes. Factores de configuración', in A. M. García (ed.), *España ¨nación de naciones?* (Madrid: Marcial Pons, 2002), pp. 53–86.

Perfecto García, M. A. 'Regeneracionismo y corporativismo en la Dictadura de Primo de Rivera', in J. Tusell, F. Montero and J. M. Marín (eds), *Las derechas de la España contemporánea* (Madrid: UNED, 1993), pp. 176–96.

Pike, F. B. *Hispanismo, 1898–1936* (Notre Dame, Indiana: University of Notre Dame Press, 1971).

Pollard, J. 'Conservative Catholics and Italian Fascism: the Clerico-Fascists', in M. Blinkhorn (ed.), *Fascists and Conservatives* (London: Unwin Hyman, 1990), pp. 32–50.

Ponce Alberca, J. 'Ejército, política y administración durante la Dictadura de Primo de Rivera: los Delegados Gubernativos en la provincia de Sevilla (1923–1930)', in A. Heredia (ed.), *Fuentes para la Historia Militar en los Archivos Españoles* (Madrid: Deimos, 2000), pp. 739–58.

Portillo, J. M. *Revolución de nación. Orígenes de la cultura constitucional en España* (Madrid: Centro de Estudios Políticos y Constitucionales, 2000).

Pozo Andrés, M. M. del, *Curriculum e identidad nacional. Regeneracionismos, nacionalismos y escuela pública (1890–1939)* (Madrid: Biblioteca Nueva, 2000).

Pozo Andrés, M. M. del and Braster, J. F. A., 'The Ribirth of the "Spanish Race": the State Nationalism, and Education in Spain, 1875–1931', *European History Quarterly*, 29, 1 (1999), 75–107.

Pozo Pardo, Alberto del, 'El Libro de la Patria. Un concurso escolar vacío de matiz regenaracionista (1921–1923)', in J. Ruiz, (ed.), *La educación en la España contemporánea* (Madrid: Sociedad Española de Pedagogía, 1985), pp. 195–202.

Preston, P. *Las derechas españolas en el siglo XX* (Madrid: Sistema, 1986a).

Preston, P. 'Alfonsine Monarchism and the Coming of the Spanish Civil War', in M. Blinkhorn (ed.), *Spain in Conflict 1931–1939* (London: Sage, 1986b), pp. 160–82.

Preston, P. *La política de la venganza. El fascismo y el militarismo en la España del siglo XX* (Madrid: Península, 1997).

Preston, P. *Franco. Caudillo de España* (Barcelona: Grijalbo Mondadori, 1998).

Preston, P. 'La Guerra Civil Europea, 1914–1945', in M. C. Romero and I. Saz (eds), *El siglo XX. Historiografía e historia* (Valencia: Universitat de València, 2002), pp. 137–65.

Puelles Benítez, M. de. 'Secularización de la enseñanza en España (1874–1917)', in J. L. García Delgado (ed.), *España entre dos siglos (1875–1931)* (Madrid: Siglo XXI, 1991), pp. 191–212.

Quiroga Fernández de Soto, A. 'La idea de España en los ideólogos de la Dictadura de Primo de Rivera. El discurso católico-fascista de José Pemartín', *Revista de Estudios Políticos*, no. 108 (2000), 197–224.

Quiroga Fernández de Soto, A. ' "Los apóstoles de la Patria". El Ejército como instrumento de nacionalización de masas durante la Dictadura de Primo de Rivera', *Mélanges de la Casa de Velázquez*, 34–1 (2004), 243–72.

Quiroga Fernández de Soto, A. 'Perros de paja: las Juventudes de la Unión Patriótica', *Ayer*, 59, 3 (2005), 69–96.

Quiroga Fernández de Soto, A. *Los orígenes del Nacionalcatolicismo. José Pemartín y la Dictadura de Primo de Rivera* (Granada: Comares, 2006).

Quiroga Fernández de Soto, A. 'Maestros, espías y lentejas. Educación y nacionalización de masas durante la Dictadura de Primo de Rivera', in J. Álvarez Junco and J. Moreno (eds), *Nacionalismo español y procesos de nacionalización en España* (Madrid: Centro de Estudios Políticos y Constitucionales, 2007).

Quiroga Fernández de Soto, A. and Alonso García, G. 'Matrimonio de conveniencia. El nacionalismo español y las relaciones Iglesia-Estado durante la Dictadura de Primo de Rivera', in *Memoria e identidad. Actas del VII Congreso de la Asociación de Historia Contemporánea* (Santiago de Compostela: Universidade de Santiago de Compostela, 2004).

Radcliff, P. 'La representación de la nación', in R. Cruz and M. Pérez (eds), *Cultura y movilización social en la España contemporánea* (Madrid: Alianza, 1997), pp. 305–25.

Ramos, C. 'El nacionalismo vasco durante la Dictadura de Primo de Rivera', *Letras de Deusto*, 15, 31 (1995), 137–67.

Reig Tapia, A. 'La justificación ideológica del *alzamiento* de 1936', in J. L. García Delgado (ed.), *Bienio rectificador y Frente Popular* (Madrid, 1988), pp. 211–37.

Rey Reguillo, F. del. 'Ciudadanos honrados y somatenistas', *Estudios de Historia Social*, no. 42–43 (1987), 97–150.

Rey Reguillo, F. del. 'El capitalismo catalán y Primo de Rivera: en torno a un golpe de estado', *Hispania*, 48, 168 (1988), 289–307.

Rey Reguillo, F. del. *Propietarios y Patronos. La political de las organizaciones patronales en la España de la Restauración (1914–1923)* (Madrid: Ministerio de Trabajo y Seguridad Social, 1992).

Reyero, C. *La escultura conmemorativa en España. La edad de oro del monumento público, 1820–1914* (Madrid: Cátedra, 1999).

Rial, J. H. *Revolution from Above: the Primo de Rivera Dictatorship in Spain, 1923–1930* (Cranbury, NJ/London: Associated University Press, 1986).

Richards, M. 'Constructing the Nationalist State: Self Sufficiency and Regeneration in the Early Franco Years', in C. Mar-Molinero and A. Smith (eds), *Nationalism and the Nation in the Iberian Peninsula* (Washington/Oxford: Berg, 1996), pp. 149–67.

Richards, M. *A Time of Silence: Civil War and the Culture of Repression in Franco's Spain, 1936–1945* (Cambridge: Cambridge University Press, 1998).

Ridolfi, M. *Le feste nazionali* (Bologna: Il Mulino, 2003).

Riquer, B. de, 'Sobre el lugar de los nacionalismos-regionalismos en la historia contemporánea española', *Historia Social*, no. 7 (1990), 105–26.

Riquer, B. de, 'La débil nacionalización española del siglo XIX', *Historia Social*, no. 20 (1994), 97–114.

Riquer, B. de, 'El surgimeinto de las nuevas nacionalidades catalana y vasca en el siglo XIX', in R. Sánchez (ed.), *En torno al 98* (Huelva: Universidad de Huelva, 2000), vol. 1, pp. 91–112.

Roig Rosich, Josep María, *La Dictadura de Primo de Rivera a Catalunya* (Barcelona, 1992).

Romero Salvadó, F. J. 'The Failure of the Liberal Project of the Spanish Nation-State, 1909–1923', in C. Mar-Molinero and A. Smith (eds), *Nationalism and the Nation in the Iberian Peninsula* (Washington/Oxford: Berg, 1996), pp. 119–32.

Rubio Cabeza, M. *Crónica de la Dictadura* (Barcelona: Nauta, 1974).

Rubio Cabeza, M. *Crónica de la Dictadura* (Madrid: Sarpe, 1986).

Ruiz Acosta, M. J. 'Hacia el gran reto: la labor de la prensa en preparación de la Exposición Iberoamericana de 1929', *Historia y Comunicación Social*, 2 (1997), 221–7.

Ruiz Rodrigo, C. 'Maestros, escuela y sociedad (de la Restauración a la II República), *Historia de la Educación*, no. 16 (1997), 155–76.

Sánchez Abal, R. *La Enseñanza Militar en el Reinado de Alfonso XII* (Madrid, 1992).

Santonja, G. *Del lápiz rojo al lápiz libre. La censura previa de publicaciones y sus consecuencias editoriales durante los últimos años del reinado de Alfonso XIII* (Barcelona: Anthropos, 1986).

Saz Campos, I. *España contra España. Los nacionalismos franquistas* (Madrid: Marcial Pons, 2003).

Saz, I. et al., 'Normalidad y anormalidad en la historia de la España contemporánea', *Spagna contemporanea*, no. 14 (1998), 142–5.

Seoane, M. C. 'El régimen de censura bajo al Dictadura de Primo de Rivera: efectos secundarios', in C. Garitaonaindía (ed.), *La prensa de los siglos XIX y XX* (Bilbao: Universidad del País Vasco, 1986), pp. 233–43.

Sepúlveda Muñoz, I. 'Nacionalismo español y proyección americana: el pan-hispanismo', in J. Beramendi, R. Máiz and X. Núñez (eds), *Nationalism in Europe* (Santiago de Compostela: Universidad de Santiago de Compostela, 1994), pp. 317–36.

Serrano, C. 'Crisis e ideología en la Restauración', in J. L. García Delgado (ed.), *España enre dos siglos (1875–1931)* (Madrid: Siglo XXI, 1991), pp. 181–90.

Serrano, C. *El nacimiento de Carmen. Símbolos, mitios y nación* (Madrid: Taurus, 1999).

Serrano, C. *El turno del pueblo. Crisis nacional, movimientos populares y populismo en España (1890–1910)* (Barcelona: Península, 2000).

Smith, A. D., *The Ethnic Origins of Nations* (Oxford: Oxford University Press, 1986).

Smith, A. 'The Catalan Counter-revolutionary Coalition and the Primo de Rivera Coup, 1917–23', *European History Quarterly*, 37, 1 (2007), 7–34.

Stone, M. *The Patron State. Culture and Politics in Fascist Italy* (Princeton, New Jersey: Princeton University Press, 1998).

Stowers, S. 'The Concepts of 'Religion', 'Political Religion' and the Study of Nazism', *Journal of Contemporary History*, 42, 1 (2007), 9–24.

Sueiro Seoane, S. 'Retórica y realidades del "Hispanoamericanismo" en la Dictadura de Primo de Rivera', *Mélanges de la Casa de Velázquez*, 28, 3 (1992), 143–59.

Talamo, G. 'Riforma della scuola e sistemi politici', in F. García Sanz (ed.), *España e Italia en la Europa contemporánea* (Madrid: CSIC, 2002), pp. 419–26.

Tarchi, M. *Fascismo. Teorie, interpretazioni e modelli* (Roma/Bari: Laterza, 2003).

Tusell Gómez, J. *La crisis del caciquismo andaluz (1923–1931)* Madrid: Cupsa, 1977).

Tusell Gómez, J. *Radiografía de un golpe de estado* (Madrid: Alianza Editorial, 1987).

Tusell, J., 'Primo de Rivera, 1930. El ocaso', *La Aventura de la Historia*, no. 75 (2005), 18–25.

Tusell, J. and García, G. 'La Dictadura de Primo de Rivera como régimen político. Un intento de interpretación', *Cuadernos Económicos de I.C.E.*, no. 10 (1979), 38–63.

Tusell, J., Gentile, E. and Febo, G. di (eds) *Fascismo y franquismo cara a cara. Una perspectiva histórica* (Madrid: Biblioteca Nueva, 2004).

Ucelay, E. 'La Diputacó durant la Dictadura: 1923–1930', in B. de Riquer (ed.), *Història de la Diputació de Barcelona*, vol. 2 (Barcelona: Diputació, 1987), pp. 178–259.

Ucelay, E. 'La iniciació permanet: Nacionalismes radicals a Catalunya de la Restauració', in *Catalunya i la Restauració, 1875–1923* (Manresa: Centre d'Estudis del Bages, 1992), pp. 127–34.

Ucelay, E. 'La repressió de la Dictadura de Primo de Rivera', in *El poder de l'Estat: evolució, força o raó* (Reus: Centre de Lectura de Reus, 1993), pp. 153–210.

Varela, J. *La novela de España. Los intelectuales y el problema español* (Madrid: Taurus, 1999).

Vilar, P. 'Sobre los fundamentos de las estructuras nacionales', *Historia 16* (April 1978), extra V.

Vilar, P. 'Estado, nación, patria en España y en Francia. 1870–1914', *Estudios de Historia Social*, no. 28–29 (1984), 7–41.

Villacorta Baños, F. 'Dictadura y grupos profesionales organizados, 1923–1930', *Ayer*, no. 40 (2000), 51–78.

Weber, E. *Peasants into Frenchmen. Modernization of Rural France, 1870–1914* (Stanford, California: Stanford University Press, 1976).

Weber, E. *L'Action Française* (Paris: Librairie Arthème Fayard, 1985).

Wehler, H. U. *German Empire, 1870–1914* (Leamington Spa: Berg, 1985).

Willson, P. *Peasant Women and Politics in Fascist Italy: the Massaie Rurali* (London: Routledge, 2002).

Winston, C. M. 'Carlist Worker Groups in Catalonia, 1900–1923', in S. Payne (ed.), *El Carlismo, 1833–1975* (Madrid: Actas, 1996), pp. 85–101.

Zunino, P. G. *L'ideologia del fascismo. Miti, credence e valori nella stabilizzazione del rigime* (Bologna: Il Mulino, 1995).

Index